WEAPONS
of the
ROMANS

WEAPONS
of the
ROMANS

Michel Feugère

translated from the French by
David G. Smith

TEMPUS

First published by Editions Errance, Paris, 1993
This edition (trans. D.G. Smith) 2002

PUBLISHED IN THE UNITED KINGDOM BY:
Tempus Publishing Ltd
The Mill, Brimscombe Port
Stroud, Gloucestershire GL5 2QG
www.tempus-publishing.com

PUBLISHED IN THE UNITED STATES OF AMERICA BY:
Tempus Publishing Inc.
2A Cumberland Street
Charleston, SC 29401
www.tempuspublishing.com

British Library Cataloguing in Publication Data.
A catalogue record for this book is available from the British Library.

ISBN 0 7524 2506 4

Typesetting and origination by Tempus Publishing.
PRINTED AND BOUND IN GREAT BRITAIN.

CONTENTS

ACKNOWLEDGEMENTS

It was the author's initial meeting with Peter Connolly in 1981 that gave him insight for the first time into the technical and cultural aspects of the Roman army, arousing his interest in spite of personal pacifist inclinations; and throughout the preparation of this book, English researchers have provided much valuable support. In Germany, I owe a large debt to the Römisch-Germanisches Zentralmuseum of Mainz, where E. Künzl has never stinted in his support, but I must also mention here my deep appreciation of the Römisch-Germanische Kommission in Frankfurt, whose successive directors have always given me a warm welcome, while in Munich J. Garbsch has been most patient and helpful.

Both in France and abroad there have been many site people, researchers and museum personnel who have welcomed me and helped me beyond measure. I should mention here D. Baatz (Saalburg), F. Beck (Saint-Germain-en-Laye), R. Birley (Vindolanda), L. Bonnamour (Chalon-sur-Saône), M. Cavalier (Avignon), L. Chabot (Les Pennes-Mirabeau), † H. Chapman (London), H. Chew (Saint-Germain-en-Laye), A. Duval (Saint-Germain-en-Laye), J-M. Féménias (Lançon), F. Fischer (Bonn), A.-B. Follmann-Schulz (Bonn), M. Guštin (Ljubljana), M. Hassall (London), U. Heimberg (Bonn), O. Höckmann (Mainz), Chr. and Cl. Holliger (Vindonissa), J. Istenič (Ljubljana), H.-P. Kuhnen (Stuttgart & Aalen), F. Leyge (Lyon, then St-Romain-en-Gal), M. Luik (then in Aalen), D.J. Marchant (Leeds), St. Martin-Kilcher (Basel), F. Naumann-Steckner (Köln), M. Pinette (Autun, then Besançon), F. Rebecchi (Ferrara), A. Roth-Congès (Aix-en-Provence), B. Schnitzler (Strasbourg), I.M. Stead (London), M. Thauré (then in Saintes) and G. Waurick (Mainz). I am also most grateful to P. Villard of the University of Aix-en-Provence for his translation of the Arrian text on the *hippika gymnasia*.

Finally, I would like to thank Chr. Goudineau for his *stimulus* and F. Lontcho for the first *editio*, and I must not forget my father Joseph Feugère († 2000), who took on the thankless task of being the first reader, nor Y. Le Bohec who has improved the text through his wide knowledge of the Roman army.

PREFACE

In terms of contemporary historical research, the Roman army seems to have been the preserve of Anglo-German scholars. Certainly, the presence of a Roman frontier in Britain and the Rhine-Danube *limes* in proximity to Germany has led to a considerable number of investigations into Roman military history, organisation and associated equipment in both countries, and for the most part research results have been published either in English or German; France has found herself in recent years on the sidelines, a situation which for reasons of ancient geography does not seem to have caused her any great concern.

However it was in France, in the mid-nineteenth century under the Third Republic, that military archaeology was born, thanks to Napoléon III's passion for Julius Caesar and his glorious victory in Gaul. Many factors, including politics, were involved in his interest; but it is the results of this enthusiasm which should concern us here. From 1861 onwards, the Emperor initiated excavations into Alise-Sainte-Reine in Burgundy with the aim of discovering more about Caesar's siege of Alésia through the examination both of his siege works and archaeological finds; this project was largely successful, and led to the discovery of Roman military equipment and battle tactics which still remain at the heart of our knowledge of Roman weaponry.

Since 1867, the Musée des Antiquités Nationales – created by Napoléon III in 1862 – has assembled collections in which the Roman army features prominently in the Château de Saint-Germain-en-Laye. Its first curator, Alexandre Bertrand, intended from the outset to display a reconstruction of one of Caesar's soldiers, but this was thought to be too uncertain of success, and it was an early second century infantryman who was the model for Bartholdi's sculpture, drawing largely on the reliefs displayed on Trajan's Column.

The Musée des Antiquités Nationales has from its creation maintained strong links with the Römisch-Germanisches Zentralmuseum at Mainz, founded in 1802 and famous for the castings produced in its its workshops, and for its impressive collection of copies. This bond benefited both organisations, and was an example to a world which, gripped by political and military tensions, had little time for cultural relations in the late nineteenth century. The links were further strengthened by the exchange of information, photographs and cast copies which are now the bases of first-class research resources and material. One of the first reconstructions of a Roman war machine, made for Napoléon III, was donated by the Emperor to the Mainz museum, though it was regrettably destroyed during the Second World War.

1 Reconstruction of a Roman war machine donated by Napoleon III to the Römisch-Germanisches Zentralmuseum at Mainz

Although the 1914-18 war brought an abrupt end to the scientific collaboration between the two organisations, it was thanks to the Musée des Antiquités Nationales collections that Paul Couissin, a 'humble teacher at Rennes Lycée' to use the words of S. Reinach, decided at the start of the 1920s to devote himself to a detailed study of Roman military equipment. This was a novel project, as there had been no French studies to continue the magisterial work by J. Déchelette on the Gaulish period; and there was a need to make more widely known, and above all to update, the already ancient researches of Le Beau (1777), Quicherat (1865, 1866), Lindenschmit (1858, 1865, 1882), Hübner (1881) and even of Schulten (1911, 1914), the excavator of Roman camps in Spain.

Couissin's work *Les Armes Romaines,* published in 1926, established itself as a baseline for a number of advances; on the one hand, a closer study of existing depictions, notably the casts taken at the end of the nineteenth century of Trajan's Column, and on the other, the study of ancient texts, a large number of which had been collected and published during the same period. Finally, there was archaeological fieldwork itself, where discoveries were clarifying, although often simultaneously questioning, the results obtained by traditional 'deskwork' methods.

Since Couissin's time, there has been no overall work on Roman military equipment and weapons published in France. This deficiency, unquestionably linked to the spectacular advances in military archaeology in countries bordering a *limes*, illustrates the immense impact of archaeological excavations and researches on traditional learning. There have been so many discoveries in recent years in Britain, Germany, the Low Countries and Switzerland that our knowledge of Roman military equipment and weapons has been completely revised.

In the past few years, however, there has been a reappearance of military archaeological programmes in France. The excavations carried out on Roman camps at Arlaines, Mirebeau and Aulnay-de-Saintonge, and the recent identification of a new camp at Saint-Bertrand-de-Comminges, remind us that the country has been pushed aside perhaps too rapidly from a discipline to which we too can make a large contribution.

We therefore have to play catch up, and the new excavations at Alésia, the projects in the valley of the Saône and other regions, all show that archaeological teams are hard at work. This book has only one purpose: to provide these teams with a handy reference work which is as complete as possible.

INTRODUCTION

Among ancient societies, war appears to have been indissolubly associated with the evolution and even the definition of the groups waging it. Starting from a simple spontaneous clash between two clans with different views, war developed in step with cities and townships. In France, the earliest conflicts between groups go back to the Neolithic period, the time when populations were starting to lead a settled existence, with livestock, pastures, cultivated fields and permanent buildings. From that period, war, property and power became interwoven, and it is only in our own times that society has realised that political differences can be resolved by other means, and that war is a very primitive way of settling disagreements between communities.

As a political and social act in itself, war in ancient times played a major role in the technical and cultural evolution of classical societies. It has recently been shown that in ancient Greece an increased mastery of metalworking techniques swiftly followed military equipment requirements. War, which Lenin justifiably called the accelerator of history – increasing and resolving conflicts simultaneously, even if only partially – is at the same time an important force for technological progress; and this is still true today. Like its Greek forerunners, the Gaulish fortress with its ramparts and towers showed not only military presence and power, but also the strength of the community within it. Military capability was an integral part of political reality, and military leaders used it to consolidate and demonstrate their strength. A military victory, celebrated with monuments and triumphs, impressed not only those outside the community but also the community's own citizens.

Among ancient cultures, it was in Rome that ideas of military organisation and equipment were first developed to a high level. Our contemporary culture is now at the point where we are examining and assessing not only the direct military effects, but also the political and technological impacts of the Roman army on society. So this book intends, drawing in part on recently acquired knowledge of Roman military equipment and arms, to examine the extent to which this affected societies under Rome's control or influence.

As the instrument and symbol of centralised power, did the Roman army push the development of new weaponry further than its neighbours, or, as one sometimes reads, did it rather adopt their arms without being a real inventor or innovator? What was the technical basis of Rome's military successes – and setbacks?

2 With helmet and shield put aside while he gets on with construction work, the legionnaire works still wearing his breastplate and with his weapons within easy reach to be ready for action (photo D.A.I., Rome)

This investigation is limited to land-based forces, as naval warfare seems to the author to be based more on the sailing performance of the ships and the determination of the fighting sailors rather than on their equipment as such. Also, it would appear that such equipment was for the most part borrowed from the land forces (with certain rare exceptions such as the 'crow' used for the first time at the Battle of Myles in BC 260, and described by Polybius (I.22)).

The equipment generally used by land forces, on the other hand, will be examined in detail, and placed as securely as possible in its historical perspective in order to highlight its technical and functional developments. This approach will lead us on occasion to cover a wide timespan, as certain items can be understood only over a long period. Finally, this book will show how profoundly our perceptions of classical soldiers have been revised in the light of the research of the last few decades. It is clear also that future discoveries and study will affect the conclusions drawn in this book. Even if our reconstructed soldier cannot be presented with certainty as a living portrait of his ancient predecessor, he will resemble him as closely as our work to date permits. Let us hope that among our readers will be some who are stimulated to analyse and refine our work, so that they may show us an even more accurate picture.

1 MILITARY THINKING AMONG THE ANCIENTS

To try to understand what war meant to the ancients, we need to examine their collective subconscious attitudes. Over and above the differences, which enable us to distinguish Rome from Athens in this respect, war was one of the essential components of a city or state's dynamism. Every imperialist society used war to demonstrate the moral and technical superiority of its culture, and we shall see that in Rome there was also a need to expand, forcing successive emperors to keep a costly permanent army. This situation changed only under the pressures of the political and moral crisis of the third century AD, and later writers show war as an affliction to be suffered rather than as an inspiring conquest, even for the victors. The history of war in ancient times can thus be seen to include a turning point in outlook; from seeing a 'campaign' – victorious or not – as part of a dynamic process, to perceiving it as a state of continuing troubles affecting one region or another until the end of the antique period.

The idea of war was built on previously accepted attitudes, and the characteristics peculiar to Rome can be understood only after also examining what war meant to peoples outside the eternal city before the third century change in attitude outlined above.

ATHENS

The image of war portrayed in the *Iliad* is one of a formalised conflict, finally resolved by a symbolic duel to the death between two heroes, a concept which shows the wish of a community to play down the stupid and murderous realities of a general battle. Such a war recognises more values common to the two antagonists than reasons for confrontation.

The situation was quite different when the Greeks were fighting barbarians; the rules of war for two opposed cities no longer applied, and such conflicts became more numerous with the passage of time. It was only with Alexander the Great that war became the main instrument of imperialist policy, the normal expression of the ambitions of one state over another. This was the concept adopted by the Roman Republic of the third century BC to build its territory.

Long before, there had appeared in Greece the first beginnings of a military organisation which was to last, with some modifications, for more than five centuries. The phalanx, originating in the eighth century BC, seems to have evolved into its classic form before the Persian

3 Hoplite of the fifth century
BC (after P.Ducrey, 1985)

invasion. Little is known about its earliest form, but the Chigi vase
(mid-seventh century BC) shows several groups of hoplites drawn up
in closed ranks ready for a concerted charge. Such soldiers were armed
only with a lance, its length being increased over time to two or three
metres, which they thrust before them, and which replaced the two
short throwing javelins previously used. They had a round shield, fitted
with an arm loop and a handgrip, on their left side, and this protected
not only its bearer but also his companion to the left. The hoplite was
also armed with an iron sword, which he drew after the first assault
with lances. As time passed, and by the fifth century BC, the metal
cuirass gave way to a much lighter woven garment which was almost
as effective and certainly much cheaper.

Phalanx tactics were simple. The hoplites advanced by files, the
leading man taking the first shock, and the length of the lances meant
that three lines of hoplites could between them present a solid wall of
lance points to the enemy. A hoplite killed or injured was immediately
replaced by the man behind him. Marching in close formation, the
phalanx formed an almost unstoppable mass, which ordinary infantry
could not resist. The overlapping shields of the front rank formed an
impregnable solid wall. Several Greek writers attest to the effective-
ness of such phalanx charges against less well-organised adversaries.

Although a redoubtable force in a frontal attack, the Greek phalanx
also had its weaknesses. It was vulnerable to a cavalry charge and sudden guerrilla attacks, and the 'argovian' shield's design caused the ranks
to open up dangerously when the phalanx moved to its left. There was
therefore need for support by auxiliary forces; cavalry were not regu-

larly used before the time of the Peloponnesian War during the second half of the fifth century BC. Previously, as at the battle of Platées for example in 479 BC, the hoplites were supported by heavily armed infantry – the helots – and by archers, the latter being usually recruited among the Scythians and in Crete. There were also Rhodians armed with slings. A further type of auxiliary, the peltasts, was also introduced during this period, recruited from the Thracians, and notable for their wickerwork shields with a double notch cut into the top edge.

All these supporting units, initially considered only as adjuncts to the elite phalanxes, progressively acquired a growing importance. In 390 BC the peltasts showed their real value in a victorious battle against the Spartans, and were thereafter entrusted with more important tasks; so Athens sent an army against Philip of Macedon in 340 BC army which consisted mostly of peltasts, supported only by a reduced cavalry unit.

From the fourth century BC the idea took root among the Macedonians that the army should become professional. The Athenian concept of citizen-soldiers was replaced by a concept of an army designed to achieve the goals set for it by administrative authority through using recruited specialists at all levels. In his struggle against his brother Artaxerxes II, Cyrus the Younger, a pretender to the throne of Persia, was the first to demonstrate the efficiency of a corps of mercenaries. In turn, Athens adopted a system which calmed the unrest among civilians who resented the need to fight successively more distant wars, but soon discovered the other side of the coin – unless mercenaries receive their pay regularly, they lose respect for their employers, and are even likely to turn upon them. Despite these risks, however, the fourth century BC and the Hellenistic period saw a dramatic growth in the part played by mercenaries in military recruitment.

THE CELTS

In general, wars fought by the Celts figure in classical texts only when they threaten Mediterranean cultures; but despite this selective point of view this evidence does reflect an ancient outlook, and give us vital information both about the objectives and the mentality of the Greco-Italians. Such sources generally present an ambivalent view, a combination of sincere admiration with total incomprehension of Celtic bravery. The astonishment of armoured and disciplined Roman soldiers at being charged by totally naked colourfully-tattooed screaming Gauls brandishing swords transfixed many ancient historians from the earliest times. The complete disregard of death shown by these strange warriors, who put the sons of their most noble families into the front ranks, hardly made sense to the Romans, who put into their front lines the *velites*, soldiers chosen from among the poorest and youngest members of the army (Polybius, VI.21).

Added to their fundamental incomprehension of the Celts was the scorn shown by the Romans for their opponents' ignorance of classic strategic principles, by this time raised to a science by the Greeks. For the Celts, above and beyond their communal determination was the

4 Celtic shield of gilded bronze (Northern Italy, second or third century BC?) (Württembergisches
Landesmuseum Stuttgart, Photo Röm.-Germ. Zentralmuseum, Mainz)

individual's attitude that battle gave the risk-taking hero the chance of dining with the gods. It is not surprising, therefore, that from the second century BC any confrontation between Celts and Roman soldiers gave the advantage to the Romans. Both the military concepts and social imperatives (individual bravery, hero-worship, an after-life) of the two groups were so far apart that neither could really assess the other; they were not even fighting the same sort of war.

However, the situation evolved considerably between the fourth and first centuries BC, as is shown by comparing the writings of Caesar with those of preceding authors. By the middle of the first century BC the Celts of 'long-haired Gaul', like the rest of the contemporary Germans, did at least fight in some sort of order, in a formation which Caesar called a phalanx (*B Gall.* I.25.52). When they needed to defend themselves against archery fire, the soldiers closed ranks and overlapped their shields to form a continuous wall. Caesar also noted however both that the point of a *pilum* would often transfix several of these shields, thus exposing two warriors simultaneously, and that while Gaulish assaults were better organised than formerly, Roman superiority continued due to their soldiers' determination and training. The Romans were also able to react immediately to a surprise Gaulish attack sprung while Caesar's forces were building a camp (*B Gall.* II.20-1).

For Caesar (*B Gall.* VI.24), as for other ancient writers, Gauls outclassed the Germans when it came to bravery, but it was the latter who were supreme in their level of pugnacity, a sentiment which held good among the Romans throughout the Empire after the loss of Varus' legions.

The Gaulish warrior's equipment was traditionally a long iron sword, worn on the right side, hanging from a belt made of chain. This heavy weapon played an essential role in the Gaulish way of fighting, individually or in a group, and the scabbard was painstakingly decorated. Lances were equally important symbolically, often buried with the soldier on his death, and their leaf-shaped blades came in a variety of shapes, sometimes large enough to suggest that they were intended for show as well as for combat.

The Gaulish shield, either oval or sub-rectangular, was basically a lattice of wooden planks, reinforced at its centre by a spine *(spina)* of which the central boss was hollowed out for the soldier's hand. This *umbo* was protected by a shaped piece of metal, usually in the form of an omega. The edges of the shield were reinforced with metal strips.

Helmets were very rarely used in Gaul until the second century BC. During the final La Tène period iron helmets started to appear in the West, notably used during the Gallic Wars, and variants are known to have existed in Slovenia and Poland. A slightly later model, the Port type, was the basis of the Roman legionary Weisenau type helmet, which became so widely used by the Roman army in the course of the first century AD, that it becomes difficult to say whether such a helmet from a burial had a Roman or a Gaulish owner. Gauls of the Second Iron Age only used daggers very occasionally. In the final La Tene period, these weapons – always very carefully made – are sometimes found with a cast bronze hilt in the shape of a human form.

THE ETRUSCANS
AND OTHER ITALIAN PEOPLES

The artefacts developed by Rome's neighbours stemmed from the Villanovian culture, which prevailed in the area between the Valley of the Po and Campania where, especially in Etruria, hierarchical societies arose in which military prowess was associated with high social standing. During the time of the Roman kings and at the beginning of the Republic there was no appreciable difference between Rome and its neighbours in military matters; it was only with the formation of the first legions during the fourth century BC (see chapters 3 and 4 below) that specifically Roman traits became evident.

It was partially under Etruscan influence that the first primitive Roman army incorporated a number of Greek elements into its tactics and equipment. Among the Etruscans, such copying did not prevent them from making their own types of weapons, whether or not these were Greek-inspired. One of the most widespread helmet types from the second half of the sixth century BC onwards – the Negau type – was the basis for several variants in Italy, the central Alps and Slovenia. This was a simple bronze skull-cap with a rib running from the front to the back, with a lateral depression at its base. The descendent of a long-established indigenous tradition, it had no cheek-guards and was held in place by a simple strap under the chin. Its various forms (Belmonte, Volterra, Vetulonia, Italo-Slovene and others) prove the existence of workshops or groups of workshops, supplying equipment of this type for a given region.

The *situlae* votive plaques and other decorated artefacts of the Este region show interesting representations of the weapons of this area during the fourth to sixth centuries BC. The foot soldiers, protected by a crested helmet, a round shield and two greaves, usually carried two lances, though some of them held a battleaxe instead. Cavalry troops, similarly helmeted, were issued with a long rectangular shield which remained in use over a long period, notably among the Gaulish cavalry; their preferred choice of weapon was the lance.

ROME

The Republic
The first military concept adopted by the Republic was designed to consolidate and strengthen its territory. Following the example of the Greek cities, Rome first established a group of colonies around the city then, from 338 BC, in enemy territory, a policy which in itself contained the seeds of a permanent army. The heavy demands imposed on the Roman State by the various Punic Wars led those citizens fortunate enough to be able to do so to distance themselves from their civic duty, and at the very moment when it needed to raise new forces, Rome was forced to revise its recruitment system, a task carried out no doubt by a number of people but generally credited to the consul Marius.

The spirit of conquest was not the only driving force behind military activity. The Roman army still felt the bitter pain of the invasions

5 Trajan's Column (photo D. A. I., Rome)

by the Cisalpine Celts and the Gauls in the fourth century BC, actions which led to vicious reprisals by Rome in the second and third centuries BC involving the massacre of great numbers of Celtic civilians as well as warriors – the reconquest of the Po Valley after Hannibal's invasion is just one example. A similar attitude, composed of fear tinged with a certain respect, existed towards the Spanish at the end of the Republican era, then against the 'elusive Germans' under the Empire. The barbarians were as mysterious to the Romans as they were dangerous, and their physical extermination was for them the most tangible form of Romanisation.

The necessity of conquests was never questioned until much later Roman times, and this moral certainty was doubled by a genuine confidence in the superiority of their army and its equipment. Thus Polybius, writing toward the middle of the second century about the behaviour of the Gaulish chieftains who, at the battle of Telamone (225 BC) appeared naked in the front ranks, wrote 'The Gaulish shield not being able to cover the body entirely, the larger the warrior's body, the better the arrows could hit the exposed parts'; and, later, ' . . . their shields were much less effective for protection, and their swords less effective in battle, as the Gaulish sword could be used only for slashing' (II.30). A frequently quoted passage, almost comic in tone, describes in detail the weakness of these swords 'Their swords, due to their design . . . could strike only one effective blow, after which they were blunted and bent, so that if the warriors were not given time to straighten them with their foot against the ground, any second blow was completely useless' (II.33). A similar criticism appears later in Livy (XXXVIIII.1.49), and in Tacitus' description of German weapons (*Ann.* II.4).

The case of Flavius Josephus, who wrote in the last quarter of the first century AD, is somewhat different. A leader in the Jewish War, defeated and subsequently pardoned by the emperor, he was appointed as an official historian and transferred to Rome, where he was given an apartment in Vespasian's private house; it is therefore not surprising that he spoke well of Roman power. However sincere he may or may not have been, his writings all praise the care shown by the Romans when it came to military equipment: throughout its history, the Roman army was very careful to equip its troops with weaponry that was tough and effective, and could meet the needs of a long-established strategy.

This strategy was based not only on general experience but also on practical, theoretical and what one might call 'scientific' considerations, developed particularly since the time of Alexander the Great. Whole books, like the 'Treatise on Military Arts' by Aeneas of Stymphale (beginning of the fourth century BC), the 'Treatise on Tactics' by Polybius, the later, 'On Military Matters' by Celsius, now lost, and again Vegetius' 'Epitome of Military Affairs' in the fourth century AD, circulated in the appropriate quarters on the way a campaign should be conducted, in the light of the troops present, the terrain and the time of day, and on how battles should be fought. Historians analysed the decisions taken by such and such a tribune at which decisive moment in the battle, and their writings often reflected the bitter arguments which must have taken place in Rome about these matters. The importance of the battles themselves is not sufficient to explain the interest in such debates; for Romans, it was a man's bravery and the wider political development of his character which was of overriding interest, particularly when he was in the heat of battle. A victorious general always had greater prestige than even the most conscientious administrator.

The Honour of Rome

Individual honour, the honour of the legion and the honour of its commanding officer all came together within the ancient hierarchical society. As Yann Le Bohec so aptly put it in his recent work, the army was, in conjunction with the central and provincial governments, one of the three pillars of the Roman state, and if its main function was war against outside forces, it was much more than just a machine for conquest. The trauma experienced by all Romans after the Teutoburgerwald disaster of AD 9 is proof of this; above all, the Roman army defended the honour of Rome. Throughout the Empire many military excursions had no purpose other than to demonstrate to the barbarians the consciousness of a 'naturally imperialist' state of its own destiny. To recover legionary standards lost in a previous skirmish, for instance, was sufficient reason to put in motion a campaign which would cost the lives of hundreds of legionaries. It is very revealing to read the works of such ancient historians as Suetonius and Tacitus in this area, and to see a mentality which, from the end of the Republican era, saw the Mediterranean lands as its own, and which would soon see the Alps, and later the valleys of the Rhine and Danube, as its own possessions as well.

2 THE ROMAN SOLDIER FROM EARLIEST TIMES

THE SOURCE MATERIAL

From the Middle Ages to the eighteenth century

The picture of the arms and equipment of the Roman soldier which we have today seems accurate to us, as it is based on a wide diversity of sources, all tested by learned criticism and practical experiments. This state, however, is the result of scientific research and has taken several centuries to evolve. From the end of the Middle Ages until the seventeenth century, no one saw any incongruity in portraying the Roman soldier dressed and equipped in a style contemporary with the writer or illustrator. Furthermore, paintings and engravings of such soldiers show splendid helmets, exquisite breastplates and superb leg-armour, all handmade to the highest standards. This is because the whole of Europe after the Renaissance laid claim to a classical cultural heritage from which emerged quite naturally a flattering portrait of the Roman soldier. It was of no importance that the arms were contemporary or that details of the equipment in no way resembled 'archaeological' reality – such a practical approach was not even considered; and what really mattered was the idea that the Roman soldier was the standard-bearer for civilization and culture. It was only with the advent of impartial historical analysis in the eighteenth and (particularly) nineteenth centuries that people began to seek a more realistic representation of military equipment and Roman armament.

The cost of illustrations and the technical constraints imposed by reproducing engravings were certainly part of the reason for this situation, but modern archaeology finds it difficult to understand how one of the first works treating of Roman arms, that of Albert Gentilis published in Latin in 1599, could be produced without any depictions at all; it is in fact based on the study of texts and takes no account even of the illustrations in them nor of archaeological sources, which did not exist at that time. One has to wait for the numerous seventeenth and particularly eighteenth century engravings to see another approach to ancient realities. A good example of this change in attitude is the engraving of a Roman cavalryman, published in 1787 as part of a series of etchings, which shows his equipment and the details of his horse's harness based on actual observation of ancient reliefs such as Trajan's Column, and not as a subjective reconstruction.

6 The Roman soldier as portrayed in the sixteenth century (Andreae Alciati Emblemata, 1581)

7 Roman cavalryman as shown at the end of the eighteenth century (from a series of engravings by Saint-Sauveur, after Labrousse, printed about 1787)

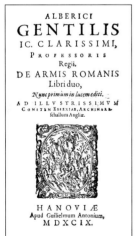

8 One of the first works published on Roman arms (1599)

Trajan's Column

Encouraged by this new approach, academics started to look closely at this extraordinary 'ancient cartoon strip', obviously a first-class documentary source of information on the Roman army; and accordingly engravings based on scenes depicted on the column predominate in the majority of nineteenth-century works, such as *Dictionary of Roman Antiquities* by Rich (1861), the *Dictionary of Greek and Roman Antiquities* published under the direction of Daremberg and Saglio (1877-1919) and *The Roman Army* by L. Fontaine (1883). This almost exclusive use of the Roman reliefs was further exposed by Cichorius' reproductions at the end of the nineteenth century, and by the detailed plaster casts prepared at that time for the Latran museum in Rome (now the Museo della Civiltà Romana), the Museum of Casts in Berlin and the Victoria and Albert Museum in London.

Ancient reliefs – the hidden danger

Unfortunately, not all the historic reliefs used to reconstruct military equipment are as reliable a source as one might think. It has long been

Trajan's column

Dedicated on May 12th., AD 113, seven years after his victorious campaigns had ended in 106 with the creation of the province of Dacia (approximately today's Romania), Trajan's Column was immediately accepted as one of ancient Rome's principal monuments. Its very form, its size, the richness of its sculpted reliefs, all made it a remarkable piece of work from the outset, and it set the precedent for such later works as the column of Marcus Aurelius in about AD 180-90, and the columns erected in Constantinople by Theodosius (AD 386-94) and Arcadius (AD 404-10). Nearly two thousand years later, it was also the inspiration for the column which Napoléon had built in the Place Vendôme in Paris (1806-10).

Placed between the two buildings of the Rome library, which since AD 102 had bordered the Basilica Ulpia, the column was intended to be both the tomb of Trajan and an illustrated book of his campaigns. It is this second purpose which interests us, with its continuous band of illustrations of the Dacian wars having been described as a 'documentary film' or even as a 'cartoon strip'. The reliefs are so precise that not only do they show us the arms and equipment in use during the height of the Roman Empire, but also detailed information on the conduct of a military campaign, and on ancillary works such as camps, bridges and trenches, as well as offering an insight into the defeated enemy, in this case the Dacians. An 'official document', the column is no less valuable as an historical document, as the illustrations must have been based on eyewitness reports by people actually present at the events portrayed.

Further reading: Cichorius 1896-1900 (photographs of casts taken from the column); Settis (ed) 1908 (photographs of the originals).

9 Trajan's Column, a highly accurate documentary source for our knowledge of Roman military equipment, though somewhat stereotyped in parts

noticed that differences occur between, for instance, funerary reliefs and military memorials, whether they were intended to record for posterity either a person or an event. In a recent study, G. Waurick has been able to show a very marked difference between the two types during the first century AD; this diminished during Trajan's reign only to reappear later as an undeniable fact.

This ancient bias shows up regularly in the use of Greek weapons of the third and fourth centuries BC, particularly with helmets, swords and armour. Can we bring together these anachronisms and the 'new Greek' fashion which appeared in particular in Rome among the ruling classes under Augustus and his immediate successors? The answer is very likely 'yes', as exceptional arms were probably produced in early Imperial times for princes and senior officials. Suetonius (*Cal.* 52) tells us that Caligula appeared in a cuirass which was a copy of that belonging to Alexander the Great, and the emperor Maximinus of Thrace (AD 235-58) had a gilded breastplate modelled in Ptolemaic style.

In fact, the images presented on the official reliefs were intended to convey an official message – the illustration of an event to preserve it for posterity. There was no thought of helping future archaeologists, and not realising this, several researchers have been led up blind alleys. The case of A. Comarmond is worthy of mention; a collector and antiquary in the best sense of the word, Comarmond was appointed Conservator of Archaeological Museums in Lyon in 1841. He was a man with an enquiring mind whose remarkably wide-ranging interests stretched from prehistory (then known as 'antediluvian antiquities') to the Middle Ages, and under his leadership the collections increased to equal those in many more important cities. Noticing that among the bronze artefacts there were some circular plaques with rings attached, Comarmond concluded that these were linked with

10 Relief on the Column of Aurelius (photo D. A. I., Rome)

11(left) Helmets with rings as shown on Trajan's column (photo D. A. I., Rome). (above) Helmet from Jard in the Vendée region of France, undoubtedly a nineteenth century fake based on reliefs on Trajan's Column (after Daremberg and Saglio)

the reliefs on some ancient monuments, such as the columns of Trajan and Marcus Aurelius, which featured helmets topped with a ring. On this evidence alone Comarmond described these objects as helmet-crests in his catalogues, though today they are known to be parts of the harnesses fitted to horses and other animals; and having acquired a Republican period helmet with the top missing, he did not hesitate to mount one of the locally found rings onto it.

Another example also shows the need felt by some nineteenth-century researchers to make archaeology conform to accepted theories. In 1878 the 'tomb of a Roman legionary' was discovered at Jard in the Vendée area, the contents of which were to intrigue the specialists. Alongside some of the finds which are now known to have been fabricated from a range of different objects, and other more or less successful forgeries, was an intact bronze helmet which lacked cheek-guards and did not seem ever to have been worn. Despite some peculiar technical and typological characteristics, the helmet seemed to resemble very closely the illustrations sculpted into Trajan's Column, and with reason, as it is very definitely a copy, made for a collector of antiquities. Illustrated in Daremberg and Saglio's *Dictionary*, the Jard helmet is to this day, with its 'Comarmond mounting', the only known example of helmets with rings as shown on second century reliefs.

Happily, other theories and discoveries have been based on a more rigorous examination of ancient illustrations in conjunction with actual artefacts. These often drew on noteworthy finds, news of which was rapidly disseminated by the growing number of local antiquaries interested in such matters. For example, the 'Sword of Tiberius' found in 1848 was published by L. Lersch in 1849, and Otto Jahn was equally prompt in publishing in 1860 a group of *phalerae* found at Lauersfort in 1858. In 1882 L. Lindenschmit, founder of the 'Römisch-Germanisches

12 The face-helmet from the tomb at Chassenard (Allier, France), dating from around AD 40, as it looked shortly after its discovery in 1874

Zentralmuseum', published in Mainz a fundamental study of the dress and equipment of the Roman soldier, based on the large collection of funerary columns *(stelae)* from the Rhineland, and on the numerous discoveries made at that time. Lindenschmit's research was to have a considerable influence on the development of military archaeology in Germany for many years.

In 1892, the creation of the Imperial Commission on the *Limes* (the frontier between the Romans and the indigenous German natives), made possible by the unification of Germany (1871), rewarded the perseverance of Theodor Mommsen (1817-1903). Site exploration, excavations and publication were the main tasks assigned to the Commission, which for the areas of Upper Germany alone published no less than thirty-nine volumes in the period leading up to 1914. The many discoveries made in the Roman camps were thus brought to the notice of the scientific community, and there is no doubt that military arms and equipment featured prominently.

The vital role of archaeology

It was clear by the end of the nineteenth century that the literary and iconographic source material on the Roman army could only be fully understood, and in many cases interpreted, with the support of archaeological material. Although excavation had started very early (from 1820, for instance, in the case of in the legionary camp at Bonn), it now increased rapidly, both in the Rhine-Danube frontier areas (where the 'Obergermanisch-rätische *Limes*' publications (ORL) appeared regularly right up to 1937) and in other Western provinces of the Roman Empire; in Africa and the Middle East, military archaeology developed a little later.

The discoveries made in the course of these activities, supplemented by casual finds, notably when dredging rivers or quarrying gravel (in the valleys of the Rhine and Saône particularly) increased progressively to build up a mass of documentation which even today remains the core of our typological and technical knowledge of the subjects which concern us in this book. This steady accretion of knowledge built up over several decades has also been supplemented by some particularly spectacular casual finds as well as by planned excavations, and it is of interest to look at some of these here.

Newstead Fort in Scotland was excavated at the beginning of the last century by the Scottish archaeologist J. Curle, who published his full results in 1911. The abundant and sometimes spectacular discoveries, such as several bronze and iron parade-helmets, generated a subsequent wide interest which was fully justified as much by the significance of the finds as by the excellence of the publication itself. A room in the headquarters building yielded the fragments of a full set of shoulder plates from a suit of *lorica segmentata* armour, from which the local pattern of such equipment was reconstructed; only the hoard discovered at Corbridge (see right) has further increased our knowledge of such material.

Excavations under F. Cumont started in 1922 at Dura-Europos in Syria, and brought to light traces of the siege of the town that took place in AD 256. The besieged Romans had dug their own tunnels where the Parthians were attempting to undermine the town walls and watchtowers, and in one of these which had collapsed onto its excavators were found the remains of several soldiers who had perished still wearing their full armour. Among the most spectacular discoveries were some wooden shields which still retained their painted decoration; their splendour, together with the actual shape of some of them, led such shields to be considered as parade accessories rather than mere practical objects (see right). Other fully preserved perishable objects such as arrows and catapult artillery bolts helped to make Dura-Europos into a documented record of which the full implications are still not completely assessed. New Franco-Syrian excavations have also started to produce new information of great importance for ancient military history studies.

Finally, at Corbridge (Great Britain) the excavations carried out by the University of Durham between 1947-73 concentrated primarily on the series of forts built between approximately AD 80-163 on the site now occupied by the modern city. In 1964 these digs

13 The Corbridge Deposit: exploded view of chest as it was when buried
(P. Connolly) (after Allason-Jones and Bishop, 1988)

brought to light a deposit of metallic objects which probably came from a military workshop; among these, in a chest, were several pieces of segmental armour from which it was possible (with the addition of some new basic parts) to reconstruct several sets of the armour in use during the first century AD. These Corbridge cuirasses, studied by H. Russell Robinson, were first published by G. Webster in 1969 then by Robinson himself in his notable 1975 publication. Previously, our knowledge of segmental armour had been based on comparisons between depictions on Trajan's Column and a few rare broken components found at Carnuntum, Newstead and London: now, the Corbridge deposit has enabled us to put together an accurate picture of these cuirasses which are so characteristic of the Roman army.

These three examples show how technical research into military equipment since the beginning of the last century has been able to develop only with the support given by archaeology. This development, however, has not been to the same level everywhere, and we should add a few words before closing this chapter about the particularly stimulating and innovative role played in this area by British research.

The English School

Since the end of the 1960s, Great Britain has seen a resurgence of interest in the Roman army, as much among the general public as among specialist researchers. The roots of this reawakened interest lie in the excavations carried out along Hadrian's Wall and on a number of military sites since the early 1900s; but the work of the archaeologists, however interesting their discoveries, would never have been sufficient in itself to generate the expansion which has taken place in the last few decades.

The resurgence was probably sparked off by the Corbridge discoveries in 1964 and Robinson's reconstruction of segmental armour in the years following. Initially as a researcher, and subsequently as Keeper of Armour at the Tower of London, he was first and foremost a very skilled craftsman combined with an indefatigable researcher. His study of ancient helmets and cuirasses, published in 1975, was regrettably brought to an untimely end by his early demise, but thanks to his skills as an illustrator his friend Peter Connolly was able to continue the work of these last years of research, which have given us a completely new insight into the Roman army (to mention only the area which concerns us in this book).

Founded in 1972, the Ermine Street Guard is an example of the spectacular heights and impact achieved by the English School. This group of amateurs, passionately enthusiastic about the Roman army, now has around one hundred members who recreate, manufacture and experiment with the equipment of a Roman legion, the *Leg XX Valeria Victrix*, which had been involved in Claudius' conquest of AD 43. As is typical in such reconstruction work, the Ermine Street Guard regularly comes up against gaps in our current knowledge – the colours, decoration and external appearance of objects which usually come to light in an advanced state of decay, for instance. Nevertheless,

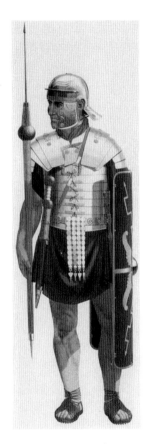

14 Legionary towards AD 100, fully equipped (P. Connolly; photo Röm.-Germ. Zentralrnuseum, Mainz)

15 Standard-bearer, *optio* and *cornicen* towards the end of the first century AD (reconstruction by the Ermine Street Guard)

by working in close contact with researchers as expert as H. R. Robinson or P. Connolly, the Guard has already made a by no means insignificant contribution to our knowledge of equipment: it is thanks to them that we have been able to understand and reconstruct the purpose of a certain method of suspension, and the precise movements of a legionary in a particular manoeuvre.

Furthermore, when we see similar groups working in other countries, notably in Holland and Germany, we can assess more clearly the influence of this generation of English researchers on contemporary advances. From now on, one will be looking not only at the form and development of weapons, but also at the ways they were made, which leads to consideration of their cost, handiness and ergonomics; implications which will in future be an integral part of archaeological study. As a result, typological evolution is now understood to be simply the result of ancient developments and advances, whether in manufacturing methods or tactics in battle.

16 Infantry auxiliary; reconstruction by P. Connolly from the funeral column of Firmus (photo Röm.-Germ. Zentralmuseum, Mainz)

By looking through the eyes of the legionary or auxiliary – bearing in mind that two thousand years have passed – the archaeologist can more easily understand the thinking of those men who conceived, used and developed Roman military arms and equipment. A good example of English initiative in this area is the series of seminars on Roman military equipment (ROMEC), which since 1983 have injected new life into European researches; and we should also welcome the recent synthesis by M. C. Bishop and J. C. N. Coulston (1993) which clearly shows the value of these meetings.

THE SOURCES OF OUR CURRENT KNOWLEDGE

All that we know today about Roman arms rests essentially on the work of several generations of researchers; but when one is confronted by the large increase in archaeological discoveries, the continuation of this tradition is leading us to take a fresh look at the sources of our knowledge. We cannot therefore reach the heart of the subject without examining, even cursorily, the major archaeological contexts on which our publications are based.

17 Legionary with his full equipment, towards AD 200 (P. Connolly, photo Röm.-Germ. Zentralmuseum, Mainz)

Military camps

Without exception, camps yield only a small number of actual arms and items of military equipment, as every soldier took the greatest care of his personal kit; thus finds are usually only of small objects. Every *castellum* had its own workshop, differing in size from camp to camp in relation to the number of men stationed there, so it is clear that the most spectacular discoveries will be in association with these workshops (*fabricae*). Accordingly, the Corbridge chest of pieces of armour and associated tools appears to be linked with either a craftsman or a small workshop, dating from the early part of the second century AD, At Künzing in Bavaria it was a group of third century daggers and swords which showed the specialist nature of these workshops.

On occasion, though not frequently, discoveries can be linked to the abandonment of a camp after a military defeat. The Rhine camp of Niederbieber fell in AD 259 or 260 for example, and rare documents of equally exceptional standards have been recovered (see below).

Theoretically, the equipment recovered from a camp should enable us to identify the types of military personnel stationed in it, but as we shall see below, whilst one may thus identify a cavalry camp, it is not always easy to distinguish camps for legionaries from those of auxiliaries by equipment alone. The authors remain wary therefore of identifying military units solely from the equipment found, though it is hoped that we shall progress in this area in the light of current work.

Battlefields

The enthusiasm – sometimes tinged with chauvinism – of learned men in the nineteenth century was often directed towards looking for

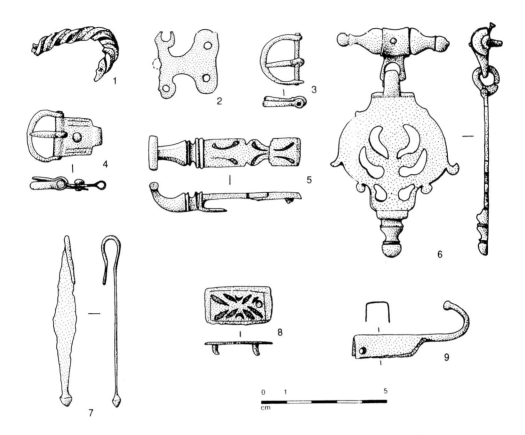

18 Military equipment from the military camp at Aulnay-de-Saintonge, c. AD 20-30 : 1. Fragment of silver armilla; 2-4. Hinge and buckles from segmental armour; 5-6. Hook and harness pendant; 7. Pendant; 8. *Cingulum* decoration; 9. Stiffener from a *dolabra* scabbard

and researching the sites of great battles mentioned in ancient sources. These researchers often cited fragments of equipment to support their hypotheses, but in practice, closer examination of these objects has often shown them to be the results of agricultural activity – parts of tools, horseshoes and harness components, for instance. The documentary evidence was often taken as self-evidently contemporaneous with the event described, but a closer critical examination frequently reveals different periods of time. Past excavations at Alésia – the site of Julius Caesar's crushing defeat of the Gauls – support this, since in addition to obviously late-Republican material the excavators unearthed both Bronze Age and Merovingian objects as well.

'Battlefield Archaeology', is thus a discipline which largely remains to be developed very cautiously and taking into account foreseeable difficulties; for example, what archaeological remains can one expect to find on the actual site of an armed confrontation? Some answers to this question can in fact now be given, based on the confirmed location of the actual site of the battle near Osnabrück in Germany at which the Roman legate Varus lost three legions to enemy native troops in AD 9. Thanks to this, Theodor Mommsen's hypothesis in 1885 now has strong supporting arguments.

The area of Kalkriese, to the east of the present town of Bramsche, has yielded some remarkable coin finds since the eighteenth century. The latest find, in 1987, was a hoard of Republican and early Augustan *denarii* scattered over a 100m² area. Since 1780, at least 15 *aurei*, 600 further silver coins and 121 bronze coins have been discovered in the vicinity, none them later in date than AD 9, and 4 bronze *asses* struck at the mint of Lyon are counterstamped VAR. Among the many metallic artefacts also found are examples of all the types of fibulae used in the Roman army around this time, plus one Germanic type; fragments of legionary equipment are also particularly well represented.

Features of these discoveries bring to mind the items found at the neighbouring camp at Haltern, excavated since the beginning of the last century – but the widespread area of the battlefield finds shows that they are not to be linked to a camp. Only one structure was found during the excavations, a hastily constructed wall built by the Germans to entrap Roman troops who were drawn into a dead-end passage. We are thus dealing here with the only battlefield of which the remains – particularly ephemeral and unusual to the eyes of the archaeologists – have so far been identified and correctly analysed.

We shall have occasion to come back to the spectacular discoveries made at the end of the nineteenth century at the base of the *oppidum* at Alésia; many of the questions currently posed about the ancient finds could be tackled in a more scientific manner if one knew precisely where these finds were made. Taking into account that there are too many gaps in the reports of old excavations, we cannot say for certain that the weapons were lost during the siege; it could be that they were grouped together after the battle, either as trophies or for some religious purpose.

Military tombs

If so few finds are to be expected from excavating military camps, except in exceptional cases, what about military tombs? Will they yield finds of military arms and equipment? Sadly, no, as the Roman soldier – unlike his Gaulish counterpart – was usually buried without his kit, though historians are not in agreement as to why this should be the case. However, one small group of Early Empire tombs, of which more than a hundred are known in Western Europe, has provided Roman arms. Paradoxically, the reasons for this are uncertain. For some (Brenner, E. Bonis), they are witness to the ethnic origins of their occupants, as in later times deposits of arms can be found in Germanic areas; these writers therefore think that these tombs belong to German auxiliaries serving with Roman regulars. For others (H. Schönberger, A van Doorselaer), the presence of weapons with the deceased indicates that he was of high social rank and a hunter. These writers' reasoning is based on an exceptional document, the 'Testament of Lingon', in which the last wishes of the deceased stipulate that he is to be buried with his hunting arms– lances, swords and sabres. The reality is that several separate groupings can be defined, each doubtless corresponding to its owner's way of life, in different geographical areas.

In the major group in Northern Gaul (today's Belgium, Luxembourg and the Ardennes), the tombs containing arms are relatively modest and the weapons found in them – sword, lance or shield – do not seem to show any 'external signs of wealth'. In these cases, an

19 Roman weapons from a tomb at Verdun, Slovenia (after D. Breščak, 1989)

31

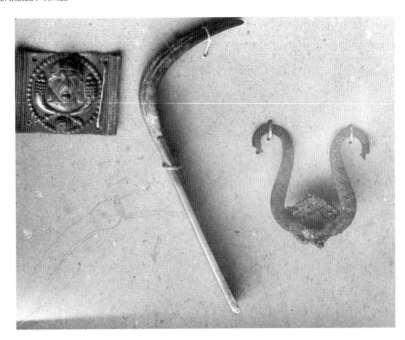

20 Plate from a *cingulum*, strigilis, cuirass hooks (*lorica hamata*) from the Chassenard tomb, shortly after its discovery in 1874 (tomb dated towards AD 40)

interpretation based on auxiliaries keeping their arms is often the more likely. In Central Gaul, on the other hand, where the tombs are more widely dispersed, there are 'privileged' burials in which weapons are accompanied by funerary objects. Three examples will suffice to show the problems presented by burials.

At Berry-Bouy in the Cher department a complete bronze toilet set, 10 amphorae of wine and a bronze *simpulum* clearly tell us that the owner had adopted the habits of the Roman upper classes; but the presence of a sword, lance and shield are not enough to prove that he was soldier (tomb dated *c*.20 BC). At Neuvy-Pailloux in the Indre department *c*.AD 40-50, there are the same indications of a Roman way of life: a decorated bronze washing kit and lamp. A sword and two lance-heads, poorly preserved, represented arms but there were also two bronze face-helmets, items which would not be used in hunting. On the grounds of these finds alone, should we say that their owner was a cavalry auxiliary?

A probable breakthrough comes with the burial at Chassenard in the Allier department, dated *c*.AD 40, where the deceased clearly showed ties with Rome. Not only was he buried with toilet objects (jug, cup, and two razors), the grave also contained four dies for striking coins, showing that he had held a responsible post in the Roman administration. Also present were a sword with *cingulum,* a chain mail vest, a face-helmet and a torque (a *donum militare?*), all of which could have belonged only to a soldier, perhaps a *decurion*.

The burials are therefore the exceptions if they yield weapons, and we are still waiting for answers to the questions which such equipment poses; so we shall in future use tomb evidence primarily to determine chronology and obtain well-preserved objects only.

Ritual deposits

During the period when Gaul was independent, ritual deposits were made containing thousands of weapons belonging to Gaulish faithfuls; the one at Gournay-sur-Aronde, at present the best known of these, was however abandoned before the end of the second century BC, and so far we know of no arms deposits which include Roman weapons. From the end of the first century BC, rural deposits usually take the form of a *fanum*, but these rarely contain arms, and we know of no instances where weapons which could have been used by Romans were included.

It is a different story when we turn to the deposits discovered since the nineteenth century in Scandinavian peat bogs. These 'burials' take the form of objects which were probably thrown into marshy areas or shallow water, perhaps as part of a tribal ceremony or when making vows. Hundreds of spear heads, swords, often complete with their suspension straps and belts, harness trappings and more have been recovered from the peat-bogs of Thorsberg, Nydam, Vimose, Kragehul, Illerup-Å and Ejsbøl. It is not always easy to distinguish items of Roman manufacture from those of Germanic origin, but in spite of this uncertainty, the Jutland peat-bog deposits are an irreplaceable source of information both for their early period – roughly third century – and subsequent periods.

It is significant that a third-century sword, complete in its wooden scabbard, was included in a ritual deposit in Western Gaul (Mézin, Lot-et-Garonne department). In temperate Europe, however, discoveries like this are exceptional towards the end of the Empire and disappear completely with the coming of Christianity.

We should also consider the origins of the numerous finds made since the eighteenth century in some river beds, as a very important part of our information on Roman armament, notably on large objects found complete, comes from such sources. All those regions where there was a sizeable number of travellers, such as the valley of the Saône, or which were close to frontiers, such as the Rhine and the Danube, have yielded large quantities of Roman arms. The earlier theory, that these were casual losses during river crossings or in battles, has now been discarded. Regardless of date, most of the swords found seem to have been put into the water complete in their scabbards, and we are talking here of a custom continued over a long period of time, from the end of the

21 Votive plaque describing the offering of a sword and a shield by a centurion (after M. Bishop and J. C. N. Coulston, 1993)

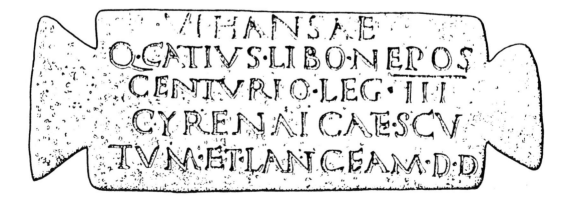

Prehistoric era to the Middle Ages. We tend today to see these deposits as part of religious or magical practices, and to think that they continued until recent times. There is also nothing surprising in the idea that Roman soldiers, perhaps of Celtic origin, judging from the nature of the deposits, should have observed these rites; in offering a helmet or a sword to a deity they were soliciting his protection in a coming campaign.

Could there have been a connection between these offerings to river-gods and the symbolic offerings found in numerous Gallo-Roman ritual deposits? If actual weapons are rarely found in temples, miniature reproductions of weapons are discovered frequently. The Flavier deposit at Mouzon in the Ardennes region turned up 578 roughly made reproductions of swords, lances and shields, forged from sheet metal. Were these imitations, mostly dating to the first century AD, connected with offerings of real weapons made on other sites? The rare inscriptions which have been found do not help very much; a bronze tablet, for instance, found at Sint Huibrichts Hern near Tongres describes the gift of a sword and a shield to the goddess Vihansa made by the centurion Q. Catius Libo Nepos of the Third Legion Cyrenaica (**21**).

Tomb memorials

If the items within a grave – even if placed there on purpose – are not always identifiable, the tomb memorial itself can in some cases serve as a reliable document from which to reconstruct a deceased Roman soldier. Some combine a statue, on occasion finely detailed, with a text describing not only his identity and his postings but also sometimes his service career. These individual posthumous portraits are naturally an outstanding item of documentary evidence.

On standing figures – the earliest (Italian) representation of this type appears to date from the Civil Wars – the soldier is characteristically portrayed from the front; on first century memorials from the Rhine area the infantryman is shown fully equipped, and the sculptors have faithfully reproduced all the details of his clothing and weapons. Some memorials, such as that of Annaius in the museum of Bad Kreuznach, have an almost photographic precision, even down to showing the details of sword scabbards and belts.

If the closeness of the sculptor to his subject guarantees the accuracy of the details, can we take these stone statues as a faithful reproduction of reality? Ordered by the soldier during his lifetime, or based on information from his close companions, the funerary statue obviously reflects personal choice or cultural traditions. It is certainly not by chance that the most splendid weapons appear on the memorials of auxiliaries and not of legionaries or even officers, as one might have supposed. All the same, from the third century AD we see a more civilised representation of the soldier, so we must add a touch of reality to total accuracy – the image we see is a reflection of the image which the deceased wished to leave to posterity.

Official commemorative memorials

Whether erected by victors to show their supremacy, to celebrate a victory, or in honour of an important person, official reliefs take different forms not only because the reasons for their erection vary, but also

22 Memorial to Largennius of the Second Legion (Strasbourg-Koenigshofen, photo Musées de Strasbourg)

because of the individual interpretations of those who built them. The iconography of a memorial may well be decided at the highest level, but the actual work will be carried out much lower down the chair of command, using local resources. One has only to compare, for instance, the reliefs on Trajan's Trophy at Adamklissi in Romania with the reliefs on Trajan's Column in Rome to be convinced of the sculptor's importance in not only the basics but in the details which interest us here.

Above all, these memorials were intended by their instigators to put across a message which would be immediately understood, and the resulting simplification can cause problems of interpretation for today's researchers, especially if the usual accompanying text is missing or if the monument has been damaged. This is the case, for example, with the

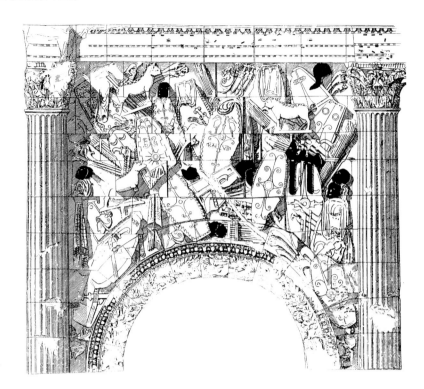

23 Cavalry equipment on a panel of arms on the Arch at Orange: five face-helmets, three Weiler-Guisborough helmets and a saddle (after R. Amy et al. 1962, modified)

arch at Orange in Southern France, erected in the reign of Tiberius (**23**); does it commemorate the suppression of the Gaulish uprisings in AD 21, as G.C. Picard proposes, or is it in honour of Germanicus for his pacification of Germany and Gaul, as P. Gros would have it?

When considering the first hypothesis we must look at the Roman weapons used by both sides. Tacitus (*Annals* III.43) states clearly that one-fifth of the 40,000 Gauls led by Sacrovir were armed 'like our legionaries', but why is there no reference on the Arch to the *crupellarii*, those armoured gladiators from Autun who are also expressly mentioned? In the second case there are similar difficulties – the German contingent, which must have been at least equal to the Gaulish participation, does not appear to be shown; and neither hypothesis properly explains why there is a panel on the Arch's northeast face showing the spoils of war taken by the navy, nor why there is a preponderance of cavalry equipment on the section showing weapons.

In short, taking just this one example, it is clear that we are lacking some vital clues, no doubt obvious to the contemporary population. Even those monuments which seem most clear, such as Trajan's Column, contain meanings and refer to common knowledge lost to us today. In fact, as with other sources, official commemorative reliefs must be subjected to close critical scrutiny before conclusions may be drawn; the images which they portray depend to a large extent on our knowledge of their historical contexts.

3 THE STRUCTURE OF THE ARMY

SCHOLARSHIP AND ARCHAEOLOGY

Our knowledge of the Roman army comes from a number of different sources. First, there is the textual evidence, some of which contains detailed descriptions of particular campaigns, occasionally including information on equipment or arms; however, ancient texts are more usually an indirect aid, supplying details of how such and such an army unit was used, based on its tactical capabilities. Second, we have inscriptions, which in some cases describe a military man's career, his postings and the ranks he held. Finally, we have archaeology, which with its various techniques – aerial photography, excavations of camps, reconstructions – can provide concrete examples of actual military equipment.

Some major reports have been prepared covering different parts of the Roman Empire – L. Le Roux, P. Holder on Britain, R. Cagnat, Y. Le Bohec on Africa, J. Lesquier on Egypt and more recently, P. Le Roux on Spain – but surprisingly, even in the most modern publications archaeology plays a minor role, and it is ancient texts and inscriptions which are more usually used as source material. As excavations increase in number, there is a growing division between historians and archaeologists, even though the two should logically complement each other. Misunderstandings probably arise because the historians see archaeology as supplying evidence to support their theories, whereas the findings of archaeologists may produce evidence which conflicts with theory, and may even disprove it, forcing a complete reappraisal, as was clearly seen by R. Davies, for example.

For this reason, M. Reddé has recently undertaken a global review of the military situation in first-century Gaul. It had been generally supposed, following Ritterling and on the basis of incorrectly interpreted texts, that Gaul, pacified from the end of the reign of Augustus, did not play a major role in the military history of the Roman West. The cohort based at Lyon, together with the proximity of the Rhine *limes,* from which troops could rapidly be drawn in case of emergency (such as the crisis and uprising in AD 21 for instance), should have been sufficient to maintain law and order. Reappraisal of both traditional dates and of previous hasty interpretations of insubstantial records (the case in Néris) forced the possibility of a more complex situation to be considered.

Thanks to the series of excavations at the site of Rocheroux (Aulnay, Charente-Maritime department) by D. and F. Tassaux, followed by P. Tronche, we now know that this camp, perhaps set up during the crisis of

AD 21, was occupied only for a few years, certainly less than ten. On the other hand, the second half of the first century saw the establishment and the relocation of several camps in the East and Centre-East, suggesting a distinctly more complex structure than previously had been thought; we will make no comment about the archaeology of the Caesarian conquest period, sidelined for nearly a hundred years but now active again, and which will certainly overturn a number of established ideas.

Military history has thus reached a turning point: by taking on board archaeologically-established facts it now has the chance to make the most significant advances since the beginning of the last century. There can be no doubt that this challenge will be taken up by the current generation, and as we wait for this to happen, let us recall some of the more firmly based facts.

From the time of Augustus onwards, the Roman army as a whole was organised into legions supported by more or less equal numbers of auxiliaries – but in certain regions the army could consist solely of auxiliaries. Before reviewing the different numbers known to be on the ground during the Empire, let us look at the overall organisation of the armed forces, and how it evolved after the Republican period.

THE REPUBLICAN ARMY

In the beginning, the Roman army was merely a group of citizens with spare time and independent means responding to a threat from an outside force, and there was only a small State levy, which was reduced over time. One of the first steps towards a 'classic' army came at the end of the fourth century BC, during the course of the ten-year war which culminated in 396 BC with the capture of Veii, Rome's Etruscan rival, by M. Furius Camillus. The total strength, 4000 to 6000 men, was composed of three groups – those fully equipped, those without cuirasses and those without leg-guards. To offset this reduction in armour, it was no doubt at this time that the typical hoplite round shield was replaced by the *scutum*, a long oval shield.

However, Rome had not yet seen the end of her troubles in Italy; immediately after the weakening of the Etruscans, the Gauls made an attack on the Po valley, and Rome herself was threatened in 390 BC. These events without doubt hastened the development of the Roman army, which until then had followed the somewhat rigid tactic of the phalanx. As a first step, the phalanges were split into more flexible maniples, whose soldiers formally adopted the *scutum*, and a lighter javelin replaced the heavy lance used by the hoplites. In 362 BC the Roman army comprised two legions, which became four in 311 BC, originating a military organisation which was to last as long as the Roman era itself.

Generally speaking, at the beginning of the Republic the hierarchy of the soldiers was based on their own financial means, as were their arms and equipment. In the absence of any administrative structure to maintain a permanent army, troops were disbanded after each conflict; every citizen between the ages of 17 and 46 was liable

---

The Republican Army based on forces brought together in 225 BC by the Romans to oppose the Gauls:

As well as the Consuls, four Roman legions, each with 5200 infantry and 300 cavalry, joined in the campaign; they were also supported by troops of auxiliaries, bringing the total force to 30,000 infantry and 2000 cavalry . . . [Details of additional troops attached to this force to protect various points in the threatened area]. . . In this way the forces involved in the defence of Rome rose to 150,000 infantry and nearly 6000 cavalry, and taking into account those prepared to take up arms [against the Gauls] the number of Romans plus their allies exceeded 700,000 infantry and nearly 70,000 cavalry.

(Polybius, II.24)

Even though we are seeing here one of the few known calculations of the Republican army, the total number of troops reached by Polybius appears to be erroneous. For a critique of the figures and their possible different interpretations, see F. W. Walbank, *A Historical Commentary on Polybius,* Oxford, 1957-6.

---

for service, serving for a maximum of 16 years. The small allowances paid to those enlisted in no way covered the losses suffered by the soldier through being removed from his normal occupation, be he farmer or businessman.

The various campaigns launched in the second and third centuries BC necessitated prolonged absences in theatres of combat further away from Rome. Because of this, it became ever more difficult to enlist troops for long periods of service, as those citizens who had already participated in one campaign made every effort to avoid being called up for a second. At the end of the second century BC, at the time of the second war against the Numidians, not enough recruits could be raised, the situation became critical, and Rome had to review its entire military organisation. This was to be the object of Marius' reforms.

A consul of plebeian origin, responsible for military affairs, Caius Marius (156-86 BC) adopted the only plan which could ensure a comfortable reserve of fresh troops, and extended the approach which had first been set in motion at the beginning of the second century (Polybius, VI.19.2) and later implemented by C. Gracchus about 123-2 BC: he extended recruitment to every citizen, regardless of his financial means. Although it is questioned by some historians, the most probable date for this essential reform seems to be 107 BC.

From this point poorer citizens flocked to join the army, showing a radically different attitude from their predecessors who could not wait to return to civilian life after a campaign; these new recruits, far from seeing the army as a disruption to their normal lives, saw it as a steady job, or even as a life-enhancing permanent career. The professional army was thus launched, based on egalitarian principles formed following the decision taken after the Social Wars to accord Roman citizenship to all citizens south of the Po. So the previous distinction between *legio* and *ala* (this latter formed from 'allies of Rome') was ended, and the corps of *velites* and the legionary cavalry were disbanded.

In addition to its direct impact on recruitment, the new military policy had a further, unforeseen, effect on army morale – in future, every legion would be building up its own personal history and devel-

24 The military diploma from Geiselprechting, dated mid-June AD 64, sheets 3 and 4 (photo Prähist. Staatsammlung, Munich). The systematic study of the military diplomas given to soldiers at the end of their service (*missio*) enable us to follow a military career in detail, and to learn of the movements of the different units in which the men served. The accompanying lists of witnesses are also a valuable source of information for students of names

oping its own idiosyncrasies. The new legions were given their own emblems, together with eagle standards to symbolise their fidelity; individually numbered under Julius Caesar, little by little they took individual names as well, which enhanced their *esprit de corps*. In a future section we shall look in more detail at the indirect effects of the 'Marian' reformation on military arms and equipment.

The military organisation continued to evolve throughout the first century BC. To relieve the army of the task of organising baggage trains, which slowed it down, Marius made the soldiers responsible for carrying their own effects. In the first half of the first century BC, soldiers received only a symbolic payment, hardly enough to buy their food, and they relied on booty captured from defeated enemies, a situation which Caesar remedied by doubling the basic pay at the start of the Civil Wars. At the same time, the very structure of the troops was completely reorganised: the number of *triarii* was increased to equal that of the *hastati* and *principes*, and the legion increased its speed of deployment through forming up in one, two, three or four ranks as the occasion demanded. Each soldier would in future be armed with a sword and a *pilum*, and the maniple was changed from being a tactical unit into simply an accounting unit when counting strengths of forces. Under Caesar, the cohort comprised six centuries, each of about sixty men, commanded by a centurion supported by an *optio* (second in command chosen by the centurion), a *signifer* or standard-bearer and a *cornicen* or bugler. The legion was made up of ten cohorts, each of approximately 400 men. These figures represent the theoretical norms and naturally changed as the circumstances required; for instance when Caesar embarked seven legions at Brindisium to challenge Pompey, he had only 15,000 troops, barely more than 2000 men per legion. (*B Civ.* III.2)

THE IMPERIAL LEGIONS

With a strength of the some 5500 men, the legion at the beginning of the Empire hardly differed from that under Caesar, and was strictly hierarchical; the basic unit was the maniple, about 160 men, or the century of around 80 men. Centuries were grouped into cohorts of about 500 legionaries.

In the second half of the first century, the fighting strength of the first cohort in each legion was increased to 800 men, formed into five centuries instead of six. Each legion also had a cavalry squadron of about 120 men, who acted as scouts and messengers between the various units during a campaign.

Proof of Roman citizenship was always demanded of any man who appled to become a legionary, as in the case of recruits from the Narbonne area and Spain when they fought in Germany and on the Western frontiers. In the Eastern Empire, however, citizenship was accorded more slowly, making recruitment more difficult, but this problem was solved when it was agreed to give every recruit citizenship when he joined a legion.

THE AUXILIARIES

The origin of auxiliary troops lies in Republican times, when Rome, following Greek tradition, started to call for a growing number of mercenaries. Towards the end of the Republic, Roman legions were frequently supported in campaigns outside Italy by levies of local troops also taken from among Rome's allies (*socii*), or from defeated kingdoms. Marius' reform, which disbanded the legionary cavalry, led Rome to exclusively use auxiliaries as mounted troops; from then on, they continued to develop. This was particularly the case in long drawn-out conflicts such as the Gallic War, in which Caesar called on a growing number of auxiliaries from different origins: Gauls (e.g.

25 (top) Tile stamped with the name of the IIIrd Legion Italica: Eining (photo Prähist. Staatsammlung, Munich). (bottom) Tile stamped with the name of the VIIIth Legion Augusta: Néris-les- Bains (?) (Photo Musée de la Civilisation Gallo- Romaine, Lyon)

41

III.18), Numidians (II.7,10,24), Spaniards (V.26), slingers from the Balearic Islands (II.7,10,19), and Cretan archers (II.7,10,19). Only in Book VII (13), that is to say in 52 BC, does Caesar take on 400 Germans, whom some saw as a personal guard although they were in fact auxiliary troops (and they were discharged after the Gallic War began). A little later in the same year, Caesar levied further troops of auxiliary cavalry in Germany, as the German races were especially renowned for their horsemanship (VII.65).

The most marked characteristic of the auxiliary troops in the Roman army was their capability in specific specialist areas, each group usually fighting with its own arms and in its own way. For example, in 52 BC the Romans were in difficulties outside Gergovia (*B Gall.* VII.50) and called on a detachment of Aedui for support. Auxiliaries were widely used in the Civil War, and fought as infantry cohorts and cavalry squadrons in the army of Augustus. Their importance continued to increase, and it is known that there were auxiliaries recruited even in Italy, some of which perhaps included Roman citizens.

Alongside the auxiliaries, and initially at least at a lower level in the military hierarchy, the Roman army also used ethnic groups which were neither part of a legion nor organised into squadrons or cohorts. These were the renowned *numeri* or *gentiles* recruited on the frontiers of the Empire. They played an increasingly prominent role among the fighting troops, and can to be seen from the end of the first (or early second) up to the third century as a major factor in the barbarianisation of the Roman army. These groups of 'natives' were recruited from widely differing backgrounds, but they possessed a common feature in that they were well-respected for their equipment and fighting techniques. M. Speidel has clearly shown through 'snapshots' of Moorish soldiers at three different times – the transition from BC to AD (Strabo, 17.3.7), the start of the second century (Trajan's Column) and the end of the second century (the column at Neapolis in Palestine) – an excellent example of the retention of a tribal style which was respected throughout its history by the Romans; they

---

The Roman army in Gaul

[The Gauls accepted the Roman yoke] not out of weakness of character or lack of valour, this people which had endured a 24 year war for their liberty, but rather because they were shocked and astonished by the power of the Romans and their self-assurance which contributed to their success even more than their weapons. This is why they obeyed 1200 soldiers, they who had almost the same number of actual towns.'

(Josephus, BJ, II.373)

This extract from a speech by Josephus was intended to show the Jews the wide-ranging power of the Romans before they rebelled against them, and ties in with contemporary inscriptions and a passage in Tacitus concerning two cohorts, the XVIIth and XVIIIth, which were based in Lyon. However, whether he was unaware of the real situation in Gaul in the last quarter of the first century, or whether he conveniently 'forgot' it in order to make his speech more impressive, Josephus makes no mention of several camps in Gaul which have been revealed by archaeology, such as those at Arlaines (Aisne department) or at Mirebeau (Côte-d'Or department).

Description of a Roman army in AD 69

There he [Titus] found his father [Vespasian] with his two legions – the most famous ones, the Fifth and the Second – together with the Fifteenth which he had just brought. Following these units were 28 cohorts plus five cohorts and a cavalry wing from Caesarea and five further cavalry wings from Syria, also newly arrived. Ten of these cohorts each comprised 1000 infantry and 120 cavalrymen. Strong reinforcements had also been furnished by the kings Antiochus, Agrippa and Sohemos, who had each sent 2000 infantry archers and 1000 cavalrymen; for his part, Malchos the Arab sent 1000 cavalry and 5000 infantry, most of them archers; counting the kings' own troops, these additions amounted to a force of 60,000 men, infantry and cavalry. This is without taking into account a very large number of valets and servants who, although they could not be counted as combatants because their duty was to look after their masters in peacetime, nevertheless shared the dangers of battle, so much so that they ceded first place to no-one in their enthusiasm and devotion to their masters.

(Josephus, BJ, III. 65-9)

The order of march in Titus' army in AD 69

In this advance by Titus into the enemy's territory, the kings' contingents led the way, accompanied by all their auxiliary corps, followed by the pioneers and surveyors and the generals' baggage. After the troops responsible for guarding the baggage came Titus himself and his elite force, notably the lancers, followed by the legionary cavalry. Behind them came the war machines, the tribunes, the senior soldiers and the cohort prefects; following these were the standard bearers around the Eagle, preceded by the trumpeters. Finally came the main column, six abreast. The legionary domestic servants followed, in front of the legionary baggage train, and at the very rear were the mercenaries under the watchful eye of a rearguard.

(Josephus, BJ, V.47)

always wear a short tunic, their hair in plaits and ride bareback on small long-tailed horses.

Even if these troops did not benefit from the same status as the auxiliaries (and so received lower pay, etc.), there is no doubt that their growing importance contributed to the cultural mix, shown also by its arms and equipment, of the whole Roman army as it developed.

THE CAMP

From the time of the Republic, the design and layout of a Roman camp was rigidly and precisely defined, for a number of practical reasons. By having a standard layout, a camp could be built more rapidly – essential when in enemy-held territory – and each troop knew its appointed place within it and where to find the other units and services such as command posts, workshops and horse-lines. The standard layout also made it easier for visitors to a camp to find the equipment or unit for which they were looking. Each soldier also knew at all times where he should be and what he should be doing, and Polybius during the second century BC correctly underlined the saving of time and increased efficiency gained by this careful organisation. The Greeks, on the other hand, always tried to take advantage of the natural

26 Off-duty legionaries in front of a camp; note reinforcements on the helmets hanging from their shoulders (Trajan's Column, photo D. A. I., Rome)

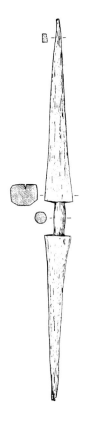

27 Oak element of a *palisade* (?) from the 1971 excavations at Welzheim (after J. Beeser, 1979)

lie of the land when setting up camp, but noted that the Romans did not shirk the formidable task of building a new camp every day, complete with earthworks and palisades. This work, however, gave the Romans not only the benefit of greater security but also the satisfaction of seeing a routine operation carried out to perfection.

The camp was a fundamental part of Roman strategy at this point, and famous generals were quick to seize on easy victories as providing time to devote themselves to improving its defences. The basic layout hardly varied from the time of Polybius onwards (though we know from archaeological researches that they were some regional variations due to the local terrain), and comprised a quadrilateral with rounded corners, encircled by a ditch and a palisade on the top of the banked-up earth excavated from it. This improvised enclosure had four gaps or gateways through which to bring in wood and water, and which were wide enough to make a sortie in any direction.

Square-section wooden stakes found on a number of military sites (**27**) have been interpreted as being part of a 'collapsible kit' which could be used to form a palisade or, if used separately, to make a defensive *chevaux-de-frise* in front of the entrances, for instance. The two usual types of defences for a camp gateway were the *titulus* (frontal wall) and the *clavicula*, an angled defence which forced the attackers to expose their left flank; both demanded a collapsible but sturdy palisade-type structure. In the absence of any explicit written documentary evidence on how these stakes were used, however, their precise function is still a matter for conjecture.

Within the camp, tents were probably erected in the same pattern as was used in permanent stone-built camps. Two main axes, starting from the gateways, crossed at the centre of the camp; one of them, the *via praetoria*, led from the gateway of the same name to the *porta decumana*

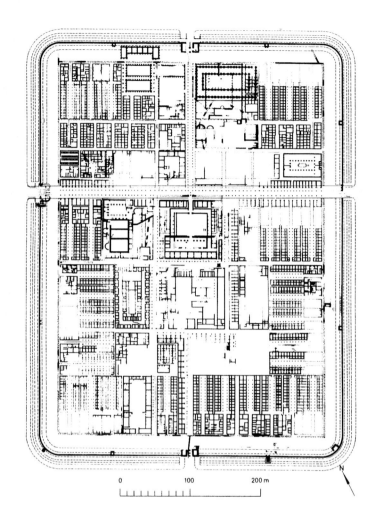

28 The legionary camp at Neuß (after C. Koenen)

(under the Republic it passed close to the 'tenth' maniples); the other, at right angles to it, was the *via principalis*, interrupted at midpoint by the camp's central headquarters, which usually comprised the *principia* and the *praetorium,* back to back. The tribunes' quarters ran the length of the *via principalis*, and the surrounding areas were occupied to a standard pattern well-known to all the troops – the soldiers' tents, the sick-bay and the workshops, together with all the other essential units and services needed for the communal functioning of a military force. Running along the inside face of the palisade was a clear space 30m wide, used for parking baggage trains and heavy armament, and serving as a partial protection against incoming arrows and missiles.

Our knowledge of the tents used on campaigns has increased considerably in recent years thanks to archaeological excavations, and we now know their basic design and construction. The regulation tent (*papilio*) was composed of 25 cattle hides and could accommodate eight men and their equipment, with enough headroom inside to enable a man to stand up.

The earthworks constructed when setting up a campaign camp were not so developed as those of permanent camps, and from the second half

29 Reconstruction of a regulation eight-man tent (after C. van Driel-Murray, 1991)

45

of the first century AD – or a little later, in Britain – such camps were rebuilt in stone, turning into veritable towns, with warehouses, shops and often their own public baths. Civilian communities grew up alongside these camps to accommodate the soldiers' women and children, and other traders attracted by the military presence. The camp at Neuss, 430x570m, is the best known Western example of a permanent camp (**28**).

THE MILITARY CAREER

Throughout antiquity the army always offered an individual a career, and one which became ever more attractive as time passed. Enlistment attracted those to whom the life of adventure combined with danger and the possibility of substantial rewards appealed, and Livy relates a typical career followed by a Republican-period volunteer. Spurius Ligustinus enrolled in 200 BC and fought with the army in Macedonia for two years against Phillip; catching the eye of his superiors during his third year, he was promoted to centurion in the tenth maniple of the *hastati*. When his unit returned to Italy in 195 BC and was disbanded, he at once signed on under the command of the consul Marcus Portius who was off to Spain, and he was ranked centurion in the first century of *hastati*. In 191 BC he enlisted again, this time to fight against the Aetolians and King Antiochus; after the Roman victory, he was posted back to Italy with the rank of centurion to the first century of *principes*. Two further years of service in overseas legions were followed by two more in Spain in 181-0 BC, where his bravery won him a place in the Triumph celebrated in Rome by Q. Fulvius Flaccus. Four times named as *primus pilus*, in other words legionary centurion, Spurius Ligustinus could look back on 34 awards and decorations and six civic crowns when he retired at the age of 50 after 22 years of army service.

From Caesar onwards, and particularly under his immediate successors, what the military career lost in variety, it recouped in security. The army became an administrative organisation in which the soldier learned a trade which could be, for those who were suitable, highly technical and so useful when he rejoined civilian life. For example, maintaining and repairing military 'artillery' – catapults such as *ballistas* and onagers – involved learning about precise carpentry, the principles of pulleys and the fabrication of metal components, all valuable skills in civilian life in such constructions as cranes, wind- and watermills and presses for grapes and olives. The Roman naval services trained a man to be a seaman and perhaps even a navigator, and gave him a familiarity with pumps. The military medical services, introduced after the Republican era (during which soldiers had learned to suffer with fortitude), were not slow to develop, and from the Principate onwards permanent camps had their own *valetudinarium*, in effect a simple hospital.

In spite of its hazards, the soldier's life was a social and intellectual introduction to other societies and countries, even if his profession required him to conquer them. Garrisoned far from his homeland, the soldier would discover a multitude of unsuspected situations, and few other careers, perhaps with the exception of the travelling trader, could so widen a man's horizons. Whatever the circumstances, often admitted-

30 Republican silver denarii (82 and 49 BC) showing a legionary eagle between two standards marked H and P respectively (*hastati* and *principes*) (after L. Keppie, 1984)

ly brutal, of encountering foreign societies, when the soldier later retired he could pass on what he had seen and learnt abroad to friends and family.

For the higher social classes, a military career was the swiftest – and often most spectacular – way of climbing up the social ladder. A proconsul basking in the glory of a long political career, Cicero discovered this to his cost when the young Octavian, the adopted son of Caesar but, more importantly, a military hero who was also one of the Triumvirate, had him proscribed and assassinated in 43 BC. The *cursus honorum* of a lucky soldier might start under the protection of a powerful patron, but it was taking part in foreign military victories that opened the doors of the highest positions of power in Rome.

INSIGNIA, BADGES AND STANDARDS

The standard was at the heart of Roman military tactics, not only serving as a rallying point to enable soldiers to regroup during the changing phases of a battle in response to rallying cries and trumpet calls, but also symbolising the pride of a unit and the honour of Rome. Because of this, to lose a standard was the ultimate disgrace for a defeated cohort or legion. As a corollary, the standard-bearer (and in the first place the *aquilifer*) played a considerable part in battle; he was the man who led hesitant troops forward, and many a dangerous moment was turned to Roman advantage by a heroic standard-bearer (e. g. *B Gall*, IV. 25). Those memorials which have come down to us testify to the importance attached by the army to these men and their duties, which were as thankless as they were prestigious.

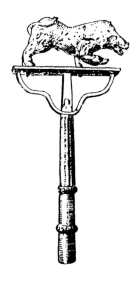

31 Roman standard with boar (British Museum: after Daremberg and Saglio)

The adoption of the eagle as the symbol of the legion took place under Marius, and according to Pliny the Elder, who dates its adoption as 104 BC, previous symbols such as the lion, minotaur, horse and boar were dropped; instead, each legion had its own eagle. This did not mean other standards of lesser importance disappeared; silver coins (*denarii*) struck in 82 and 49 BC show an eagle between two standards which carry the letters 'H' and 'P' respectively, which can almost certainly be interpreted as referring to the *hastati* and the *principes* (**30**). Such standards, decorated with discs and other symbols, but not crowned with a token animal as they were in the time of Polybius, were used throughout the Principate. Several later references, such as that by Ammianus Marcellinus to the loss of a standard in Persia recovered in AD 363, clearly demonstrate the importance attached by the army to its standards throughout its long existence.

Because of their symbolic importance, standards were very rarely lost, let alone abandoned, in circumstances which would enable us to find them today. We only know what legionary standards looked like from the many illustrations of them on coins and sculptures, and we can reconstruct their appearance and interpret their symbolism only by drawing on a range of sources. The bull, for instance, the zodiacal sign associated with Venus, the legendary founder of the *gens* Julia, was adopted by legions founded or restored by Caesar. The capricorn identifies the legions created by Augustus, and legions involved in a naval victory might portray a dolphin, or even Neptune, on their standard.

Winning back the eagle

Mallovendus . . . said that one of Varus' eagles was buried in a nearby wood, guarded by only a handful of men. A detachment of troops was sent at once to lure the natives forward, while another detachment went round behind and dug up the soil. Both detachments carried out their tasks successfully.

(Tacitus, Ann., II.25. Episode during Germanicus' campaign in Germany)

32 Considered until recently to be a legionary standard, this bronze Capricorn, found near Wiesbaden, is now thought to be a chariot mount (photo Röm.-Germ. Zentralmuseum, Mainz)

The signal of the *vexillum*

Seeing a band of armed men approaching, the standard bearer of the cohort accompanying Galba (said to be Atilius Vergilio) tore off the Galba medal and threw it to the ground; at this signal, all the soldiers showed their support for Otho.

Tacitus, Hist. I.41: The assassination of Galba)

33 Reconstruction of the *vexillum* found in Egypt (Limesmuseum Aalen, photo Würtembergisches Landesmuseum Stuttgart)

We know from reliefs that awards made to a military unit were placed on its standards; a crown would be placed in the talons of an eagle, or on its wings, and *phalerae*, torques and bracelets, tassels and fringes were placed above each other on the standard's shaft.

The *vexillum*, the emblem carried by cohorts and *alae* when the main troops stayed in camp, was, as its name implies, a small square of cloth, attached to a lance point by a crosspiece; on it, in brightly painted colours or in gold, were the symbols and perhaps the name of the unit. The imperial *vexillum* had heavy gold fringes and usually two straps also laden with pendants.

The exceptionally dry climate of Egypt has preserved a *vexillum* almost intact, published by Rostovtzeff in 1913 and 1942. It is roughly square, 47cm high by 50cm wide, and still has the transverse piece of wood in a pocket at its top so that it could be suspended from the tip of a staff; its edges were hemmed, and the lower edge must have had a fringe. Bright red, this unique object has even retained its painted decoration, enabling it to be dated with certainty to the early part of the second century AD. Four angled motifs in the corners frame a Victory on a globe, who holds a triumphal wreath in her right hand and a palm frond in her left (**34**).

During English excavations in Egypt in the late 1980s, a second *vexillum* was found, roughly similar in size to the first and made from fairly coarse material. This flag is much less elaborately decorated, with a simple cruciform motif based on a geometrical pattern or a floral design.

Towards the end of the first century AD, or the beginning of the second, a special form of standard appears, with a design very probably

34 (above) *Vexillum* found in Egypt (after M. Rostovtzeff, 1942)

35 *Vexillarius* from Dura-Europos, second/third century (after M. Rostovtzeff, 1942)

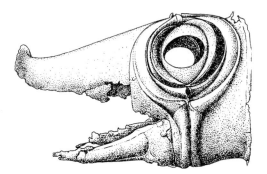

36 All the traditional metalworking skills and vivid fantasies of Celtic design are to be seen in this bronze head found at Deskford in Scotland and for many years considered to be a *carnyx* or ceremonial trumpet: current thinking now inclines to the view that it is the standard of a cohort (drawing after MacGregor, 1976, photo National Museum of Antiquities of Scotland, Edinburgh)

37 Bronze sheetmetal *draco* from Niederbieber, third century AD (photo Röm.-Germ. Zentralmuseum, Mainz)

49

38 Military standards, decorations and mascots (?) on the memorial of M. Pompeius (after A. von Domaszewski, 1885)

39 Silver disc from the standard found at Niedebieber: emperor (Tiberius or Caligula) in front of pile of German weapons (photo Röm.-Germ. Zentralmuseum, Mainz)

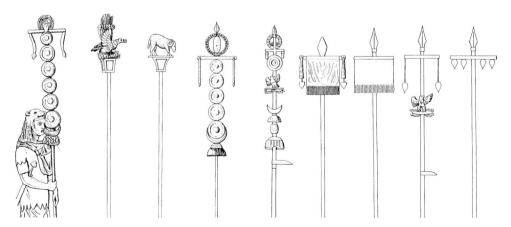

40 Reconstruction of Roman standards (after P. Filtzinger, 1975)

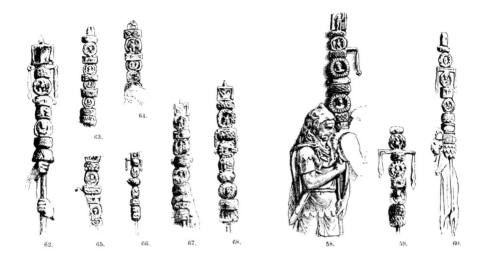

41 Carved standards as represented on various memorials (after A. von Domaszewski, 1885)

taken from the Parthians or the Sarmatians: the *draco*. Thanks to several written references, confirmed by a discovery at the Niederbieber site, we know that this had a sheet-metal bronze head to which was attached a sort of cloth sleeve, which billowed out behind it like the waving body of a monster when it was carried on horseback. These *dracones* grew in popularity during the third and particularly the fourth centuries and became the emblem of every cohort.

Because they were highly treasured at the time, the actual number of legionary standards which has come down to us is very small, and museum examples are of *signa minora*, small objects which are sometimes difficult to identify with certainty. For instance, the Capricorn found by a Roman road north of Wiesbaden, long thought to be the top part of a legionary standard, is now considered to be a chariot mount. On the other hand, resulting from the final destruction of the Niederbieber camp in AD 259 or 260, two typical components of a legionary standard have come to light, and the body of a *signifer* was found in close proximity. These two objects clearly reveal the appearance of what could be a third-century standard; the first is the left-hand portion of a silver plaque with the unit's name, COH. V (II RAET), the seventh cohort of the Raetians, and the second is a disc, also in silver, which by its style dates from the first century AD. We can recognise, trampling on Gaulish and German spoils of war, the figure of an emperor who could only be Tiberius or Germanicus. Taking into account the lapse of time, this disc must have been seen by the cohort based at Niederbieber as much a representation of the imperial image as a specific reference to a Julio-Claudian event.

Much more plentiful in excavations and museums are objects described since the early 1900s as the standards of *beneficiaries*; these objects, of different types and sizes, are to be seen represented on carved reliefs and funerary memorials, and there can be no doubt as to their identities. The *beneficiaries* were special units in the Roman army with a specific, generally non-combatant, function, such as administrators, police and transport specialists, and they were issued with standards whose point was more slender and often longer than a normal

42 Fragment of silver standard of the Seventh Cohort of Raetians COH. V (II. RAET) found at Niederbieber (photo Röm.-Germ. Zentralmuseum, Mainz)

43 Beneficiary's standard from Ehl (Bas-Rhin) (Wiesbaden Museum, photo Röm.-Germ. Zentralmuseum, Mainz)

44 Beneficiary's lance found at Künzing (photo Prähist. Staatsammlung, Munich)

lance-head and had a characteristic transverse cut in it. The most impressive of these, found many years ago at Ehl (department of the Bas-Rhin) reached a length of 93cm, and lengths of 40-60cm are not exceptional for these objects, some of which have on occasion been confused with real lance-heads because of their simplicity of design. They may in addition have adorned the tops of some minor standards such as *vexilla*. Some of these perforated lance-heads also have two apertures side by side which might have served to secure a horizontal mount or a *tabula ansata*.

One series of artefacts, for many years of unknown purpose, consists of a large perforated bronze disc with two round holes, around which are fixed various religious objects. They were at first identified as standards; E. Künzl now suggests that they should be considered as connected with religious ceremonial rites foreign to any military context, and that the two apertures are a wish for protection against the 'evil eye'.

Other items of military equipment may also have served as focal points in battle. When the Gauls made their surprise attack during the battle of the Sambre, Caesar saw that the soldiers who were building the camp did not have time to put on their helmets, take off their shield covers or hoist their standards (*insignia*), and it is thought that the cockades found attached to some helmets (though removed when on the march) helped the troops to find their comrades more easily in a battle.

AWARDS AND DECORATIONS (*DONA MILITARIA*)

As in all armies, one component of a soldier's heroism is his desire to receive due recognition for his bravery. Although promotion in the Roman army came primarily through years of loyal service, a soldier's status in his unit and the charisma of the senior officers were based also on their bravery and individual acts of courage.

Accounts of a particular action, as recounted by Caesar for instance, who frequently mentions individual soldiers by name (often posthumously), show that outstanding feats of arms were recognised in front of the whole unit. Fundamental to the attitude of the Roman soldier, such recognition compensated to some degree for the severe punishments which were meted out for any dereliction of duty.

Under the Republic, loot and booty were at the heart of the soldier's pay. While a victorious general could certainly ensure that a major part went to the bravest, there could be difficulties. The booty might be small or of low value, for example, and although the reward system persisted under the Principate, there was a growing recognition of the need for a definite system which would reward years of service and rank, as well as individual exceptional acts.

It is significant that several of the *dona militaria*, whose symbolic value was intended to replace the actual value of booty, did in fact consist of items that could be captured in battle. Torcs, for instance, the symbol of the Gauls, perhaps recalled the occasion in 225 BC when the victorious consul returned to Rome following the battle of Telamone and decorated the Capitol with the standards and gold torcs taken from the defeated

Pay parade in Jerusalem, AD 70

As was their custom, the infantry, having taken their weapons from the storage chests, advanced in their full equipment, and the cavalry led forward their magnificently-adorned horses. A large space in front of the city sparkled with gold and silver, and nothing pleased the Romans more than this sight, but it terrified their enemies.

Josephus, BJ V.350-1

A parade – Vitellius enters Rome

In front of the eagles marched the prefects of the camp, the tribunes and the centurions of the first rank, all dressed in white; the other centurions marched with their respective centuries, bearing their arms proudly and showing off their decorations; as for the other ranks, they sparkled with phalerae and neck torcs'.

Tacitus, Hist. II.49

Military rewards : honourable decorations not recognised by the Germans

Flavius described what he had received: an increase in pay, a torc and a crown, plus other military gifts, whereupon Arminius mocked him for becoming a slave so cheaply.

Tacitus, Annals, II.9

Written towards the end of the first century, relating an event which took place during the reign of Tiberius.

45 (left) The Bonn Monument: C. Marius, cavalryman in the Legio I Germanica, with carved representations of all his military awards. He is wearing a harness with *phalerae*, and a second harness with nine *phalerae* and two bracelets is shown below; there are also two torques in the upper corners of the monument (photo Rheinisches Landesmuseum Bonn)

46 Details of the decorations received by M. Caelius who died in AD 9: torques and *phalerae* (photo Rheinisches Landesmuseum, Bonn)

47 Four of the silver *phalerae* from Lauersfort (photo Röm.-Germ. Zentralmuseum, Mainz)

49 Chalcedony phalera, first century, mediaeval mount, Musée des Thermes de Cluny (after M. Feugère, 1989)

48 Chalcedony phalera of a chubby child; provenance unknown (photo British Museum)

50 Harness of *phalerae*. 12 *phalerae*, probably in chalcedony (see buckle on left) surrounding a figure of Victory; memorial from Ribiera, period of Augustus (photo Soprint. Arch. Emilia-Romagna)

51 Silver centrepiece of a harness of military awards found near Pola in Istria (after J. Evans, in Archaeologia, 1886)

Gauls (Polybius, II.31), and bracelets (*armillae*) and *phalerae* come into the same category. The crown, too, of which the *dona militaria* included various types relevant to the heroic action performed, was also of classical origin, and some awards were based on Roman arms such as the lance (*hasta*) or the ensign (*vexillum*). From the end of the first century BC there was a recognised list of awards, including:

corona obsidionalis	siege crown
corona civica	civic crown
corona navalis (classica, rostrata)	naval crown
corona muralis	walls crown
corona vallaris	ramparts crown
corona aurea	gold crown
hasta pura	ceremonial lance
vexillum	pennant
torques	torcs (Gallic)
armilla	bracelet
phalera	round decoration (harness)
patella	small cup
corniculum	small bugle

52 Blue glass medallion showing Drusus and his sons: perhaps a military decoration? (Röm.-Germ. Museum, Cologne)

With the exception of the *corona civica* these awards reflect the recipient's rank, and only senior officers could hope to receive the highly prestigious *corona aurea*. Below the rank of centurion the most frequently awarded *dona militaria* were torcs, *armillae* and *phalerae*.

Worn on parades and no doubt also on important public occasions, decorations were attached to a sort of leather harness, frequently depicted on funerary memorials. It is very rare to find objects in excavations which can be identified with certainty as *dona militaria*, and the most complete find known is the Lauersfort *phalerae*, which consists of ten round plaques and a crescent moon shape. More frequent are carved reliefs depicting nine or twelve *phalerae* carefully arranged on their backing.

An Augustan period relief from Rubiera (Reggio Emilia) has however enabled us to identify as *dona militaria* some of the chalcedony objects – circular medallions with two vertical apertures on the back

53 Bronze *phalera* (military decoration ?) showing head of a putto (photo Röm.-Germ. Museum, Cologne)

54 Reconstruction of an *optio* with his military decorations (Ermine Street Guard, 1992)

55 The torque from the Chassenard tomb: military award or ethnic artefact? (Musée des Antiquités Nationales, Saint-Germain-en-Laye)

and a representation of a chubby faced child on the front – which are fairly common in museums, but whose purpose until now was unknown. On the Rubiera relief, these *phalerae* are arranged around a diamond-shaped plaque, probably metal in the original, decorated with a Victory. A similar item, in silver, found near Pola in Istria around 1855, almost certainly refers to the conquest of Britain. This shows a Victory erecting a trophy with the words *devic(ta) Britta(nia)* above a figure of Mars; the several rings around this plaque must have been fixed to straps supporting the actual decorations.

Apart from these finds, *dona militaria* are only rarely identified in excavations, but this rarity stems only from the difficulty of distinguishing between functional objects and symbolic rewards; a fragment of a silver twisted bracelet, found at the camp of Aulnay-de-Saintonge, could thus be part of a Tiberian period *armilla*, though one cannot be certain. Similarly, F. Beck sees the torque from the tomb at Chassenard (department of Allier) as a military decoration rather than an ethnic artefact.

The Roman system of *dona militaria*, derived from Republican customs, operated particularly during the first and second centuries AD; after the reign of Severus (AD 193-211) it fell into disuse, replaced during the

third century by internal promotion and, more importantly, by monetary awards. It was only much later, under the reign of Julian in AD 363, that we start to find once more references to the *dona militaria,* obviously inspired by the old ways; but with the exception of a few fleeting reappearances, rewards in the High Empire style did not survive the changes in thought and opinion which are characteristic of the later period.

56 Bronze *lituus* from Saalburg (Rheinisches Landesmuseum Bonn, photo G. Füssenich-Hintzen)

MUSIC AND MUSICAL INSTRUMENTS

'Military music' in the Roman army was primarily a means of passing commands to the troops, as in modern armies; but this practical aspect, and the limited number of instruments used, should not overshadow the extensive penetration of such music into civilian and religious life as well. At entertainments and public spectacles – circus, theatre, and even amphitheatre – as well as at home, the Roman citizen had plenty of opportunities to hear music.

57 Reconstruction of a *cornu* (after P. Barton, 1987)

In the Roman army, it was the wind instruments which played the major role. Since the time of the Republic, three successive calls controlled the departure from a camp: at the first call, wake up to start the day; at the second, dress and stand by; at the third, move off in the regulation fashion. Different calls, accompanied by visual signals such as the raising of the standards, would sound the alarm (Caesar, *B Gall.,* II.20) or order a retreat (*B Gall.* VII.47). Widely used in camp, music also added a stimulus to the field of battle. When the troops launched their attack, the trumpet calls added to their shouts (*clamor)* to encourage them as well as to frighten the enemy, and different calls, audible over the noise of the battle, passed on the officers' orders.

Archaeological discoveries and sculptures give us an idea of ancient instruments and their capabilities. The simplest, the *tuba,* was a straight tube with a bell end; the *lituus* differed in that it widened out laterally, somewhat resembling the Gaulish *carnyx*; the *cornu* was a tube bent into almost a full circle with a transverse bar to strengthen it; and finally there was the *bucinum,* similar to a modern trumpet, and adapted for cavalry use, perhaps by modifying a *cornu.* However, M. Speidel suggests that the instrument of this type, as shown on the monument to the cavalryman Andes and on a fragment from Remagen, is not a *bucinum* but simply a *cornu,* and it is true that when an instrument is depicted on memorials to *bucinatores* it is a straight tube, not bent as are modern trombones or trumpets.

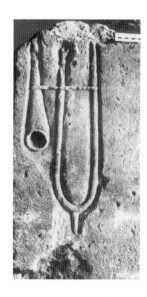

58 Fragment from the Remagen monument: *cornu?* (photo Rheinisches Landesmuseum, Bonn)

59 Aurelius Suro, *bucinator* of Leg I Adiutrix in the
Archaeological Museum of Istanbul (after J. Oldenstein, 1976)

60 *Cornu* brace or *vexillum*
component? (photo Musées de
Strasbourg)

61 *Cornu* brace (?) from Murrhardt
(photo Württembergisches
Landesmuseum, Stuttgart)

62 Bronze *cornu* brace (?)
(photo Landesmuseum Trier)

Although a *lituus* like the one preserved at Bonn was capable of playing six different notes, it must be noted that these instruments could have been played singly or in groups, and for all we know, Roman musicians may have known nothing of polyphony. Their instruments were obviously chosen for their loud clear notes, but it may well be, judging from discoveries at sites such as Vindonissa, that other wind (*tibias*) or percussion instruments such as tambourines were used as well.

An important part of our knowledge of these ancient musical instruments comes from carved reliefs which show them being played (notably Trajan's Column), and the funerary memorials of *tubicines, cornicines* and *bucinatores* which sometimes show their instruments – that of the *tubicen* Sibbaeus in Mannheim museum for instance. One of these memorials, of M. Julius Victor, *ex collegio liticinum (et) cornicinum*, showed that his beneficiaries played both instruments, but in the absence of more specific information, how the *lituus* was actually used by the military remains controversial.

Although the majority of funerary memorials showing musicians come from the Rhine valley, a very fine monument, that to the Syrian Aurelius Surus, *bucinator* of the First Legion *Adiutrix*, has recently been discovered in Istanbul. This monument, dated by Speidel to between AD 210-15, shows that recruitment continued in the East at the turn of the second/third centuries and thus the persistence of functions better known, in the West at least, at the start of the Principate.

To conclude this section, archaeological documentary evidence showing the instruments of the Roman army is far from plentiful; apart from these rare intact finds shown here (the *lituus* from Saalburg for example), our understanding of them is not yet complete. This is particularly the case with the tubular sleeves or sockets interpreted as *cornu* reinforcements. Objects like these have notably been reported from Murviel-Les-Montpellier, Trier, Murrhardt, etc; the best example of these, found at Strasbourg, has been thought since R. Forrer to be a brace from a standard or a *vexillum*. The reliefs on it (Hercules, Dionysus, Diana and Mercury) are not sufficient for us to decide one way or the other.

PERSONAL EFFECTS AND EQUIPMENT: TRANSPORTATION

From the time of Marius onwards, every legionary carried with him, in addition to his military kit, a good part of the equipment previously divided among the chariots and the baggage trains which accompanied an army on the march. These *impedimenta* were hung from a form of cross-shaped framework, the *furca*, of which the carvings on Trajan's Column give us a general idea. Numerous written sources show that this system put a considerable burden on the infantryman; Cicero, for instance (*Tusc* II.XVI.37) says that the soldier carried not only his weapons (helmet, shield and sword) but also rations for 15 days plus all that he would need in camp, by which is understood tools for making ramparts, digging trenches, cutting wood, etc. Adding the rations to the weight of the military equipment alone – some 18–26

63 *Cornu* brace (?) from Murrhardt (photo Württembergisches Landesmuseum, Stuttgart)

The importance of the impedimenta: a testing time during the return of Germanicus' expedition in Germany

.... the misery continued; there were still the ramparts to be built and the material for building them to be collected. The proper tools for digging and for cutting turf had for the most part been lost. There were no tents for the troops, no medication for the wounded. While the survivors shared out the mud-splashed bloodstained rations, the whole camp was filled with lamentation throughout that dreadful night, and all waited for the coming day to bring death to thousands more.

Tacitus, Ann. I.65

---

kilos based on modern reconstruction – one is already looking at a load of more than 40 kg. Taking an average of 11 days' rations, N. Fuentes arrives at a figure of 40.8 kg, while F. Junkelmann calculates a weight of 54.8 kg for each legionary. For comparison, a French Zouave in the mid-1800s carried a total weight of 35kg. Loaded down like this, the Roman soldier regularly covered 20-30 miles (48km) at a stretch, roughly the same distance expected of the eighteenth or nineteenth century French or English soldier, who was only slightly less burdened.

Despite the account of Cicero and that, a century later, of a writer like Flavius Josephus, one must retain one's sense of perspective; not every soldier was overloaded all the time with such a miscellaneous burden. The individual's load, as shown for instance in the crossing of the Danube depicted on Trajan's Column, does not seem to have been extraordinary – a bronze frying pan and cooking pot, a leather satchel with two crossed straps and at least two further bags or less conventional items (the pear-shaped object must be a gourd in a skin); is the apparent uniformity shown on the Column perhaps only a reflection of the limited range of sketches given to the sculptor as a guide?

On the practical side, it seems that there was a regulation type of package, doubtless less uniform in reality than on the reliefs, plus additions shared out by the NCO's; not every man carried the same tools, as only a few of some would be needed. A Byzantine text (Leon, *Tactica*, IV), which must describe the situation in the High Empire quite accurately in spite of its later date, states that 16 men had between them 2 pickaxes, 2 shovels, a saw, a sickle and a basket; only four out of the sixteen would be carrying a long-handled implement, which perhaps explains the absence of such tools (Cich., 12-14) on Trajan's Column, where only ten individual packages are shown.

However, whatever it might have contained, the loss of the baggage, individual or communal, was always a disaster. Although the individual's load had increased considerably at the end of the Republic in order to reduce the baggage train, draft animals and chariots still travelled with the armies of the High Empire. The pattern followed in the first and second centuries AD was thus a compromise between convenience and efficiency; in an emergency, the soldier had to be able to divest himself very rapidly of his baggage, and take up his weapons. Tents, artillery, reserve rations and ammunition were essential bag-

64 The Roman army on the march, with weapons and baggage; relief from Trajan's Column (after Daremberg and Saglio)

gage, which had to be protected as well as transported. All in all, we can understand how the Roman army developed the same operational pattern in this area as modern armies.

65 Ivory reliefs from Palestrina

4 REPUBLICAN ARMS AND EQUIPMENT

How would a soldier of the third century BC have dressed? Can we deduce his appearance from certain reliefs, such as those carved in ivory from Palestrina which show two heavily-armed warriors, apparently in full formal dress? They are both wearing a 'muscled' cuirass over a short thigh-length tunic under a cloak fastened at the neck. Their highly elaborate helmets have crests and plumes, and a pair of *cnemides* (greaves) and a lance completes their outfits; one of them is holding an oval shield behind him, but neither has belt or sword. Such representations are rare, however, and, more importantly, there is no firm evidence that we are looking at Roman soldiers. This is also the case with the numerous third-century BC bronze statuettes found in Italy, which usually depict a helmeted infantryman brandishing a sword and a small almond-shaped shield, with *spina*. As a result, we can only reconstruct a regular legionary's equipment by drawing on other complementary sources as well.

TEXTS

Of all the writings on the Republican army, the best and the oldest is the description given by Polybius (VI. 19-42) around 160 BC. Unfortunately, the complete work has not come down to us, but it is still an extraordinarily detailed source of information on the army as it was prior to Marius' reforms on Roman camps and on the arms and equipment in the various army corps. A cavalry officer himself, Polybius describes an army which he knew well, but he probably draws on other sources also, and descriptions would appear to be accurate for the period 220-160 BC. Looking at the extract on the next page one can see the essential information which Polybius gives us, while emphasising the archaeological problems when one tries to identify precisely some of the objects described.

Julius Caesar himself, particularly in his *Gallic War*, is another specially qualified source of information about the last years of the Republic, firstly because he himself lived through and witnessed the events about which he writes – though one may doubt his impartiality on occasion – and secondly because of his direct military experience, which gives even his passing references to weapons an accuracy not found in the works of contemporary civilian writers such as Cicero.

Later sources, interesting though they may be, suffer from their timing; Livy and Vitruvius, in the Augustan era, had difficulties giving accounts of historical events without confusing them with events in their own times. Their testimonies can only be used therefore after a critical analysis which may itself not be free from error. One is thus forced to accept only those parts of these writers' works which are firmly based on facts which can be verified, such as Vitruvius' descriptions of artillery, actual datable examples of which have been discovered by excavation.

SCULPTURES

Several commemorative reliefs from the Republican period show, in varying degrees of detail, items of military weaponry and equipment. For the period prior to the reforms of Marius, the major examples are the frieze from the monument to Paulus Æmilius at Delphi, erected after the death of Perseus at the Battle of Pydna in 168 BC, and the reliefs on the frieze set up by Eumenus II between 197-59 BC.

For the period of Marius to the reign of Augustus, the list is a little longer, but still limited. The oldest relief, known as variously the 'Louvre Altar', 'The Census', 'The Founding of Narbonne', or, most frequently, 'The Altar of Domitius Ahenobarbus', probably dates from around 100 BC; its origin is unknown, but it was in a collection in Rome from the seventeenth century. Just one sculpture seems to date from the first half of the first century BC, a Roman relief from the time of Sulla with a frieze of weapons which appear to be from the period. One of the oldest military memorials shows a Roman soldier, a centurion in the *Legio Martia* (IIIrd, XIIIth or XXIIIrd?), known from Padua. Its date, which must be before the disappearance of the legion at sea in October, 42 BC,

---

The altar of Domitius Ahenobarbus

The fragment of the relief bearing this name, preserved in the Louvre museum in Paris, is one of our most explicit sources of information about Roman troops for the period from just after the reforms of Marius to the end of the second century BC. It formed part of a rectangular monument from which three carved sides are now in the Glyptothek in Munich. From the seventeenth century, the reliefs from this monument were in Rome, in the Palazzo Santacroce and the Campus Martius; this collection of antiquities was dispersed on the death of its owner, Cardinal Fesch. It seems probable that the reliefs came from a monument previously discovered, perhaps under the S. Salvatore church in the Campo, and removed during the Italian Renaissance. The section acquired by the Louvre is now in the museum's Department of Greek and Roman Antiquities, Reference Number 975.

Whilst the long wall-section in Munich shows a procession of marine deities in Hellenistic style, the Louvre section is strictly Roman in style and depicts an official religious ceremony. Surrounding a statue of Mars dressed in a military officer's uniform, close to the altar, are people dressed in togas on the left, looking at a list, while on the right, animals are being readied for a sacrifice. Mingling with the civilians are four infantrymen in chain mail vests and a cavalryman, all wearing crested helmets and apparently armed only with a sword in a scabbard hanging on their right side and a long oval shield similar to the one from Fayoûm.

66 The Battle of Pydna, 168 BC; detail from the monument to Paulus Emilius, Delphi (after L. Keppie, 1964)

67 The altar of Domitius Ahenobarbus

68 Memorial to the centurion Minutio of the IIIrd (?) Legio Martia; Padua, towards 44-42 BC? (after L. Keppie, 1991)

is a particularly valuable source of information about Caesar's soldiers; but unfortunately for us, it depicts an NCO in equipment which is very different from that of his men. Just a few years later (around 40-35 BC is the accepted dating) are the reliefs from the Julii Mausoleum at Glanum; a little after this are some rare early-Augustan era reliefs from Italy itself. All the other examples, funerary or commemorative, belong to a later period, notably the statue of a warrior from Vachères (Alpes-de-Haute-Provence), which was probably taken from an Augustan funerary monument; we shall refer to this further below.

The sparsity of this documentation is such that it is very unsafe to take parts of it as fixed reference points and then to fit our ideas on the evolution of equipment between them. There is nothing to prove that some of the known sculptures are not depicting items from an earlier period – often the case with 'historical' reliefs, it would seem – or are showing new equipment which had not yet been widely adopted by the contemporary army. We should therefore compare these representations with actual archaeological material, taking into account the differences between the two forms of evidence.

ARCHAEOLOGICAL DISCOVERIES

These are still relatively rare, but there are certainly many finds which are waiting to be properly identified, restored and published, particularly single examples, and notably from Italy, Greece and Yugoslavia. We shall limit ourselves here to mentioning the most important of these.

One of the oldest collections in our possession is the result of the excavations carried out at Numance by A. Schulten, particularly his discoveries to the east of the sites and in the camps at Renieblas. The interpretation of these finds is not always certain, as Camps I and II were probably covered first by Camp III in 153-2 BC, and then again by Camps IV and V, which definitely date from around 80 BC. Additionally this chronology, based on Schulten's work on these sites between the wars, may need to be reconsidered in the light of current knowledge when work on them is resumed (current research of Martin Luik).

G. Ulbert's recent study of the camp at Cáceres el Viejo in Estremadura concludes that Schulten's interpretation and dating are probably correct based on work at Castra Caecilia, Q. Caecilius Maetellus' camp during the early years of the first century BC. The military equipment recovered from this site is unfortunately fragmentary: points from a few *pila,* tanged and socketed types, fragments of daggers, butt ends and fittings from lances, plus 15 stone balls, probably *ballista* ammunition. There was a noticeable absence of sword or scabbard remains.

One of our best sources of information about late Republican weapons results from the excavations carried out at the instigation of Napoléon III in the nineteenth century at Alésia (Alise-Ste-Reine, Côte-d'Or department – see inset below). However, although the finds have been preserved at the Musée des Antiquités

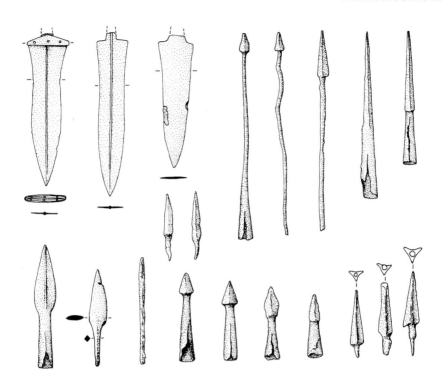

69 Republican weapons from Numantia (after A. Schulten, 1927)

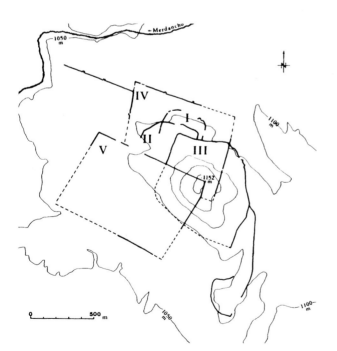

70 Successive Republican camps at Renieblas to the east of
Numance (after A. Schulten): Camps I and II, early to mid-second
century BC: Camp III, certainly 153-152 BC: Camps IV and V,
perhaps from the 80s BC

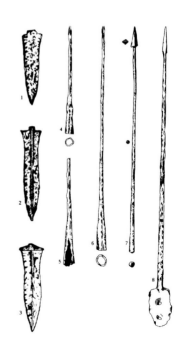

71 Republican weapons from Numance (after
L. Keppie, 1984)

Nationales since their discovery, they did not receive the attention that their importance merits, in spite of the high hopes placed on them when they were found. It was only in 1992, as part of the preparatory work for an exhibition, that a scientific study was carried out, and in spite of the inevitable deterioration over 150 years, we now have at our disposal the precise information which we have hitherto lacked.

Whilst the weapons from Alésia will in the near future greatly enhance our knowledge of the equipment of Caesar's soldiers, there is no similar collection of material to inform us about those Roman troops who between 125-1 BC overcame the warlike peoples of Southern Gaul. A few sporadic finds in different settlements in the valley of the lower Rhône are the only testimony to the bitter fighting in some localities, but these discoveries have never been evaluated as a group. One small village in the countryside inland from Marseille, the *oppidum* of La Cloche at Les Pennes-Mirabeau (Bouches-du-Rhône department) was totally destroyed when Marseille fell in 49 BC, and its excavator, L. Chabot, recovered several *pilum* points, the circular boss from an *umbo* and a number of stone

---

The weapons from Alésia

The weapons found in the vicinity of Alésia during the excavations in the time of Napoléon III form one of our rare sources of information on Roman arms at the end of the Republican period. The finds comprised 38 *pila*, 138 points and about 139 butt-ends of lances or javelins, 11 swords or sword scabbards, 5 daggers, 41 arrowheads and 11 *stimuli*. Among the protective equipment there were 2 helmets and paragnathides, 17 shield-edgings and 11 *umbones*. To this already impressive list may be added 10 catapult bolts, 6 stone balls and one lead slingshot. All told, this whole collection of material, confusing at first sight, presented several problems.

Some of the weapons could definitely only be those of Roman troops – this is the case with the pila and the artillery projectiles; some others are certainly Gaulish – the swords, the iron helmet, and most, if not all, of the paragnathides and the omega-shaped umbones. Finally, the circular umbones must have belonged to the German auxiliaries expressly mentioned by Caesar (B Gall. VII.80). One must thus ask how this collection came together.

From the notes left by the excavators and from the archives of the Musée des Antiquités Nationales, where the finds are now, one group of the Alésia weapons was found in a trench, which the recent excavators have unfortunately not yet found. If it formed part of the counterscarp, an accumulation of weapons from both armies could be a trophy, to which there are contemporary textual references. Alternatively, if what is described was a trench or an enclosure, then we cannot rule out the possibility of a religious observance during the Caesarean attacks or just after. Such an accumulation of weaponry cannot be explained simply by actual battle conditions; one, or perhaps several, specific deposits were made, the purpose of which is as yet unclear.

Whatever the solution may be, it appears that the analysis of the weapons found at Alésia must be closely linked to a wide-ranging search on site if we are to find it, and this is the objective of the programmes carried out since 1991 by a joint Franco-German team led by M. Reddé (CNRS) and S. von Schnurbein (RGK).

Bibliography: Verchère de Reffye 1864; Quicherat 1865; Duval 1987; Brouquié-Reddé 1997 [1999]; Sievers 1997 [1999].

Infantry Equipment During The Second Century BC

The regulation equipment of the youngest soldiers comprises a sword, some javelins and a light shield, quite sturdy and large enough to give protection, circular, with a diameter of three feet. The velite also wears a plain helmet without a crest, sometimes covered with wolf skin or something similar to protect it and to catch the eye of the junior officers so that they can see whether their men are fighting bravely in the front line. The velites' javelins have shafts two cubits [approx 20in/50cm] long, as thick as a man's finger; the point measures one empan [approx 20in/22cm] and is filed down and sharpened so much that it bends on impact so that an enemy cannot throw it back; otherwise, both sides could use it.

The next class of soldiers, by age, are called hastati and are fully equipped, with a convex shield 30 inches wide and four feet long, a palm's breadth thick at the edges, made from two planks stuck together with cows' hoof glue and covered with cloth or wolf skin. The top and bottom edges are reinforced with iron strips to resist sword blows and to protect it when standing it on the ground. The shield also has a central iron boss to give protection against stones, spear thrusts and other assaults. The shield is accompanied by a sword worn at the right thigh, and called 'Spanish'. It has a sharp point and a strong blade, sharpened on both edges. In addition, the soldier has two javelins, a bronze helmet and shin guards. The javelins may be either thick or thin. Of the heavy javelins, some have a shaft a palm's width in diameter, others have square shafts with a cross-section of a palm's width also; the light javelins, carried in addition to the heavy ones, are of medium size, resembling a hunting spear.

All the javelins have shafts about three cubits long and carry a barbed iron head as long as the shaft. The heads are so firmly riveted to the shafts that in action they will break rather than be torn loose from the shafts, even though they are an inch and a half thick at the base end where they join the shaft, showing how much care goes into their construction. In addition, every javelin is adorned with red or black plumes about a cubit long, making the soldier seem twice as big and frightening to the enemy. Most soldiers also wear a bronze plate about 22cm², which they called their 'heart protector', to complete their equipment; those soldiers, however, who have more than 10,000 drachmas wear a chain mail shirt instead of the 'heart protector', and the principes and triarii are similarly equipped, except that the triarii carried a lance instead of javelins.

Polybius, VI.22-3

balls – showing that the Romans used artillery – from the sacked ruins of the dwellings. All the weapons recovered from this site were of Roman origin, perhaps implying that the Roman troops had not hesitated to attack an undefended village.

THE TYPOLOGICAL ROUTE

In addition to the information derived directly from group finds and individual discoveries, a good part of our knowledge of Republican weapons is deduced by working backwards from the best understood objects and sources using the 'typological development' technique. As we shall show below for each type of weapon, the most clear-cut and reliably-dated developments during the Principate are often merely a further evolution within an established progression. This is particularly the case with the sword and the dagger, two weapons whose forms during the Empire can be clearly seen to be developed from a common original – Iberian, according to Polybius. The case is similar for the *pilum* and for various types of helmet, and one can draw on known steps in their development to formulate an evolving progression in which the weapon's form is closely linked to its function.

DEFENSIVE EQUIPMENT

Pre-Roman helmets

The Roman army inherited a long-established cultural and technical tradition that the helmet was a soldier's most important piece of equipment. Originating in the Bronze Age, when they were very rare, helmets based on Eastern designs spread steadily across Europe, with Italy being among the first to adopt them, and they are to be seen also on Greek vases of the eighth century BC. From the sixth century onward, bronze helmets grew in acceptance, though they were still not numerous (Snodgrass, 1964), and the first well-established series, the bronze Negau helmet and its variants, was developed between the end of the sixth century and the fourth century BC.

Among the Celts, helmets of native manufacture are scarcely known before the fifth century BC. At that time (the Berru helmet), and in the fourth century, they were worn primarily for show. The helmets from Anfreville and Canosa, and the recently found examples from Agris and Montlaurès, are all witness to their use as status symbols. The appearance of iron helmets in the Cisalpine region in the fourth century, however, perhaps indicates a more democratic use among Celtic troops, and during the same period the Celtic style of helmet – a skullcap topped by a button or a plume-holder – was being produced in bronze by the Etruscans. It is this type of helmet, sometimes called the 'Montefortino' type, or jockey cap, depending on the shape of its rear-peak, which was issued to the first Republican legion.

Although they disappeared in the Celtic world during the La Tène B-C period, simple skullcap helmets with a button on the top

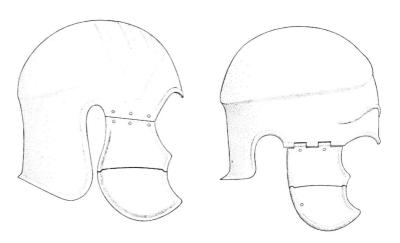

72 Attic helmet from the third or fourth century BC: Yorkshire Museum at York (after Robinson 1975)

were being produced in quantity in Italy by the fourth and particularly the third centuries. Helmet bodies were polished and decorated in simple style, with often no more than a few lines and patterns incised into the reinforcing band. Some of them, perhaps like those depicted on the 'Altar of Ahenobarbus', had a plume on top, which probably served to distinguish the officers in battle – these were, perhaps, the *insignia* to which Caesar makes several references. Other interpretations have been proposed, however, and G. Waurick sees those helmets with their archaic design as based on Greek rather than Etrusco-Roman models.

The helmets worn by the officers of those first legions followed Greek originals – Attic, Italo-Corinthian – whilst those worn by lower ranks were mass-produced types, conical with a button on top. After Marius' reforms, and even more so after the reforms of Augustus, Roman army helmets were produced in large numbers in factories (State-owned? privately-owned?) set up to manufacture military equipment.

The conical helmet with a button on top, still worn by the officers in the early first century BC, was soon replaced by a simpler smooth version. These types, without paragnithides (replaced in the Mainz and Vieille-Toulouse examples by a pair of large oval rings narrowed at the waist) are known in two versions, a heavy, relatively carefully produced type, weighing more than a kilogram, and a lighter one (500-800g), often of mediocre quality. The heavier are generally referred to as 'Mannheim Type', and the lighter as 'Coolus Type', but German archaeologists use the former to refer to both types. Specimens of both were found in a well in Vieille-Toulouse, and it is difficult to explain this as either a difference in date of deposit or in origin; actually, it may be that there were different series for legionaries and auxiliaries. The oldest example so far known is that recovered from the Roman ship of the Madrague de Giens, which sank around 70 BC.

The conical type of helmet with a button on top – 'Montefortino' type – may have been less frequent in the middle of the first century

73 Terracotta statue from a vase from Canosa (Röm.-Germ. Zentralmus. Mainz) helmeted and cuirassed warrior, late fourth / early third century BC.

74 Bronze helmet (British Museum) showing method of securing this type of helmet; on a statue of Pyrrhus (Naples Museum) (P. Connolly in Robinson 1975)

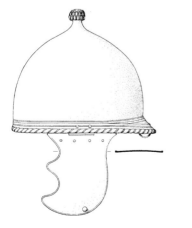

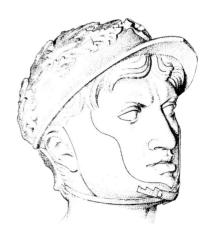

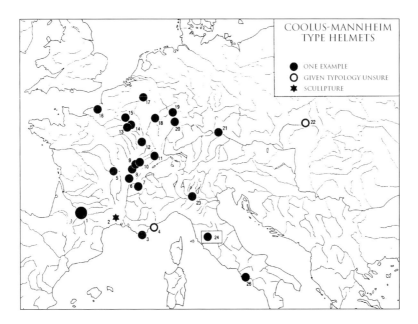

75 Distribution of Coolus-Mannheim type helmets: 1. Vieille-Toulouse (Haute-Garonne); 2. Corconne (Gard); 3. Madrague de Giens (Var); 4. Dramont A; 5. Lusigny (Allier); 6. Belleville (Rhône); 7. Les Avenières (Isere); 8. Montbellet (Saône-et-L.); 9. Verjux (Saône-et-L.); 10. Ciel (Saône-et-L.); 11. Lacollonge (T. de Belfort); 12. Breuvannes (Haute-Marne); 13. Coolus (Marne); 14. Vadenay (Marne); 15. Variscourt (Aisne); 16. Bracquemeont (Seine-Maritime); 17. Tongres (Limburg); 18. Trier-Olewig (Rheinland-Pfalz); 19. Mainz (Rheinland-Pfalz); 20. Mannheim (Baden-W); 21. Straubing (Bayern); 22. Zips (Slovaquie); 23. "Lombardy" (?); 24. "Toscana" (?); 25. "Italy"; 26. Pompeii

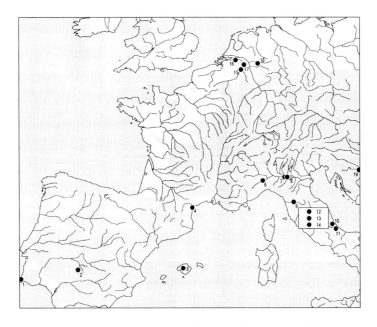

76 Distribution of Buggenum-type helmets; Buggenum: 1. Aljezur; 2. Alcaracejos; 3. Llubi; 4. Gruissan (Aude); 5. Dramont A (Var) (Buggenum type?); 6. Alessandria (Piemont); 7. Castenuovo Bocca d'Alda (Milano); 8. 'Lombardy' ?; 9. 'Bed of the river Arno'?; 10. Loreto Aprutino (Pescara); 11. Monterodomo (Chieti); 12-14. 'Italy'; 15. Buggenum (Limburg); 16. Millingen (Gelderland); 17. Waard-Luttingen (Nordrhein-Westfalen); 18. Olfen (Nordrhein-Westfalen); 19. "Bed of the river Kupa" near Sisak (after G. Waurick, 1990, completed)

BC than earlier, but it led to the development of a simpler type with a hollow button, which is known collectively as 'Buggenum Type' after a discovery at a place of that name in Holland. Few in number, these helmets are particularly found at the mouths of the Rhine and Meuse rivers, and can be associated with the attack on the Germans in these areas in 12 BC. However, a helmet of this type, found near to Sisak in Croatia, is engraved with SCIP IMP, from which G. Waurick and U. Schaaff deduce a mid-first century BC date. In this case (see also the discovery at Dramont A above), some Buggenum helmets could also have been used in Caesar's legionary forces.

77 Bronze helmet of Mannheim type, from Vadenay, Marne (photo Röm.-Germ. Zentralmuseum, Mainz)

The origins of metal armour

Although metal armour had been used in the Middle East even earlier, the first known example from the Mediterranean area dates from the fifteenth century BC, and was discovered during the excavation of a tomb at Dendra by a Greco-Swedish team, so the armour that later developed in Greece and Italy goes back to Bronze Age Greece itself. Made as an assembly of tubes, in which the wearer had very little freedom of movement, such armour very soon gave way to a style which only covered the ribcage; this was known from the end of the Geometric era onwards and remained unchanged until the end of the sixth century BC. Armour of this type was subsequently copied in much of Europe from as early as the end of the Bronze Final period, as instanced by the armour from Čaka in Czechoslovakia, which dates from the thirteenth century BC.

78 Buggenum-type helmet from Duisburg (Photo Röm.-Germ. Zentralmuseum, Mainz)

Later, in the Classical and, particularly, the Hellenistic periods, 'ribcage' armour developed into a more anatomically correct form; hinged parts allowing freedom of movement appear from the fifth century, and there are symbolic and mythological decorations in relief on the breastplate. These Hellenistic types were the prerogative of senior officers in Roman times.

Whilst these types were particularly prized for more than a thousand years, other types of armour met with varied success. An Italian model, consisting of two discs only 20-5cm in diameter, was used in Italy from the start of the seventh century to the fourth at least, and this rudimentary protection, called *cardiophylax* as it protected only the heart, was held in place by a form of harness (shown by a statue from Capestrano, seventh century BC; and a painting from Ceri, late sixth century BC). Even though these discs did not give much protection, this type of armour has been found at considerable distances from its regions of origin, in Ancona for example, and in Caserta in Campania, Aléria in Corsica and even Agde in the Languedoc (Southern France, west of Marseille).

This type is probably the basis of Samnite armour, which from the beginning of the fourth century comprised three symmetrical discs placed on the chest and back, giving a greater degree of protection. From the end of the fourth century, this type evolved under the influence of the Greek muscled type, and we see rectangular plates corresponding to the chest musculature, even though they covered only a part of the chest. This armour, in use during the second and third centuries BC, was no doubt worn by Republican-period legionaries

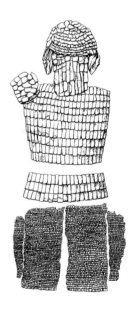

79 Scythian armour with iron scales; warrior's tomb from L'Ingul: fifth century BC (after Saposnikova)

before the reforms of Marius, and seems to have been manufactured throughout central and southern Italy.

The origins of 'scale' armour

Originating in the Middle East, where it had been in use since at least the seventh century BC, scale armour was used by the Roman army throughout its whole existence, and one of the reasons for its long life was probably its ease of manufacture and repair . Consisting of metal plates sewn to each other and to a backing, it offered an acceptable degree of protection at a modest cost, the wearer could move freely while wearing it, and, suitably cleaned and polished, it would shine brightly on parade like a snake's skin or a freshly caught fish. For an army like the Roman army, with its large numbers of auxiliaries, it was also ideal for equipping second-rank troops and cavalry at minimal cost.

Although used very little in ancient Greece – the scarcity of archaeological finds is matched by the scarcity of depictions – scale armour must have come to Italy via Greece in the first instance. Its widespread adoption under the Principate must have been the result of the massive recruitment of Eastern auxiliaries into the Roman army during the first century AD.

The origins of chain mail

With its remarkably complicated construction, chain mail was a late arrival on the battlefield. Based on the principle of combining strength with supple flexibility, it consisted of alternately riveted and plain iron rings, each being linked through its four neighbours. With this design, the force of a sword blow was spread over a wide enough area for the wearer to be no more than bruised. The chain mail wearer was thus protected against most of the usual injuries arising in hand-to-hand fighting, though not against artillery arrows – but no ancient form of armour could really withstand such projectiles. Chain mail's major problem was its weight, around 12 kilos, making it the heaviest commonly-used armour since the Bronze Age.

It would seem that the honour of making and popularising the first chain mail armour should go to the Gauls; equally as skilled as their Roman counterparts, the Gaulish weaponsmiths had devised a form of iron armour efficient enough to continue in use in the West until the Middle Ages. The scarcity of finds of Gaulish chain mail is undoubtedly a reflection of its high cost of manufacture right from the outset. It had long been thought, following J. Déchelette, that a 'La Tène' tomb found in the Marne department and dating from the fourth century BC had yielded the most ancient known fragments of chain mail; but a recent study has now re-dated this tomb to the fourth century AD. As a result, the oldest archaeological evidence is the example found at Ciumesti in Romania, which dates from the third century BC; but it was not until the middle of the second Iron Age that this new technology appeared, right at the heart of the Celtic world.

Dating from the second century BC, several statues, thought to be of heroic ancestors, have been found in the territory of the Salyens who lived in the lower Rhöne valley; many are depicted wearing chain mail.

80 The 'Gaulish Style' of the chainmail coat on the Pilier de Mavilly (Côte-d'Or); early first century AD (after Robinson 1975)

There has been much hesitation about interpreting this type of armour in some representations, so that there are many literary references to 'leather armour' and 'semi-rigid tunics'. Actually, the ancient sculptor who wished to depict chain mail had technical problems in showing thousands of interlaced rings, and had to resort to tricks to achieve his results – tricks common to a wide range of periods and places.

The first method, seldom used because it was only a partial solution, was to exaggerate the size of the links; but even by enlarging them four or fivefold, the sculptor soon realised the extent of his difficulty. This technique, the most realistic solution, is found in only few cases, such as the frieze of the temple of Athena at Pergamum in the second century BC and on a column at Mavilly (Department of Côte-d'Or) from the early first century AD. To show only the backing for the rings was somewhat simpler, but still time-consuming; this was the technique used on the Altar of Ahenobarbus around 100 BC, and for the Vachères Warrior at the end of the first century BC. Another trick was to punch holes all over the surface of the representation of the cuirass, as was done on some of the statues at Entremont and on a second century statuette now in the British Museum. More usually, it seems that the sculptor left it to a painter to add detail to the basic statue; and on such works, the actual sculpted surface of the cuirass is left completely smooth.

81 General view of the Vachères Warrior (Alpes-de-Haute-Provence); end of the first century BC (photo CNRS, Chéné-Réveillac)

It is therefore useful when analysing ancient reliefs not to look so much at their surface appearance as the characteristic 'cut' of the chain mail garment; there appear to have been two designs in use during the last century of the Republic. In the older type, perhaps a Celtic speciality, the arms and shoulders of the wearer are protected by a sort of open cape, the two corners of which are simply folded outward and back, and which must have been held in place by a system of laces. Such is the traditional chain mail coat worn for instance by the statue of 'Gaulish Mars' on the column from Mavilly. Various representations during the Imperial period show some soldiers, probably those of Gaulish origin, wearing a garment in this style in the middle and even at the end of the first century AD; typical examples are the numerous monuments to cavalrymen in the Rhineland – Reburrus, Togitio, Annauso, C. Romanius, L. Faustus, Val. Secundus – and again, the *imaginifer* Genialis at Mainz, to mention only the clearest examples. The most frequently found design, however, from the end of the second century BC (the Pergamon frieze) has two large shoulder protectors fastened at the front on the chest and held in place by a transverse fixing. In the early second century BC this fixing was rectangular, but from the Augustan period onward it comprised two S-shaped fasteners and a central button. Later, the chain mail coat had short sleeves emerging from under the shoulder protectors. We can appreciate the benefits of the new design of fastening by looking at the representation of soldiers in action, for instance in the frieze on the Arch at Orange; not only did it give excellent freedom of movement, it gave greater protection as well, notably to the shoulders and arms of its wearer.

A transitional model, probably of Gaulish manufacture, is known from an early first century AD memorial now in the Musée Borély in Marseille. On the cuirass worn by a cavalryman, the cape covering the shoulders is lengthened by vertical shoulder pieces fixed both by hooks at the lower ends and folded back on themselves transversely by what appears to be a system of chains; but this 'mixed' pattern does not seem to have been widely adopted.

Greaves

Less frequently used than in Greece, greaves, or shin-guards, were however worn by centurions and the higher ranks (Vegetius, I.20) in the Republican army. They rapidly fell into disuse (with a few exceptions) at the start of the first century AD, reappearing occasionally as part of the sporting equipment worn by the cavalry in the third century.

The origins of the Roman shield

During the Bronze Age and the Archaic period in Greece, shields were circular, usually fitted with a central *umbo;* in the West, the whole shield was often made from bronze, whereas in the archaic Greek version, only the projecting part, the *umbo,* was of metal. It was in Italy, in the eighth century BC – doubtless because of new ways of fighting – that the need arose for a shield which was better suited to the body shape of the infantryman, taking first a leaf shape and then becoming oval. The circular version soon acquired a tapered reinforcing rib, the *spina,* leading to modified forms of *umbo,* shell-shaped then omega-shaped.

The oval shield moved from Italy into Celtic Europe during the transition from the First to the Second Iron Age. One of the oldest Gaulish representations of an oval shield has just been found at Vix, on one of the two statues recovered from the ditch of an enclosure dating from the first half of the fifth century BC, and it was certainly the Celts who were responsible for the widespread diffusion of this type of shield among the native Europeans from then on. The Celtic presence in Italy – attested by stelae from Padua and Bologna – combined with ancient traditions to ensure the adoption of the oval shield with a *spina,* with or without a metal *umbo* covering the central reinforcement. Finally, in Gaul, this style continued until the shields themselves were no longer used. At Nîmes, for instance, where weapons are relatively well represented in tombs of the late Iron Age, the omega-shaped *umbo* is found in the last tombs to contain arms, towards the middle of the first century BC.

A Republican shield

It was therefore only natural that the first Roman legions should be equipped with an oval shield with *spina,* combining the established pre-Roman Italian model with that of the traditional enemy. This type is clearly recognisable on the Altar of Ahenobarbus, and can be found in the descriptions of Polybius, but we also have a much better source of information in the complete example from Kasr-el-Harit in Egypt, perfectly preserved in the dry sands of Fayûm.

This infantryman's shield is in a remarkable state of preservation, just slightly distorted by desiccation, and measures 120x64 cm; it is composed of three layers of thin laths glued together, which give it its curved form. It was originally covered with a layer of felt carefully sewn round its circumference, though unfortunately any colour or

83 Miniature reproduction of a shield (Celtic? Roman?) found in Greece (RGZM Mainz, inv. O. 7095)

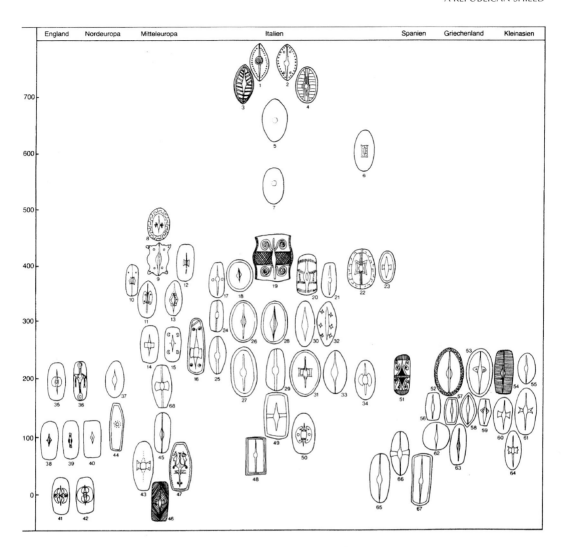

84 Evolution of the oval shield during the Iron Age (after P. Stary, 1981)

decoration which may have been present has now disappeared. The only reinforcement is a solid *spina* in three sections, and the interior of the central boss has been hollowed out and has a horizontal handgrip, which enabled the shield to be moved in any direction.

The shield has no metal components except for the nails used to secure the *spina*; there is neither a sheet metal *umbo* nor the octal edging strips at head and foot to which Polybius refers in his description of shields from this period, though minor modifications could have been made during the two or three centuries during which such shields were in service. Found by people looking for papyrus documents, the Fayûm shield cannot be accurately dated, but it seems probable that this type of shield was used during the whole duration of the Republican era until the introduction (under Augustus?) of a rectangular model which was itself only a shortened version of this design.

The discovery on the west bank of the Rhine, and also in non-

84 Republican-period shield from Fayûm, Egypt (after W. Kimmig, 1940)

85 Front and back of a miniature reproduction: Gaulish shield of the second century BC, found in Italy (RGZM Mainz, inv. 0. 7093)

occupied Germany, of oval iron *umbo* reinforcements which could come from late versions of this Republican type of shield has in recent years laid to rest the problem of the origin of these metal *umbones*. In fact, the principle behind this form of reinforcement goes back to the Gauls in the fifth century BC, both in Champagne and in Central Europe. It is therefore quite possible that its later adoption by the Roman army was a result of borrowing from the Celts or Germans.

Shields with a round umbo

The influence of native types on Imperial – and even late Republican – equipment is clearly shown in the case of shields with a round *umbo*, and we are looking here at a weapon based on a quite different tradition, as the vertical axis has no reinforcing rib. This type of shield, usually oval, has a central boss (*umbo*) with a corresponding cavity on its inner face to accept the user's hand. Contrary to what might have been expected, the round *umbo* is fairly common in Gaul in the first century BC. Several examples have been found at Alésia, and another, clearly associated with the battle, was in a group of broken Roman weapons left over from the destruction of the village of La Cloche near Marseille in 49 BC. Other discoveries have been made at less likely places, such as the deposit at Larina (department of Isère) or the tomb at Sigoyer (department of Hautes-Alpes) where a Celtic *umbo* with wings and a round *umbo* were found in association with a Gaulish sword.

Though rare in the West, the round *umbo* is very well represented in Germany and Northern Europe at the end of the Iron Age. Nevertheless, it was also well distributed to the South, as examples are often found in tombs containing arms in Slovenia. As in Belgian Gaul, placing weapons in a tomb goes back to a pre-Roman tradition kept up by native auxiliaries in the Roman army in the late first century BC and the early first century AD.

OFFENSIVE WEAPONS

Sword and dagger

The Republican-period sword has posed an irritating problem for historians and archaeologists for a long time – why is it that an abundance of early Empire swords has come down to us, whilst there is an almost total absence of identified Republican examples? With this in mind, and taking into account that it was impossible to identify a single Roman sword in the excavations at Alésia, I even went so far a few years ago as to suggest that the pre-Augustan Roman army did not have a sword type of its own, but the in-depth research carried out for the preparation of this book, however, does not support that idea. The first Republican sword discovery, in 1986 and not yet fully analysed, was made in a dwelling in Delos, now referred to as 'The House of the Sword': a burnt sword, complete with its scabbard, was found under the courtyard paving in a layer of burnt material datable to 69 BC. This sword, 76cm long, is notable for its long sharp point and parallel blade edges; nothing was left of the handgrip – no doubt made from wood, as was the pommel – except seven fixing rivets. When it was burnt, the sword had been in its leather scabbard, the leather being stretched over two iron rods, apparently held in place by a system of three transverse circlets. Remarkably, the system of suspension has survived, and consisted of four rings fastened to two transverse circlets on the upper part of the scabbard. The adjustable slings of the baldrick were attached to these by small bronze buckles, two of which were found by the scabbard. The baldrick itself, or a belt, was secured by a larger buckle, which was also found.

With its sharp point and 4-ring suspension arrangement, the Delos sword shows all the characteristics of the *gladius hispaniensis*; described a century earlier by Polybius, this evolved under Augustus into the classic 'legionary sword', the Mainz type. The 4-ring system, which became the norm for Imperial-period swords, was basically Iberian in origin, and very different from the contemporary Greek or Celtic systems.

A further, more recent discovery has just confirmed that we really are seeing Polybius' *gladius hispaniensis*. Found in a tomb at Mouriès (department of Bouches-du-Rhône) in association with a group of pottery and metal artefacts, notably a bronze washing-kit with an Italic jug and *patera* and having no scientific context, this assembly can be dated to the last years of the second century BC or the very early part of the first century BC. The Mouriès sword, also 76cm long, had a system of transverse suspension circlets – two in this case – like the Delos sword, and thus could not be one of the contemporary Celtic swords so frequently found locally. Its tapered point, also like the Delos example, recalls the old form of Roman sword. The Mouriès sword had been placed upright in the tomb, and the handgrip still had a rectangular metal part, which had slipped down the tang as the perishable parts of the sword rotted away, and was probably a pommel rather than a hand guard.

The sword recovered from a Numidian tomb at Es Soumâa near El Khroub (Algeria) can now perhaps also be included among the group

86 Legionary with full equipment, towards 100 BC (P. Connolly; photo Röm.-Germ. Zentralmuseum, Mainz)

of known Republican swords. Originally 70-5 cm long (now actually 67cm) the sword found by F. Bonnell at the beginning of the last century had a leather-covered wooden scabbard, riveted along its length, and whilst the suspension system is unfortunately missing, the proportions of the weapon and the construction of the scabbard unmistakably recall the *gladius hispaniensis*, as G. Ulbert fully appreciated. The tomb dates from between 130-10 BC in the opinion of C. B. Rüger. An even older sword, from the Montefortino cemetery (tomb 30), with similar characteristics – length, tapered point – is definitely different from the contemporary local series.

In spite of their being one-off individual finds, we may hope that further Republican swords, until now thought to be Imperial weapons, may be more accurately identified in the future. It is admittedly difficult to distinguish late-Republican swords from those in use in early Imperial times, but some swords of the right length, in particular those with tapered points, are undoubtedly from the earlier series. This is the case, for instance, with the weapons found in rivers – in the Saône at Mâcon (67cm), in the Rhône at Lyon (68.1cm), perhaps from the period of the Celtic conquest, or from the Kupa near Siscia in Yugoslavia (Hoffiller 1912).

A table constructed using measurements from the best preserved swords available also reveals the archaic character of swords such as that from Berry-Bouy. There is nothing to prevent this weapon, deposited around 20 BC in this well-known grave, from having arrived in the area several decades earlier, for instance at the time of Caesar's siege of Avaricum in 52 BC.

Pilum

A weapon exclusive to the Roman army in Imperial times, the *pilum* would seem to be an individual creation amongst the many arms copied from defeated enemies. There was much intellectual discussion of its origin during the late nineteenth and early twentieth centuries, but insufficient textual and actual archaeological knowledge available; the situation is different today, and we can now be virtually certain of an Italian origin for the *pilum*.

Missiles with a small head on a long thin stem have been in use since very early times. Fifteen tombs in the burial ground of Ostoria dell'Osa in Rome itself, dating from the ninth and early eighth centuries BC, have yielded miniature reproductions of such weapons, rarely preserved due to their fragility.

In the middle of the second century BC, Polybius describes two types with wooden shafts, three cubits long (about 1.38 metres), with heavy heads as long as the shaft. This head, however, had half its length buried in the shaft where it was firmly riveted in place. From his text we can deduce an overall length of 2.07m for both of Polybius' models, the light and the heavy, which every soldier carried. From a rather obscure description – for which some past authorities proposed differing readings – we can infer that at the point where the head is attached there was a sort of 'bulb', either spherical or pyramidal in form, and it is this mounting which is prevalent under the Empire.

87 The Fontillet (Cher) *gladius*: a Caesarian weapon retained until the start of the Augustan era ? (Musée du Berry, Bourges)

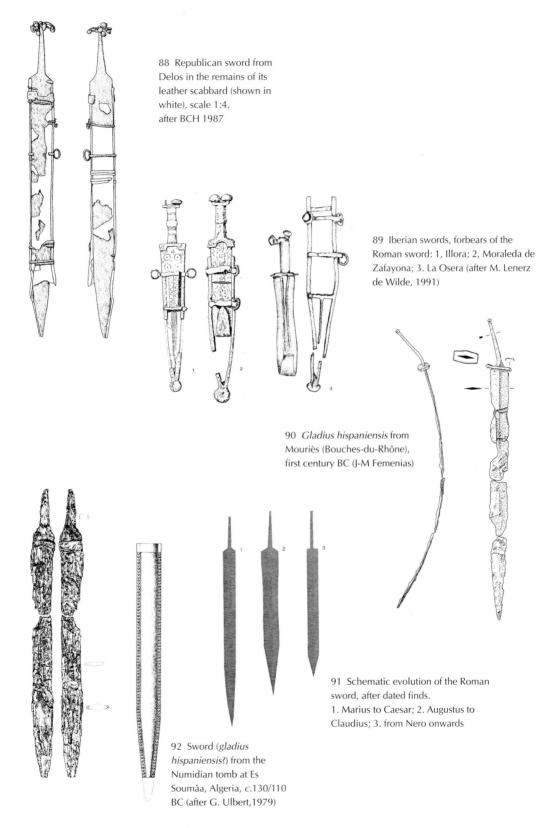

88 Republican sword from Delos in the remains of its leather scabbard (shown in white), scale 1:4, after BCH 1987

89 Iberian swords, forbears of the Roman sword: 1, Illora; 2, Moraleda de Zafayona; 3. La Osera (after M. Lenerz de Wilde, 1991)

90 *Gladius hispaniensis* from Mouriès (Bouches-du-Rhône), first century BC (J-M Femenias)

91 Schematic evolution of the Roman sword, after dated finds.
1. Marius to Caesar; 2. Augustus to Claudius; 3. from Nero onwards

92 Sword (*gladius hispaniensis*?) from the Numidian tomb at Es Soumâa, Algeria, c.130/110 BC (after G. Ulbert,1979)

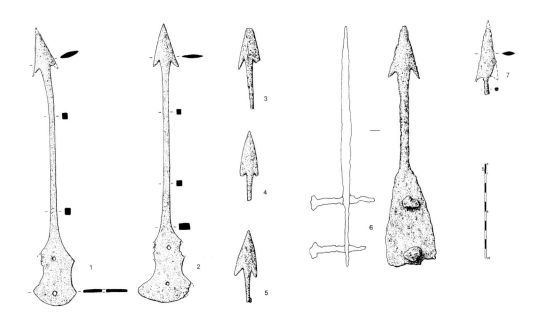

93 Examples of the riveted *pila* of the Republican period: 1-5. Ephyra, before 167 BC; 6. Entremont, towards 120-90 BC; 7. Les Pennes, La Cloche, 49 BC (1-2, after D. Baatz; 3-5 after S. Dakaris, 1964; after M. Willaume, 1987)

Although recognised as a powerful weapon, ancient writers considered that the *pilum* had the disadvantage of slow flight, and a nimble enemy could dodge it, or even throw it back at his attacker. The weapon was therefore redesigned, and the head slimmed down so that when it stuck into a shield, it bent, making the pila unusable. Plutarch attributes a further modification to Marius, which occurred to him during his battle against the Cimbrii in 101 BC; one of the two iron rivets holding the *pilum* head was replaced by a wooden peg which snapped at the first impact, to make it more certain of handicapping the shield bearer (*Vit. Mar.*, c.25). This modification was not always adopted, however, and Caesar (*B Gall.* II.27) some 50 years later writes of quick-reacting or lucky Gauls throwing *pila* back at his soldiers.

Several archaeological discoveries have enabled us to assess the Republican-period *pilum* more accurately than was possible using the information in the ancient texts, and design differences have been noticed, both in shaft dimensions and the methods of attaching the head. One model, used possibly in the third century BC and particularly in the second, is notable for its shorter head (approximately 25–32 cm) fastened to a trapezoidal plate by two rivets, the head itself also being altered to a triangular section with two wings. This model was definitely used in Greece, and examples have been found at the Nekromanteion site at Ephyra, which was destroyed by fire in 167 BC; the base of the head has a lateral groove deliberately cut into it. The same type, in this instance with a triangular foot, has been found in the destruction level of Entremont (dating from 123 BC or a little later), and this site has also yielded a socketed *pilum* point. It seems that from this time onwards the head was lengthened considerably – an Entremont example measures 78cm, and one from Numance 95cm; see also examples from Alésia and the Saône – to exceed a metre in length in some cases.

Another type of *pilum* head, well represented at Numantia (19 examples out of 26, according to Schulten) is not mounted on a riveted plate, but has a socket, and heads from this site vary considerably in length, from 15 - 95cm. This same model has been found at Alésia, where socket-mounted heads are as frequently found as riveted or tanged types. A different method of fixing, unknown from Numance, seems to have been developed at the end of the Gallic War period, though discontinued before the start of the Principate. This consists of a tapered shaft pierced laterally to accept a dowel. A well-preserved example of this type, 76.5cm long, with a ferrule in addition, was recovered from the Saône at Ouroux.

THE CAVALRY

Here again our principle source of written information is Polybius, who in Book VI of his *Histories* not only gives a fairly precise description of the cavalry in his own era, but also writes about the improvements made in his time to earlier equipment.

Although it had become widely used by his day, Polybius singles out the cuirass as a new development, though he was without doubt referring to chain mail armour, examples of which can be seen on some reliefs of his period (allowing for the problems of identification referred to previously). One of the most ancient depictions is that on the memorial to Paulus Æmilius at Delphi, which goes back to the second quarter of the second century BC. On this relief, unfortunately very badly damaged, the *equites,* like their opponents on foot, wore chain mail coats, fastened with a belt. Their round shields – as opposed to the oval design of the infantry – have an unusual transverse *spina.* According to Polybius, these cavalrymen were armed with strengthened lances which also had the butt-end reinforced so that it could be used as a club.

In Polybius' time, each legion had 300 cavalrymen, but they were recruited solely on socio-economic grounds. According to Livy (I.43), a man could join the cavalry only if he had a personal fortune of at least 100,000 *asses*, thus continuing the ancient tradition that having one's own horse was part of the aristocrat's privileges. This was hardly likely to give the Roman army particularly effective mounted troops. Unlike other races such as the Celts and the Arabs, the Latins had no local tradition of horsemanship.

The combination of these two factors resulted in several severe defeats for the Romans in the Second Punic War. During the Battle of Cannae, for instance, in 216 BC, some 50,000 troops were killed as a result of the inferiority of the Roman cavalry when they encountered the Numidians, Spaniards and Celts in the army of their Carthaginian enemy.

Having fought in Africa, P. Scipio was well aware of the importance of battle-hardened cavalry when fighting against such experienced adversaries as the Punic troops, and the skill of his mounted Numidians made a major contribution to his victory at Zama in 202 BC, which brought the Second Punic War to a successful conclusion.

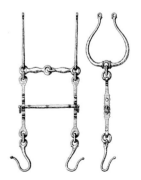

94 Bit and bridle in bronze, Italic style, with 'omega' decoration on the sides; Firenze, second century BC (after W. Krämer, 1964)

Cavalry equipment during the second century BC

The equipment used by cavalrymen these days is similar to that of the Greeks, but in former times it was different. Firstly, they did not wear armour, just a tunic, which no doubt gave them greater ease of movement and the ability to dismount quickly, but left them seriously exposed in close combat as they were unprotected. Also, their lances were ineffective on two counts: not only were they too slim and fragile for their intended use – even the jolting of the horse was often enough to break them before they could be used – but as they lacked an iron butt, they could be used only for thrusting. As a result, when their lances were broken, the riders were left holding only a pathetic stump.

Polybius VI

It was then that he gained his title of 'Africanus', and Rome started to have doubts about the way the legionary cavalry was being recruited; but it was only in Marius' time that auxiliary cavalry superseded the legionary cavalry.

This evolution was clearly visible by the middle of the first century BC, and it became the norm to recruit local native cavalry as near to the scene of action as possible, with such troops fighting in their traditional manner with their own weapons; in his Gaulish campaign for example, Caesar followed this pattern by recruiting cavalry from among the Aedui and their allies (*B Gall.* I.15). During the Civil Wars, Brutus had recourse to Gauls, Lusitanians, Thracians, Illyrians, Parthians and Thessalians (Appian, *B Civ.* IV.88), and in turn, Cassius recruited similarly in Gaul and Spain, but drew his mounted archers from among the Arabs, Medeans and Parthians.

These *auxilia* were at first only partially integrated into the Roman army, and they retained their native officers, though these were subsequently progressively replaced by young aristocrats as the regular Roman army evolved. It is very difficult when examining first century BC military finds to distinguish those weapons and items of equipment which belonged to the auxiliary troops, who under the Republican system were disbanded and sent home at the end of a campaign. The growing importance of auxiliaries to the Roman army explains why during the Principate their equipment retains strong traces of native origins. The equipment of the cavalry also developed, and the Roman army's horses were fitted out with saddle and harness types taken from the Gaulish cavalry.

THE ARTILLERY

We must distinguish here, as we shall do below for the Principate, between 'the light artillery' and the 'war machines' developed by the Greek engineers from the fourth century BC onwards. The 'light artillery' – thrown stones, slingshots, bows and arrows – was in use from the earliest times, notably in siege warfare, although it played a fundamental role in the Republican wars also. When preparing to confront Caesar in 50 BC, Pompey recruited 3000 archers from different regions – Crete, Sparta, Pontus and Syria – and created two cohorts of slingers, each of 600 men (*B Civ.* III.4). These numbers show not only the origins of these recruits but also their importance when preparing to receive a frontal attack.

War machines were also used in infantry engagements, but their use was first and foremost in siege warfare. Moreover, according to tradition, it was during a siege at Syracuse at the beginning of the fourth century BC that these weapons were invented; the principle of torsion springs, which persisted through to the Middle Ages, was apparently invented a little later, perhaps in Macedonia. This principle was very simple, consisting of winding ropes chosen for their strength and elasticity (some sources say animal tendons, others say twisted horsehair) between two metal bars firmly fixed into a stout frame. A bar passed through these twisted ropes tensioned by a winch imparted a massive force when released – see p.165 below. Using this system, arrows could be fired with much greater power than even the strongest archer could achieve.

Such machines mark the introduction into warfare of the first weapons with a destructive power greater than that attainable by human physical means alone. This advance had two immediate effects on warfare. First, it gave the Greco-Roman armies a 'quantum leap' advantage over their enemies, as they were, with rare exceptions, the only peoples able to build and use these weapons; and secondly, no defensive personal equipment – helmet, shield or body armour – could withstand a catapult arrow or a *ballista* ball. In addition, warfare became impersonal for the first time, as any soldier could be struck down at any time by a projectile, possibly without even seeing where it had come from. In short, these Greco-Roman advances in military technology revolutionised warfare.

The technical standards to which war machines were designed and constructed are based on a system of proportions described by Philon of Alexandria (late third century BC?) and in Augustan times by Vitruvius, but they were undoubtedly devised earlier, in the first half of the third century BC. At the very beginning of the second century catapults like the one from Ampurias (and also the new one from Teruel: Vicente 1997) followed these Greek standards meticulously; they continued to be followed until the end of the first century AD, enabling any size of war machine to be designed and built by making its components in fixed proportion to the length of the arrow to be fired from it. This basic measurement determined the dimensions of all the other components of the weapon.

The oldest catapult components which have come down to us do not antedate the early second century BC, but we do have two fairly complete examples from that time, both found in Spain. At Ampurias, excavations early in the nineteenth century of an arsenal close to the south gate brought to light the crushed metal reinforcements and the end pieces (*modioli*) from four rope bundles from a large wooden catapult; a reconstruction by E. Schramm in the early 1900s is still to be seen at Saalburg. Excavations at Teruel in 1986 led to a very similar find, and detailed study of this discovery and comparisons with the Ampurias evidence add much to our knowledge of Republican war machines (Vicente 1997).

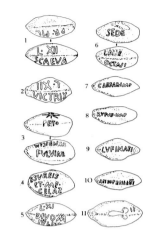

95 Lead sling shots used during the siege of Perugia by Octavian, 40 BC. References are made to the Twelfth Legion Victrix (1); the Legate Salvidienus Rufus (8); the *centurio* Fulvia (3); many carry insults to the enemy forces (after L. Keppie, 1984)

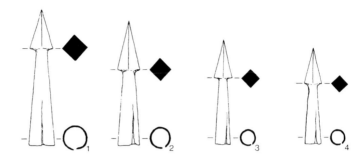

96 Points of catapult darts from Ephyra, excavation level of 167 BC (after D. Baatz, 1982)

Apart from these two catapults, we currently have nothing more than some odd pieces, which can be assessed only by comparing them with the above finds and later documents. At Ephyra in Epirus, excavators found a group of notched wheels from a tensioning system and some *modioli*, which were found in a burnt layer dated to 167 BC. These items were almost certainly intended to be used by a workshop or for repairs. The famous shipwreck at Mahdia, found off the coast of Tunisia, is probably that of a vessel lost very early in the first century BC. As well as a cargo of bronze and marble works of art, the ship was carrying a number of small useful items, amongst which were found four odd *modioli*, again probably intended for a maintenance workshop.

Finally, at Pergamon the reliefs on a balustrade erected between 197–59 BC by Eumenes II provide us with what is certainly the oldest known representation of a war machine. A frontal view, it shows the two rope bundles firmly secured in the wooden framework; one of the tensioning arms can be seen on the left, and three arrows are also visible, confirming that it is an illustration of a catapult.

In contrast to the rarity of mechanical components in our possession is the relative abundance of the projectiles used in sieges. Most arrows had relatively short solid heads, to judge for example from the discoveries at Ephyra in Greece and Entremont in Gaul. During the Transalpine conquest, the Roman army attacked the native villagers hiding behind their ramparts with war machines throwing stone balls often weighing more than ten kilos.

5 PROTECTIVE EQUIPMENT IN THE EMPIRE

Under the Principate, as at the end of the Republican era, the Roman soldier's protective equipment was the shield which he carried and the helmet and armour which he wore; after Marius' reforms, every soldier, legionary or auxiliary, had the benefit of all three. We shall look in turn at each item of equipment and trace its development during the first two centuries AD, as we are relatively well informed about this period. The third century poses other problems, and will be treated on its own. The fourth and fifth centuries will be considered together in the chapter on the Late Roman period (p.183-98).

SHIELDS

With their fabric covering and painted decoration (personal and unit emblems), shields were relatively fragile objects, easily damaged when travelling, and after Marius' reforms at least, shields were kept in leather sleeves with a hole for the projecting *umbo*. Such sleeves, mentioned by Caesar in the *Gallic War* (II.21) have been found on several High Empire military sites, such as Vindonissa and Valkenburg.

However, one must not think that the Roman soldier's equipment was totally romanised at the start of the Empire period. The auxiliary troops retained their own equipment for a long time, and clearly the army drew on this when updating its own. This is the case, for example, with shields, for which Rome initially drew on native patterns. The Republican pattern *umbo* was based on the 'winged' type developed throughout the West during the closing centuries of the Iron Age. The German type of round *umbo* is known from several early sources; Caesar first mentions the German mercenaries in the *Gallic War*, then again later when writing of the siege of Dyrrachium during the war against Pompey (*B Civ.* III. 53). Several German-type *umbones* were recovered from the trenches at Alésia and other first century BC Gaulish sites. The *oppidum* of La Cloche aux Pennes-Mirabeau (department of Bouches-du-Rhône), destroyed by Roman troops in 49 BC for having supported Marseille, also yielded a circular *umbo*. Further instances could be cited; in the Narbonensis at Lavérune (Hérault), for example, and close to the German frontier (shield edging from Augst: Deschler-Erb 1992).

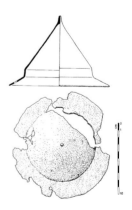

97 *Umbo* from a Germanic shield discovered at Lavérune (Hérault) in a context dating to time of Tiberius

98 *Umbo* from a round shield from a tomb at Berry-Bouy near Fontillet (Cher) (Musée du Berry, Bourges)

As an essential component of the shield, the *umbo* supplies valuable information on both how different types of shield developed through time and the requirements of its users; but other shield components can also be of use to the archaeologist. Straight lengths of edging strip tell us little, but some reinforcing corner pieces, like those from a find at Strasbourg, can help us to reconstruct the Tiberian period polygonal shields known from reliefs such as those on the Triumphal Arch at Orange.

Even if we have not yet found a complete Roman shield in the West, the fragments of leather protective shield-sleeves from sites such as Valkenburg in Holland or Vindonissa in Switzerland give us indirect information on shield shapes and sizes. Such sleeves suggest that the curved rectangular model went out of use early, from the start of the second century AD onwards, in favour of a more easily handled oval or sub-rectangular shape.

Shield types and their standardisation

In spite of the complete lack of any written documentation about shields from the beginning of the Principate, the introduction of new types, which were soon to be adopted by the Roman army, can be dated from the reign of Augustus. It appears that the Republican pattern underwent several modifications, but that these were not enough for it to be retained in service. In several tombs in the Rhineland, at Bránov and at the Magdalensberg, metal *umbones* have been found which follow the elongated shape of the wooden *spina* on the Greek pattern. Such shields do not seem to have been very numerous, and in addition we do not know whether they may not in fact have been used by Celtic auxiliaries in the Roman army. Actually, it is in Central Europe and the Champagne region, from the start of the Second Iron Age onwards, that similar *umbones* (in two parts) have been found, and these may have evolved into the solid *umbo* around the time of the change from BC to AD and up until the time of Tiberius or Claudius, the date of the latest deposit, at Urmitz.

The typical Roman legionary shield, as shown on reliefs on monuments such as Trajan's Column, was the rectangular scutum, which resembled a Republican shield shortened at the top and bottom; its pronounced curvature gave better protection, but the real reason for its development was the introduction into the army of new combat techniques, such as the tortoise. The oldest depiction of this type of shield, dated around 10 BC, is on the tomb of Munatius Plancus at Gaeta. Was the curved shield standard equipment for the first-century legions? This seems doubtful, in spite of the evidence of Trajan's Column, where rectangular and oval shields serve respectively to distinguish legionaries from auxiliaries. Apart from this famous representation, the curved shield appears only very rarely on legionary memorials; that of Valerius Crispus in the Wiesbaden Museum seems to be exceptional. Conversely, other memorials (Flavoleius Cordus at Mainz, Castricius Victor at Aquincum) show legionaries with shields, which are either oval or which have definitely rounded corners.

In spite of the difficulty of establishing fixed dating points before the change from BC to AD, it is difficult not to see the curved shield

The shield as an offensive weapon

They [the legionaries] had only to stay in their ranks and throw their *pila* then use their swords and shield bosses to kill and massacre without pause.

Tacitus, Ann. XIV.36

99 Legionary of the Augustan period (after J. Warry)

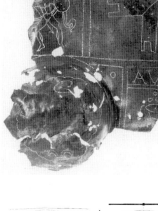

100 Memorial to the legionary C. Valerius
Crispus at Wiesbaden (photo RGZM, Mainz)

101 *Umbo* from
a shield from Vindonissa,
with the name of the
Legio VIII Augusta (photo
Th. Hartmann, Vindonissa-
Museum, Brugg)

102 Reconstruction of
the Doncaster shield
with round *umbo* (after
P. Buckland, 1978)

as the same as the shield used by gladiators, and this is especially
noticeable on figures shown in relief, even small ones in bone or, particularly, in bronze. As will be seen below, it can be argued that another part of the soldier's protection, segmental armour, was developed
for Roman army use from the gladiator's equipment, either by copying or by using it as a source of ideas, though we do not yet have any
precise information.

As might be expected, archaeological discoveries of shields are rare.
With the exception of a find at Doncaster in England in 1971, our
knowledge of the developing form of the shield comes principally
from shield fittings and sleeves from military sites where they are more
frequently discovered than shields themselves. Reconstructed from
traces on site plus laboratory work, the Doncaster shield is rectangular
in shape, slightly convex, and made from three layers of wood glued
together, like the example from Fayûm. It is notable for its applied
metal fittings (plates and rivets, in a poor state of preservation unfortunately), and particularly for its hemispherical *umbo* which protects a
large vertical reinforcement on the inside which served as the handgrip. These features seem to suggest a German or Western influence,
but the identification of an auxiliary's shield (P. Buckland, 1978) does
not fit easily into the scheme of evolution subsequently proposed by
C. van Driel-Murray.

The shield as disguise

Two soldiers risked a
stunning exploit. Taking
shields from a pile of
corpses to prevent their
being recognised, they
severed the ropes and
straps of the war
machine, a ballista of
extraordinary size,
which had been flaying
their ranks with
enormous stones.

Tacitus, Hist. III.23

103 Relief on the Aurelian Column; the sculptor has tried to avoid repetition by changing the shapes of the shields (Photo D.A.I., Rome)

The shield, a personal possession

To ensure that soldiers did not become lost or separated from their comrades during the confusion of battle, each cohort had its individual design of shield decoration, and this practice continues today; these distinctive signs are known by their Greek name of δειγματα. Furthermore, the soldier's name and cohort number were written on his shield.

Vegetius, Mil. II.17

Overall, the only site which has yielded a definite example of a shield of the type portrayed on Trajan's Column is that of the legionary camp at Vindonissa: was this type perhaps only used during a manoeuvre such as the 'tortoise', which might explain why it was used only by a limited number of soldiers. Several sources indicate the rarity of this model during the second century, and specialists are hard pressed to explain its presence at Dura-Europos in the middle of the third. This remarkably well-preserved example has richly painted decoration, and it has been suggested that it is a parade shield. Perhaps the curved rectangular type was used throughout the Empire, but only by certain corps and was never a general service issue. Other legions, in Britain and Germany, clearly used the first-century sub-rectangular type, as is shown by the Doncaster and Valkenburg finds, where two models, the oval and the sub-rectangular, were in use during the same period. A little earlier, around 130 AD, the workshop of the *Legio I Minervia* at Bonner Berg yielded only shield-sleeves and sub-rectangular shield fittings.

One must therefore abandon the idea of a strict standardisation of shield types during the first century AD. In spite of its being illustrated on Trajan's Column, the rectangular model cannot have been used by every legion, but only by selected troops when carrying out special operations. This would explain why on a monument commemorating the same victories of Trajan over the Dacians there are legionaries who are definitely carrying the sub-rectangular type.

104 Trajan's Column; illustration showing the different shapes and decor of the Dacians' shields. (Photo D.A.I., Rome)

105 An auxiliary with his oval shield: in addition to his lance, he carries two javelins in his left hand as a reserve (Mittelrheinisches Landesmuseum, Mainz)

106 Painted shield No.1 from Dura-Europos, mid third century; state as found and state after restoration (H.J.Gute)

107 Painted shield No.2 from Dura-Europos, mid-third century; state as found and state after restoration (H.J.Gute)

108 *Umbo* from a decorated shield from Halmeag, Romania (after E.Hubner, 1978)

Whatever their shape, shields at the beginning of the Principate carried a large number of metal reinforcements, both as edgings and to protect the *umbo*. On the rectangular shield this central feature was hemispherical, possibly fixed to a metal plate which followed the shield's curvature. The best example of this type, now preserved in the British Museum, was found in the River Tyne in Northeast England; it bears both the emblem, a bull, and the name of the Seventh Legion *Augusta*, as well as the owner's name, Junius Dubitatus of the century of Julius Magnus; a detachment of this legion served in Britain under Hadrian. The *umbones* of this type of shield are usually simpler, sometimes being only a simple flanged hemisphere; only the characteristic curvature of the legionary shield, composed of glued laminations, enables it to be distinguished from the pattern used by the auxiliaries.

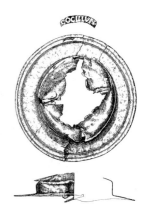

109 *Umbo* from a shield carrying bronzeworker's mark Cocillus; London (after R. Jackson, 1984)

The *umbones* on auxiliary shields can be very elaborate, as is illustrated by various discoveries in different parts of the Empire; one from Kirkham in Lancashire is decorated with a series of military subjects round the central figure of a seated Mars.

The various discoveries of leather shield-sleeves, all fragmentary, show that they could carry decorative elements, inscriptions and other symbols without reducing the shield's efficiency under normal conditions (see quotation from Caesar above). Nevertheless, even protected by its sleeve, a shield was still fragile. During one period of continuous rain, Varus' troops could not remove the sleeves, swollen as they were by water, and the shields themselves, heavy, waterlogged and warped, became difficult to use (Dio Cassius, LVI.3).

The top of a goatskin sleeve discovered in 1985 at Caerleon had had a sort of ticket, now unfortunately missing, sewn onto it, which must have carried such information. Better preserved examples from Bonn and Vindonissa enable a legionary number to be read, and on the Valkenburg and Vindonissa specimens there is a label in the form of a *tabula ansata*. It is tempting to link these labels with the texts on the shields on the Triumphal Arch at Orange, although they could also be interpreted merely as manufacturers' marks. Vegetius (1.18) explicitly states that 'formerly' – meaning at the beginning of the Principate – every shield carried the cohort's unique decoration, the soldier's name and the cohort and century unit numbers. A stamp also provides the only known reference to a manufacturer: a circular *umbo* discovered in London bears the stamped phrase *Cocillus f(ecit)* in just the same way that bronze artefact makers signed their work. The same name appears on a sword found at Nydam in Denmark, but this is perhaps just a coincidence.

110 Leather tag in the form of a *tabula ansata* from a shield cover from the XIth Legion (Vindonissa, from a photograph)

In general terms, we can now say that the curved shield was used only by legionaries, and they may also have used other shapes more close to oval; the method of construction, the glued laminations, going back to the Republican period, could be specific to the legionary shield. For their part, the auxiliaries carried flat shields of simpler construction, just layers of planks perhaps, like the Gaulish shield. Shapes vary from oval to hexagonal, without our being able to say that either form was exclusive to the cavalry or the auxiliary infantry.

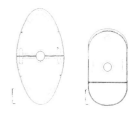

111 Two shield types based on the leather covers from Valkenburg (after C. van Driel, 1986)

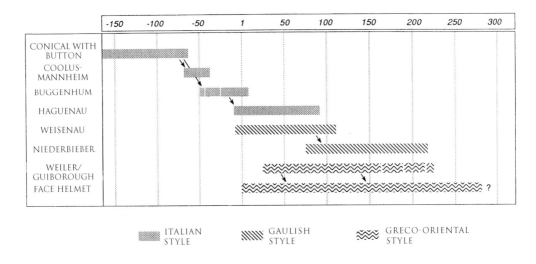

	-150	-100	-50	1	50	100	150	200	250	300

CONICAL WITH BUTTON

COOLUS-MANNHEIM

BUGGENHUM

HAGUENAU

WEISENAU

NIEDERBIEBER

WEILER/GUIBOROUGH

FACE HELMET

ITALIAN STYLE   GAULISH STYLE   GRECO-ORIENTAL STYLE

112 Table of the main types of helmets from the end of the Republic and the start of the Empire

HELMETS

In 1926, P. Couissin elaborated a first synthesis of various nineteenth-century studies of Roman helmets, and research into these has progressed very considerably since then, due in large part to the information published in England and Germany. The attribution of some Gaulish helmets as Roman, and vice versa, caused confusion for a while, but the overall situation is now much clearer.

In 1975, H. Russel Robinson classified known helmet types as representative of very large groups: the 'Coolus Type', in which he included the very early types from the group of that name as well as the later grouping which had been named 'Hagenau' by P. Couissin, and the 'Imperial-Gallic Type', corresponding to the 'Weisenau Type' defined by his French predecessor. To these he added an 'Imperial-Italic Type' which grouped together the various helmets manufactured in the Attic-Italian tradition under the Principate, and also included in this series those later examples classed by Couissin under the name 'Niederbieber', whilst recognising the influence of the 'Imperial-Gallic' model on these.

Since then German research, notably that published at Mainz by U. Schaaf and G. Waurick at the time of a major exhibition of ancient helmets in Berlin, has enabled us to consider the different types among these helmets from two viewpoints. On the one hand the craftsmen's traditions were fully integrated into the Imperial *fabricae*: the Italian traditions were superseded by what were probably Gaulish methods, then by Eastern; certainly, local manufacture was not immune to these influences. On the other hand, the refined chronology which we now have enables us to construct a theoretical 'family tree' of helmet types which can often be confirmed by archaeological discoveries.

We will now take up this family tree at the point where we left it, that is, with the army of Julius Caesar; in other words, with the Coolus-

113 Weisenau-type helmet
from Theilenhofen
(Photo Prähist.
Staatsammlung Munich)

Mannheim types. Finds at those sites continuously occupied up to the time of Drusus' campaign – notably the camp at Haltern, abandoned in AD 9 – enable us to identify new types as they appear, perhaps as a result of Augustan military reforms. First, came a bronze helmet which is a lineal descendent of the Caesarian type, and a second type which, surprisingly, seems to have developed from Gaulish originals contemporary with it. The iron helmet classified as the 'Weisenau Type' must have been made at workshops very close to the preceding ones, and in any case follows the same traditions of craftsmanship.

The evolution of the bronze Italic helmet is well-established, and only the date of some developments remains a subject for discussion. As far as is known, though the correlation between Caesar's pattern of movements and the distribution of the helmets is still a major point of

114 The Niedermörmter (third century ?) helmet, a late variant of the Weisenau type (photo Röm.-Germ. Zentralmuseum, Mainz)

115 Helmet-type from Mainz-Weisenau (photo Röm.-Germ. Zentralmuseum, Mainz)

discussion, the Mannheim-Coolus type is the most characteristic of the helmets in use in the middle of the first century BC; this was superseded by a helmet with a button on top and a guard for the nape of the neck, known as the Buggenum type. This model is perhaps the last which can be called a descendent of the Etrusco–Italic line, its successors profiting from a number of basic additions. If we accept G. Waurick and U. Schaaf's interpretation of the inscription SCIP IMP on the Sisak helmet, the Buggenum type was in use from the middle of the first century BC onwards; the number of finds in the Lower Rhine and the Lippe river indicate a long period of use up to the turn of BC into AD.

The two helmets discovered in the camp at Haltern come from around the period 9 BC to 9 AD (when the site was abandoned). The first, made of bronze, shows the development of the Italic helmet – Republican types, then Buggenum; the guard for the nape of the neck is more developed than in early types, and is at a right angle to the helmet bowl. The conical button on the top is not found on every helmet in this series, but a more important feature is the frontal reinforcement which has been added to give protection from blows from above. The eponymous helmet in this series, discovered at Drusenheim (Lower Rhine) has two tubes on sides, to take vertical plumes. The cheek covers, found for example on the example from Schaan (Switzerland), are quite large, with semicircular cut-outs in the front edge, one at eye level and one for the mouth.

The other helmet from Haltern, this one in iron, is of similar shape after allowing for the use of a different metal in its construction. The bowl is fairly well developed, almost cylindrical at its base, and the nape protector in either at right angles or rather less. Two to four grooves reinforce the bowl above the nape guard and there is similar strengthening at the front, in the form of ringlets or eyebrows. These technical modifications, which show the great skill of the weaponsmiths who produced this series, do not replace the frontal reinforcement itself, described above, which seems to have been standard. Some early examples, like the eponymous Mainz-Weisenau or Besançon helmets, are very carefully decorated, using the different colours of various materials – iron, copper, brass and silver, plus enamel and even coral. Most ancient helmets must have had a lining – leather, cloth or felt – as is proved by the lines of perforations in them, particularly the later examples. Alternatively, troops may have worn a light 'bonnet', the *pileus*, to which reference is made in the fourth century by Ammianus Marcellinus (*Hist.* XIX.8).

The study of helmets from the second half of the third century AD is handicapped both by the rarity of archaeological material and, perhaps to a lesser extent, by the surviving sculptural representations. A resulting judgement, perhaps too hastily made, was that the Roman army abandoned the use of the helmet during this time. As often happens, however, further research showed that this judgement was based on assumptions which could not be sustained in the light of the facts. Until recently, it was thought that the helmets 'disappeared' in the middle of the third century, to reappear in an entirely different form – the 'composite' (see chapter 10 below) – at the beginning of the fourth century when, for lack of any preceding types, they were attributed to the Parthians.

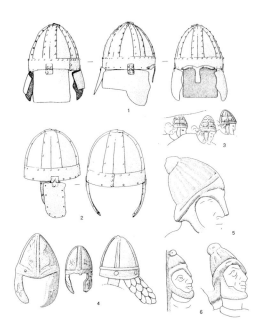

116 Trophy of Sarmatian and Dacian arms on Trajan's Column. Note the dragon-shaped standards, later adopted by the cavalry as sporting equipment, and the 'Spangenhelme' composite helmets which two centuries later were to equip a large part of the Roman army (Photo D.A.I., Rome)

117 'Spangenhelme' of the second and third centuries. 1 and 2, helmets from Der-el-Medineh and 'Egypt', in the Leyde museum; 3, Sarmatian cavalry composite helmets on Trajan's Column; 4, Composite helmets (Dacian or Sarmatian) from among the trophies at the base of Trajan's Column; 5 and 6, helmets from the Arch of Galerius at Thessalonica (after S.James, 1986)

In reality, S. James has shown very clearly that composite helmets, or 'helmets with ridges or ribs' ('Spangenhelme') before becoming widely used in the sixth century, were in use in the West from the turn of the first to second century AD. Conical composite helmets – in one case perhaps fitted with a nose-guard – attributed to the Dacians or Sarmatians, can definitely be identified in some of the scenes and on some of the trophies depicted on Trajan's Column, and are also to be seen on the Arch of Galerius at Thessalonica, erected towards 300 AD. Moreover, two helmets found in Egypt and thought to be from a much later period, can now be attributed to this time. Fashioned in the same way as 'Spangenhelme', these helmets correspond in every particular to the earlier representations, and can be distinguished from the later models by their hinged cheek-pieces, a feature which disappeared at the beginning of the fourth century at the latest.

It was due to the great economic, political and military crises around 250-60 AD that the Principate type helmets were discontinued, with their one-piece bowls and meticulous craftsmanship. From Diocletian's time, a few years later, a network of Imperial *fabricae* took over helmet manufacture to overcome the rapid decline in the traditional production system (see below).

ARMOUR

With the exception of segmental armour, Roman armour at the start of the Empire showed only minor detail developments from its Republican forbears. Senior officers continued to benefit from the 'muscled' cuirass, and many highly decorated examples must have been made for special occasions, if we are to believe the evidence of the Imperial statues studied by C. Vermeule. It is without doubt to such cuirasses that the *Notitia Dignitatum* refers in its list of 'government workshops' of the Late Empire. It is significant that these cuirasses, so frequently appearing on statues and on some coins, must in reality have been extremely rare, as none have yet come to light in our times.

Scale armour

In the East, a type of armour made from small plates was in use from the Bronze Age, though Greece, as we have seen, used it only occasionally; for instance, we know of many more examples of scale armour from the Crimea than from Greece. Unknown in the Celtic world, it was no doubt introduced into the Roman army by Eastern auxiliaries from the start of the Christian era, and many examples are to be seen in the West on statuary dating from the first to the fourth centuries AD.

The scales found in excavations – no complete example has yet been discovered – permit several comments to be made. Some sites have yielded several hundred plates (346 from Newstead for instance), and others only a few. Nothing could have been easier for a craftsman than to cut a replacement scale from sheet metal, the scales being held together by small metal rings, like tiles on a roof. Using scales from Carnuntum alone, the Austrian archaeologist von Groller in the early 1900's defined 36 different types. The most frequently occurring were rectangular, 20-30mm long by 10-20mm wide, with one end rounded; each scale was dished by a hammer blow, and the plate was pierced with several pairs of small holes for fixing purposes.

A recent discovery at Carpow in Scotland has revealed the details of how scales were fixed in the West. The scales were first laid out in rows, fastened together with short pieces of bronze wire which passed through the holes in their sides and were bent over towards the back; each row was then stitched through its top holes through a tough backing cloth to a string running the length of the row. This ingenious method required very little skill, and garments could easily be made or repaired as necessary. Other methods must have been in use as well, as can be seen from the variations in placement of the fixing holes in scales found on different sites; at Strasbourg, 'twinned' scales have been found – but this variation, which must have reduced the flexibility of the garment, does not appear to have been widely adopted. The overall design of scale armour garments is known to us only from reliefs, and we can distinguish two models, for the infantryman and the cavalryman respectively (see below). Judging from what we know at present,

118 Plate armour, a variant form of scale armour. 1 and 2, Tibetan example; 3 and 4, Corbridge. The existence of this type of armour at Corbridge probably indicates that there were auxiliaries of Eastern origin there at that time (after Robinson, 1975)

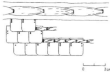

119 General view of the scale armour fragment from Carpow (Scotland), also showing the way scales were attached to the backing fabric (after J.C.N. Coulston, 1992, and J.P. Wild, 1981)

120 Scale armour, chainmail coats and segmental armour on the Aurelian Column (photo D.A.I., Rome)

scale armour seems to have been less used than chain mail among the infantry; numerous monuments show standard-bearers in such armour, particularly the *aquilifer* – one example is L. Sertorius Firmus of the *Legio XI Claudia Pia Fidelis*, in the Verona museum. Several panels on the monument at Adamklissi also portray legionaries wearing scale armour.

Apart from those to cavalry, most of the funerary monuments which show scale armour belong to centurions, for instance that commemorating Q. Sertorius Festus at Verona. On some particularly carefully illustrated cuirasses, the scales have been engraved to make them look like a bird's plumage, and one ornamented version (*lorica plumata?*), examples of which have been found at Newstead, Ouddhorp, Augsburg and Besançon, shows a chain mail coat overlaid with tiny scales engraved with a dorsal fin.

This raises the question of whether, as far as the infantry was concerned, Rome did not think that scale armour gave poorer protection than other types of armour in use at that time, or was perhaps less convenient. An important point also is that we know nothing about how it was fastened by the wearer. Funerary monuments showing scale armour, like the one to T. Calidius Severus at Carnuntum, confirm that it was never fitted with the shoulder-hooks which to a certain extent made the chain mail coat easier to put on. As scale armour was made form solid metal components, of necessity fitting closely to the body, there must have been an opening which was closed by laces or hooks. Specialist opinion is undecided between an opening at the back, which would need a helper to fasten it, and a slit on the left shoulder, which seems more likely.

121 The Vachères Warrior (Alpes-de-Haute-Provence), end of the first century BC. (Photo CNRS, Chéné-Rveillac)

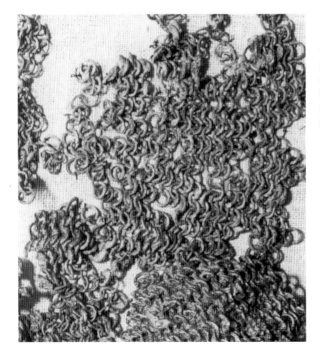

122 (left) Fragment of a chainmail coat from Künzing in Bavaria (Photo Prähist. Staatsammlung, Munich); (below) chest hook from chainmail coat from Chassenard (Allier) (Musée des Antiquités Nationales, Saint-Germain-en-Laye)

The chain mail coat

The adoption of the chain mail coat by the Romans stems from their having borrowed the idea from the Celts, among whom it had been use since the third century BC, albeit reserved for the aristocratic warrior classes. There is little to say about Roman chain mail apart from the fact that it came in two styles known to its originators, the Gaulish and the Greek. The first was very popular among the first century AD cavalry, and the second had shoulder reinforcements, accurately shown on the Vachères statue among others. It is hard to say whether either type had a specific use; in sculptures, the cavalry are shown wearing the model with either a cape or shoulder patches, and this appears equally to apply to the legionaries and auxiliaries, although we have less information in this area.

123 Minerva in 'Gaulish' chainmail coat on an armour plaque from Hrusiča (Photo Narodni Muzej, Ljubljana)

Several Roman chain mail coats, usually found rolled up, have been recovered from rivers such as the Saône, and on some of them the lower rows of rings are of bronze, probably as decoration. Apart from these river finds, chain mail coats are usually found only on military sites, and their most characteristic feature, apart from riveted rings, are the pectoral hooked clasps, usually with snake-head terminals. Some of these clasps, which are the easiest part of a set of chain mail armour to write about, carry an engraved inscription, as in the case at Chassenard for instance, where what is perhaps the name of the wearer, *A. Blucius Muci(anus),* appears on the two clasps still *in situ* on the garment.

Segmental armour

While both the chain mail coat and scale armour were of ancient origin and were copied respectively from their Celtic and Eastern users, segmental armour was a Roman invention, appearing at the beginning of the Principate (though we do not know its Roman name). The need for a new form of armour which would give better personal protection must have become apparent fairly early in the campaigns at the start of the Principate. One of the most attractive theories about its origin suggests that it was copied from gladiatorial equipment, since these fighters are known to have worn a form of articulated protection for the chest and limbs.

Being a Roman invention, segmental armour is shown on a number of monuments, such as Trajan's Column and that of Aurelian, though we cannot learn from this representation how widely it was in use. Much debate on this subject in scientific circles has led to the view that it was worn only by legionaries, although not universally; the situation is somewhat similar to that of the curved shield, which seems to have been carried by some legionaries but not by others. Is it a question of the wearer's privileged rank, or of the needs of his military role?

Segmental armour had various advantages over the chain mail coat, notably in the greater protection it afforded to the wearer. As we have seen, chain mail spread the effect of a blow satisfactorily, but could not prevent serious bruising or protect against a sharp pointed weapon or an arrow. Segmental armour was 'real armour', resistant to much heavier blows than a chain mail coat, and it also gave the wearer excellent

124 Artist's impression of a
Flavian-period legionary
(after J.Warry)

freedom of movement, particularly of the shoulders, where there was
extra reinforcement as on chain mail coats.

The introduction of segmental armour is generally dated to the
reign of Claudius, thanks to discoveries at Magdalensberg, which
was mainly occupied around AD 45, Chichester (closed context of
AD 47?) and Colchester (AD 49?). The presence of a characteristic
hinge at the Tiberian Aulnay-de-Saintonge campsite, occupied AD
20-30, should also be noted. This was used by the forces repressing
the Gaulish revolts of Florus and Sacrovir, but the hypothesis that
segmental armour was inspired by the equipment used at the gladiatorial school at Autun, the *crupellarii*, is still valid. In his *Annals*, Tacitus
describes fully the almost totally protected gladiators, so covered in
iron that it would take an axe to knock one down. It is quite possible
that this text reflects the strong impression made on the legionaries
by this equipment, leading to the creation of the new armour. The
modern reconstructions and re-enactments of the Ermine Street
Guard show the extent to which a tightly-knit group of legionaries
wearing it would seem invulnerable.

In spite of its advantages, segmental armour nevertheless had its
weaknesses. The multiplicity of hooks and hinges which gave freedom
of movement, and the fixings between the different plates, were easily
broken, which is why they are relatively abundant among site finds. In
addition – and this is another discovery based on the modern English
reconstructions – the leather straps which gave flexibility to the shoulder guards were soon vulnerable to sweat or heavy rain. Segmental
armour was therefore effective against attacking blows or in impress-
ing the enemy, but one can understand why it never became standard
equipment among the legionaries for whom it had perhaps originally
been intended.

125 Floored gladiator on first
century sculpture from
Chalon-sur-Saône; note the
articulated protection on the
arms. (Photo Musée Denon,
Chalon-sur-Saône)

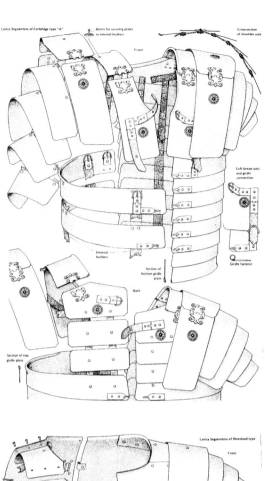

126 Segmental armour (*lorica segmentata*), Corbridge type (P. Connolly in Robinson, 1975)

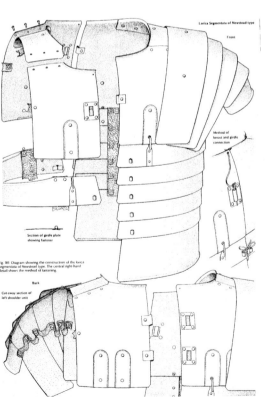

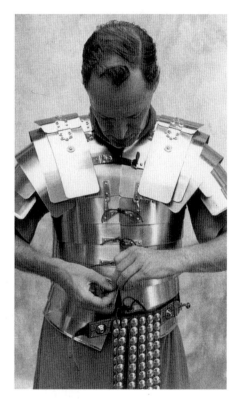

127 Putting on *lorica segmentata* (Ermine Street Guard, 1992)

128 Segmental armour (*lorica segmentata*), Newstead type (P. Connolly in Robinson, 1975)

129 Bronze statuette of a soldier wearing segmental armour (British Museum)

As we have seen, our knowledge of segmental armour is still imperfect, insofar as reconstruction has been based on the information gleaned from statues and monuments. Several archaeological discoveries, notably at *Carnuntum* and Newstead early last century, and especially at Corbridge more recently, have enabled us to learn more about the details of segmental armour during the first and second centuries AD; two types have been identified from these latest finds. Central to our thinking on the distribution of this armour are the military sites where bronze armour components – easier to identify and more fragile than the iron plates – have been recovered. The discovery of segmental armour components on sites manifestly occupied by auxiliary troops, such as the port of Fréjus in Southern France, is not enough to cause us to doubt whether segmental armour was limited to the legions; such isolated finds could be explained either by visitors' losses or be seen as coming from a group of components collected together for recycling.

The third century

One established opinion, shaped and polished by generations of historians, holds that military equipment in the third century AD is characterised by the abandonment of earlier items which had been in use during the High Empire. Examination of the Arch of Septimius Severus, for instance, generated the view that the armour used hitherto practically disappeared from the start of the third century; but J. Coulston was able to show that H. R. Robinson was wrong in this instance, and had himself fallen into the same error which he had corrected previously in others who cited older reliefs as evidence.

On these statues, almost without exception, all the soldiers in the foreground are wearing one of the three known types of armour – segmental, chain mail or scale armour. That the armour of the soldiers fighting in the background lacked detail was not due to the laziness of the sculptors but stems on the contrary from a wish to highlight the importance of the persons in the foreground. There are no more leather cuirasses on these reliefs than there are on first or second century reliefs.

The evidence of funerary memorials is less certain, and one should not conclude when seeing the representation of a soldier in a simple tunic and cloak that armour had gone out of use. Deceased, the soldier is above all just a man, and to show him in 'civilian' clothing, as more than a few memorials to military personnel do, is to continue a trend which was noticeable from the beginning of the Principate through to the second century. Several memorials, like that to Severius Acceptus of the VIIIth *Legio Augusta* in the Istanbul Museum, show the armour, and often the rest of his military kit, displayed at the side of the deceased. One cannot, therefore, use a depiction in civilian attire to 'prove' that the infantry had ceased wearing armour during the third century.

Finally, mention should be made of a funerary inscription, dated to the third century, which was discovered, used as building material, in 1876 in the church of Montceau-le-Comte (department of Nièvre). This exceptional discovery mentions an armour factory in the territory of the Aedui managed by the centurion *M. Ulpius Avitus,* whose career

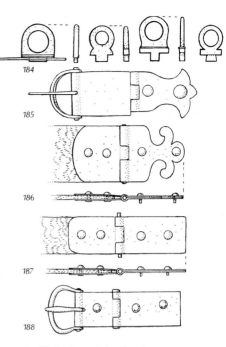

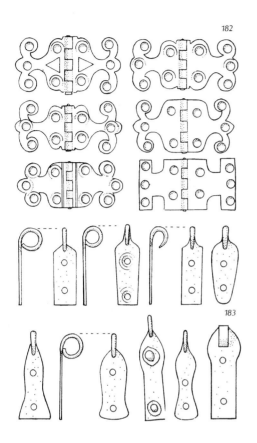

Fig. 182–184: Bronze fittings from loricae segmentatae.
182: Hinges from shoulder units showing the deterioration from the most elaborate to the most crude. The last, from Rheingönheim, may be a makeshift repair. 183: Girdle-plate tie hooks showing the known variety of shapes. The first three are the most usual. 184: Bronze loops – an alternative to hooks – known from Carnuntum and Caerleon.

Figs. 185–188: Hinged strap and buckle fittings common to 1st century loricae. 185: From Carnuntum. 186: From Caerleon. 187, 188: The common form from most military sites.

130 Hooks and hinges from *lorica segmentata* from various finds (after Robinson, 1975)

131 Third century equipment: helmet, armour and shin guards, oval shield, *spatha* and baldrick. Memorial to Severius Acceptus in the Istanbul Museum, Turkey (after J.C.N. Coulston, 1990)

132 A third-century army: helmeted soldiers wearing armour, with lance and oval shield, on the fresco of Exodus in the synagogue at Dura-Europos (after J.C.N. Coulston, 1990).

had included service with the IIIrd *Legio Augusta* and the IVth *Legio Flavia*. One cannot say whether this factory was dedicated to the ‚manufacture of chainmail coats or other types of armour, as Héron de Villefosse thought, but it seems to have been fully operational before the reference in the *Notitia Dignitatum* to the *fabrica loricaria* at Autun from Diocletian's time onwards. We are seeing here one of the few known mentions of the arms manufacturing system which Diocletian tried to establish as part of his reforms.

Armguards and leg protectors

This 'guided tour' of defensive equipment would not be complete without mentioning protection of the soldier's limbs, which were generally not covered by his body armour. The wish to protect these parts of the body as well as the chest can be seen in the addition of *pteryges*, 'winglets' which extended the body armour over the thighs and also sometimes the upper arms. From the second century BC (the Pergamon relief) the upper arms had a form of armguard – continuously articulated metal cylinders which gave perfect protection yet permitted free movement. These forms of armour were generally worn in Rome by gladiators.

While body armour would preserve the life of the soldier, protection for his limbs was intended to enable him to continue to fight; a soldier immobilised by an arrow through the leg could not continue, and was thus both vulnerable and of little help to his companions. Armour extensions like the above were particularly appreciated when the enemy were bowmen: at Dura-Europos, helmets were fitted with a chain mail extension to protect the neck.

Some of Trajan's legionaries portrayed on the Adamklissi monument are shown wearing both armguards and leg protectors. The latter could have been of genuine use, even though it has often been deduced from their appearance on monuments to officers, from the rank of centurion upwards, that wearing them was just the continuation of an old Greek tradition. Leg protectors do not appear to have been widely used in the Republican army, but seem to have been worn in the early Principate. However, it is not always easy to pick them out on reliefs, and one cannot be sure that they were always of metal; a leather leg protector found recently in the harbour at Narbonne reminds us of the possible existence of accessories made from organic materials, which are rarely preserved on land sites.

133 Chainmail coats with a hood covering the head, on the 'Battle of Ebenezer' fresco in the Dura-Europos synagogue (after J.C.N.Coulston, 1990)

6 OFFENSIVE WEAPONS IN THE HIGH EMPIRE

The equipment of the Roman infantryman was considered by his contemporaries to be a masterpiece of efficiency; time and again in the *Annals* Tacitus praises the superiority of the protection this gives him. The armour 'close-fitting to his body', 'the long shield pressed against his chest' (II.21), his helmet ... all combine to make him victorious. The short sword, as opposed to the Germans' 'long spikes', is equally deadly both in the woods into which the barbarians often lured the Roman troops and on the open ground in hand-to-hand combat. Of course, this is largely propaganda to give the reader and the soldiers a warm glow of superiority; but at the same time, this publicity does reflect a real sentiment. The barbarians always placed heroic deeds and a scorn of death above equipment and technique; in adopting the opposite attitude, Rome changes the nature and purpose of combat – and conquers triumphantly.

The offensive weapons of the Roman soldier were both hand weapons – the short sword, the long sword and the dagger – and the spear, *pilum* or lance. Roman artillery — war machines, bows and slings – are treated in a special chapter later in this book.

SWORDS

The Roman sword was generally worn on the right side, both for practical (it was thus quicker to draw) and cultural reasons: P. Couissin has correctly pointed out that wearing the sword on the right side goes back to the Iberians, and before them, to the Celts. This is the position generally seen on statues, though there are certain exceptions, which may in some cases reflect local habits. It is, for instance, tempting to bring together a passage from Flavius Josephus, which clearly describes first century legionaries wearing their swords on the left side, with several statues and reliefs from Palmyra of the first century AD, which in their depictions of warriors, the god Aglibôl, a sea-monster relief and so on, definitely show the sword worn on the left.

In the West at least, the rule in the early Empire was that all soldiers who had to carry a shield must wear their sword on the right, with the exceptions of centurions (who usually did not come under direct attack) and, for less clear reasons, some standard bearers (for instance, Pintaius of the fifth cohort Asturum in the mid-first century AD). The

---

The inferiority of German weaponry

The giant shields of the barbarians and their enormous pikes were nothing like so effective as the pilum, the sword and close-fitting body armour among the trees and thickets where a soldier had to fight hand-to-hand and go for the enemy's face with his sword point. The Germans wore neither armour nor helmet, and even their shields, without iron or leather to strengthen them, were only thin wickerwork or thin painted planks. Only their front ranks were armed with pikes, the rest of the troops were armed only with fire-hardened wooden spears, often very short.

Tacitus, Annals, II.14

In its propaganda message, the above passage expresses the Roman army's genuine belief in its technical superiority.

---

style changes in the Severan period with the introduction of the longer sword, which was to be worn on the left.

The *gladius*

The hallmark of the Roman soldier from the Republic onwards was the *gladius*, a particularly murderous weapon used primarily for thrusting but also in slashing. At the beginning of the Principate it hardly differed in appearance from the *gladius hispaniensis* of preceding centuries and was quite a long sword – examination of well-preserved examples showing a length of more than 60cm (24inches) including the handgrip, but it tended to become shorter from the start of the Empire.

A passage from Tacitus (*Ann.* XII.35) has been used as evidence to show a difference between the equipment of the legionary (*gladius* and *pilum*) and that of the auxiliary (*spatha* and lance), but the text does not tell us whether this difference applied as a general rule throughout the Roman army. Studies of reliefs, including several Rhineland memorials such as those to *Annaius Daverzus* (Mainz), *Licaius* (Wiesbaden) and *Firmus* (Bonn) show auxiliaries armed with the *gladius* and a dagger, like their contemporary legionaries. The rec-

134 The grip of the *gladius* was designed for thrusting; Mainz relief

tangular shield with rounded corners appears to be a legionary exclusive, but is shown only rarely on monuments (*C. Valerius Crispus*). On the other hand, all auxiliaries carried lances, but only legionaries used the *pilum*. For their part, the cavalry auxiliaries at this time used a longer sword than the infantry (see below, *spatha*).

Based on *gladii* found at Pompeii and on several sites along the Rhine-Danube frontier, G. Ulbert has been able to show that there were two models of *gladius*, the one succeeding the other. First came the long-pointed 'Mainz Type', whose blade alone could measure 60cm (24in), and is well-evidenced in the Augustan period and the first half of the first century AD. The 'Pompeii Type' followed this, a short-pointed type which replaced it, probably during the early principate of Claudius.

Taking into account the historical contexts, the older type is much better known in the West than its successor. Mainz Type *gladii* have been found on several occasions in rivers like the Rhine ('Sword of Tiberius') and the Thames (Fulham), and on various sites occupied when it was in use. A very fine example has recently been found, together with several parts of a silver *cingulum*, in an early shipwreck at Porto-Novo in Corsica, but its restoration revealed a transition form to the later type; some well-preserved specimens have come to light also on land, at Fontillet (Cher department) and at Rheingönheim. Apart from examples from Pompeii itself, the Pompeii Type is less well represented, though there have been a number of finds in France, notably the river Saône, and some from Mediterranean shipwrecks such as the 'Chrétienne H', as well as others in Great Britain and Germany.

The Mainz Type has a handgrip in three distinct parts slipped onto the blade tang; a metal handguard, the grip itself and the pommel. The guard is protected on its face nearest to the blade by a bronze disc, sometimes carrying an engraved or punched decoration: on the Augustan *gladius* from Comacchio there is a hunting scene showing two pairs of animals confronting each other. From Dangstetten comes an example with two oval protective discs, one silvered and the other engraved with *pelta* shapes. The actual handgrips could be of wood, bone or ivory, and typically had four grooves to ensure a firm grip. The pommel is also usually of wood or ivory, and a discovery at Dangstetten suggests that the wooden versions had a sheet-metal bronze covering, which has rarely survived.

The scabbards of this type of *gladius* exhibit a variety of styles whilst retaining the basic design features of protecting the sword's cutting edges and point and method of suspension – two circlips, each with two suspension rings. Basically comprising two thin sheets of wood, sometimes covered with bronze sheet, scabbard decor and fittings can vary considerably. The scabbard tip, for instance, with the primary function of protecting the scabbard's point and holding its lower end together, is usually a cast-bronze button, but it can also serve to hold in place a piece of bronze sheet, sometimes decorated; examples have been found which are veritable works of art, resembling decorative lace and contrasting in colour with the scabbard itself. Both types were found at Dangstetten, for example, but one from Comacchio is elongated, made from bronze sheet and has a cut-out pattern.

135 Augustan period *gladius* from Mainz (Rheinisches Landesmuseum, Mainz)

—	Measurement unknown				
?	Measurement to investigate				
>	Measurement incomplete				

Site	Gl. + grip + scab.	Gl. + grip	blade only	scabbard	Date (context)
Late-Republican gladii					
Mouriès	—	765	637	—	Ist BC
Delos	760	760	631	620	69 BC
Mainz-type					
Bonn RLM	—	765	591	—	—
Berry-Bouy	> 757	—	—	667	20 BC
Lyon	—	681	556	—	—
Strasbourg-Kngsh.	—	—	535	540	—
Mâcon	—	670	530	—	—
Chalon 102	—	642	525	—	—
Chichester	—	665	520	—	—
Wederath gr. 2215	—	628	487	—	AD 40 – 50
MAN 49824	—	610	479	—	—
Mainz (RLM 2580-81)	749	—	437	590	?
Saint-Marcel	—	559	417	—	—
Rheingönheim	—	?	?	-	AD 40-70 ?
Wederath gr. 1344	—	450	345	—	c. AD 50
Magdalensberg	662	—	—	556	20 BC – AD 20
Bijlandse Waard/Mars	—	—	—	570	—

136 Measurements of some early, well preserved *gladii*

137 Early *gladius* and scabbard from Strasbourg, marked *Q.Nonienus Prude(n)s ad ara(m) f(ecit)*; Strasbourg Museum (photo Röm.-Germ. Zentralmuseum, Mainz)

The external appearance of scabbards is known only through a few discoveries, but the example recently found at Porto-Novo is well preserved enough to show, the wooden sheath and its construction. The cloth or leather covering once described on the wood does not exist (it was merely an effect of the organoc material decay).

Two richly decorated scabbards with repoussé bronze decor carry names. An example from Strasbourg shows '*Q Nonienus Prude(n)s ad ara(m) f(ecit)*', the *tria nomina* form perhaps implying that Prudens himself was not the maker, but more likely a selling-agent or distributor. The place of manufacture, obliquely referred to as 'the altar', which could apply to any altar in any town, can in this case be precisely identified, thanks to the second example. This comes from Vindonissa, and has a more precise mark *C. Coelius Venust. Lugud.*: from its *tria nomina* form plus 'Lugud.' we may deduce that the maker or seller of both scabbards, which closely resemble each other in style, was in Lyon. The similarities between the markings – their positioning on the scabbard, style of lettering and the use of the nominative case for the name – make it highly improbable that they indicate the sword's owner or user; they certainly refer to a manufacturer or seller. Also, we know from other sources that the altar at Lugdunum, dedicated to Rome and Augustus and illustrated on contemporary coins bearing the legend ROMETAVG, was surrounded by the workshops of bronze founders and finishers, on what is now the hill named Croix-Rousse.

To these two items, one from the Tiberian period and the other from the Claudian, may be added a scabbard fragment found among sanctuary material at the Grand Saint-Bernard. The design on this – a scene of animals hunting in lush vegetation – also appears on the signed plaque

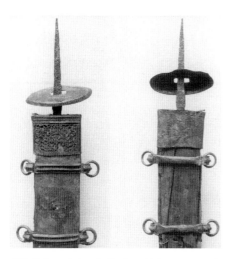

138 Grip end of a *gladius* from Mainz, preserved complete with its scabbard (Rheinisches Landesmuseum, Mainz)

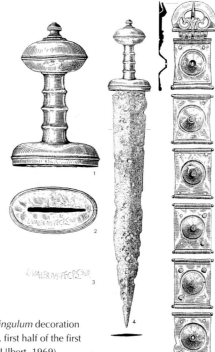

139 *Gladius* and *cingulum* decoration from Rheingonheim, first half of the first century AD (after G.Ulbert, 1969)

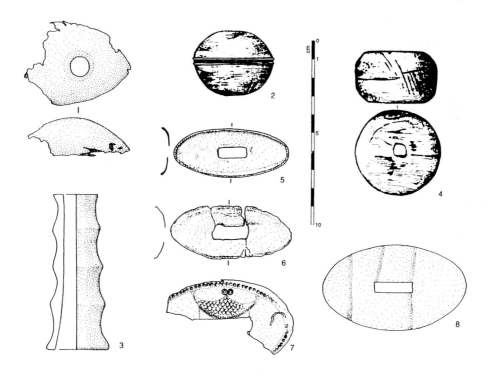

140 *Gladius* grip components: 1. Bronze cladding for the wooden pommel (Dangstetten); 2. Wooden pommel (Vindonissa); 3. Bone grip (Musée de Vienne); 4. Wooden guard (?), Vindonissa; 5-8 Metal reinforcements for handguards (Dangstetten). Illustrations - 1, 5-8, after G.Fingerlin, 1986 2,4, after Unz, Deschler-Erb 1997; 3, after J-C Béal, 1984

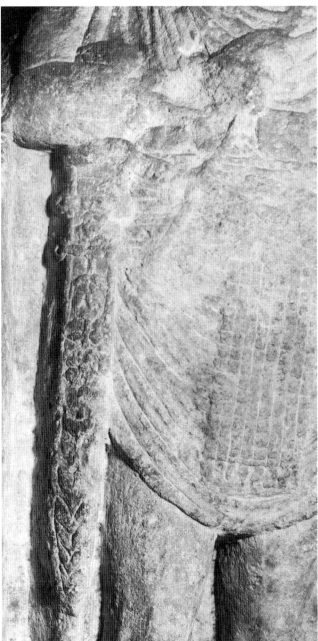

141 Early *gladius* found in the Thames at Fulham, with its decorated bronze scabbard

142 (left) Detail of the *gladius* with a decorated scabbard on the memorial to the archer Hyperanor found at Bingerbrück (photo Röm.-Germ. Zentralmuseum, Mainz)

143 Lower part of an early *gladius* scabbard found at Wiesbaden (Wiesbaden Museum; photo Röm.-Germ. Zentralmuseum, Mainz)

from Vindonissa, so we can attribute it securely to Lyon's *C. Coelius Venustus,* and we now have some information on the distribution of these high quality military items from the second quarter of the first century AD.

Within the Pompeii type of *gladius*, we can see a certain measure of standardisation. The chape, which carries less decoration, is length-ened to extend up the sides of the scabbard, ending in palmettes, as at Hod Hill. The transverse circlips follow the grooved type, which until this point was just one of a number of variants. Finally, and most noticeably, the bronze scabbard plaques are much reduced in size and the repoussé decoration which was characteristic of the finest early first century scabbards is discontinued.

The appearance of this new type of *gladius* perhaps coincides with a perceived need to improve the sword's main feature, its point, and the previous model seems to have been rapidly replaced by the new. Whilst the blade length of the Mainz type varied between 35-60cm, the blade of the new type is rarely more than 50cm, thus continuing the steady shortening of the Roman sword from Republican times, to tie in with developments in combat techniques. As will be seen below, this development was to be reversed from the third century onwards.

We know very little about the manufacture of these early *gladii*; only two stamped examples are known. The first, from Vechten, bears only the letters AE, whose meaning is very difficult to determine. The second, a Mainz Type found in the Rhine at Bonn, has SABINI on the tang and SVLLA on the blade, which H. Dressel suggests may indicate the name of a craftsman called Sabinus Sulla. As we have seen, the most useful information has come from scabbards, and we can now identify various items as coming from workshops in Lyon in the first half of the first century AD. Further consideration of style and the discovery of other marked scabbards may in the future enable us to learn more about weapon manufacture in the High Empire.

144 Fragment of *gladius* scabbard from Vindonissa carrying the stamp of its maker in Lyon (after E.Ettinger and M.Hartmann, 1984)

145 Fragment of *gladius* scabbard : Vindonissa (after E.Ettlinger and M.Hartmann, 1984)

146 (top) *Gladius* scabbard from Valkenburg (photo Röm.-Germ. Zentralmuseum, Mainz)

147 '*Gladius* of Tiberius' found at Mainz and now in the British Museum (photo Röm.-Germ. Zentralmuseum, Mainz)

148 (left) An unusual depiction of Mars, wearing a Corinthian helmet, engraved on the scabbard of an early *gladius* found at Lobith in the Low Countries (Leiden Museum, photo Röm.- Germ. Zentralmuseum, Mainz). (below) Parts of an early *gladius* scabbard from Vindonissa (photo Th. Hartmann, Vindonissa-Museum, Brugg)

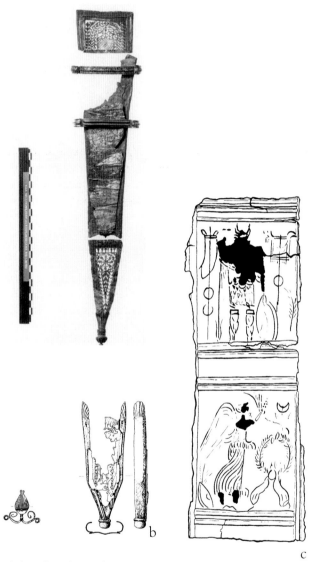

149 a. *Gladius* scabbard chape from the oppidum at Aumes, Hérault (photo L.Damelet, CDAR, Lattes); b. applique in the form of a palmette, and *gladius* chape from Rottweil (after D.Planck, 1975); ºzc. part of a *gladius* scabbard from the second half of the first century from Vindonissa (after E.Ettlinger and H-W.Doppler, 1986). d. Mainz, Brand : *gladius* from the late first or early second century (photo Röm.-Germ. Zentralmuseum, Mainz)

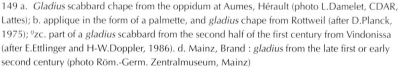

The infantryman's equipment under Nero

They move off, advancing silently and in order, each one in the place he will occupy when facing the enemy, every infantryman wearing armour and helmet and having a sword on each side.

    The sword at his left side is noticeably longer, the one at his right measures only around one empan (*c.*25cm). The elite soldiers escorting the general carry a lance and a round shield, the rest of the phalanx have a javelin and a long shield, and also carry a saw, a basket, a pickaxe and an axe, plus a sickle, a strap and a chain as well as rations for a three-day march; overall, the infantryman is almost as heavily laden as a pack-mule.

Josephus, BJ III.93-5

The *spatha*

The long sword, the *spatha*, may be contrasted with the *gladius* in the High Empire sources, but it had become a generic term from the end of the second century onwards. Late authors such as Vegetius use the terms *spatha* and *semispatha* where earlier references would have been to the *gladius* and *pugio*; because of this, it is sometimes difficult to identify early *spathae* in museums, and one sword from Pontoux (Saône-et-Loire), 84cm long, and another even longer example (102cm) from Rottweil, may be cavalry swords from the early Principate. Such discoveries, however, are the exception before the third century, and one of the first *spathae* which can be associated with an infantryman is that found in a Roman soldier's (hurried?) burial at Lyon. This discovery, which can perhaps be linked with the battle there in AD 197 (the soldier's purse contained twelve silver *denarii*, the latest being struck under Septimius Severus in AD 194), also gives us accurate information on the new method of hanging the *spatha*.

    The adoption of a long sword by the infantry entailed essential modifications to the way in which it was worn; heavier than the *gladius*, the *spatha* was worn on the left side, suspended from a baldrick whose length could be adjusted by a row of metal buttons. Several such decorated baldrick-straps have been preserved in Scandinavian peat deposits, notably at Vimose. This discovery of a baldrick and its metal components together has enabled us to understand the purpose of the bronze objects found in association with *spathae* in other tombs where only metal artefacts remain, such as the burial at Lyon cited above. In the latter case, the skilful reconstruction by J. Oldenstein, as well as demonstrating the adjustment system, has shown the purpose of a solid bronze button for adjusting the baldrick over the applied decoration.

    In examining the origin of these swords, their barbarian ancestry can clearly be seen. It is significant to note that the soldier who died at Lyon in AD 197 had obtained his kit from a region in close contact with Germanic peoples, as is borne out also by the fibula he was wearing, typical of the Frankfurt area, and the only one of its type so far found outside the Rhine-Danube *limes* area.

    The *spatha*, in no way just a 'long *gladius*', marks an important break in the evolution of Roman arms, and its characteristics do not appear to have changed very much during the third century. In any

150 Early *spatha* from Rottweil; after D.Planck, 1975

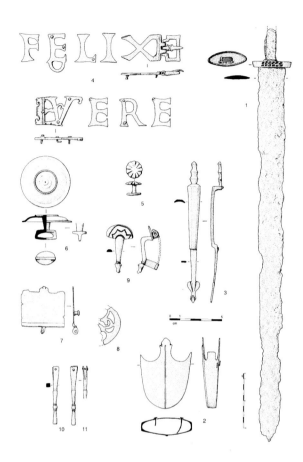

151 Contents of the tomb in the Rue des Fantasques, Lyon; AD 197 (?), Musée de la Civilisation Gallo-Romaine, Lyon

152 (above) Handguard and chape from the *spatha* (photo Musée de la Civilisation Gallo-Romaine, Lyon); (below) map showing origins of the *fibulae* found, suggesting origin of the deceased

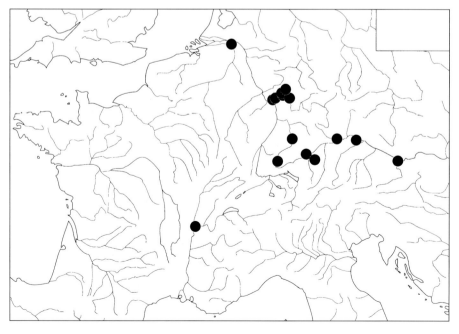

153 Distribution of knee fibulae Böhme 19 with engraved decoration

event, sword lengths cannot be seen as part of a chronological development, though the case seems to be different for the widths, which did increase over time (although only from the fourth century onwards). This criterion is, however, not sufficient in itself to permit its use for dating an older sword found out of context, as will be seen from the table below which shows the dimensions in centimetres of a number of contextually-dated *spathae*.

	Provenance	Dating	Overall length	Blade length	Blade width
Early form	Lyon	c.200	75.4	68.4	5.2
Straubing/Nydam type	Augst 2	post 273	75	59	4.2
	Augst 19	post 268	74.8	58.5	4.0
	Augst 20	post 268	74.6	60	4.4
	Augst 45	post 268	84.5	66.3	4.4
Lauriacum/ Hromowka type	Canterbury 1	c.200	87	65.5	5.8
	Canterbury 2	c.200	92	70.2	5.7
	Augst	post 268	77.2	59.4	5.6

Measurements: from the original (Lyon); Martin-Kilcher 1985 (Augst); Goodburn 1978 (Canterbury). Datings from contexts (Lyon, Augst); chape typology (Canterbury)

If *spatha* blades did tend to become wider (see Later Antiquity below), the arrival from the end of the third century of wide blades, usually grooved and having parallel cutting edges, should be noted. A sword of this 'Lauriacum/Hromowka type', which preceded the large 'rapiers 'of the Merovingian and Carolingian periods, is known from Augst and has been dated to shortly after AD 268.

A particularly remarkable *spatha* has been found in a tomb in Cologne, fitting tightly into a wooden scabbard covered either in leather or perhaps fish-skin, with an ivory handgrip and a richly decorated circular silver chape to protect the point. 88.8cm long (70.6cm without the handgrip) this very slim weapon can be dated to the second half of the third century.

A large part of our information on swords of this period comes from finds in Scandinavian peat bogs, many of which were first used around the start of the third century, such as those at Thorsberg, Vimose, Illerup-Å and Nydam. This last site, in East Jutland, has yielded at least at a hundred swords of this period, all imports from the Roman world, and these discoveries have enabled an individual type to be identified, the Straubing-Nydam, which is characteristic of the third century. Usually 71-85cm long overall, these swords have a blade which tapers slightly towards the point, unlike earlier types. Some of these Straubing-Nydarn *spathae* carry a maker's mark, a practice which had become more widespread since the beginning of the Principate and which increased in subsequent years. Often in

154 Memorial of the praetorian M. Aurelius Lucianus, third century; after J. Oldenstein, 1976

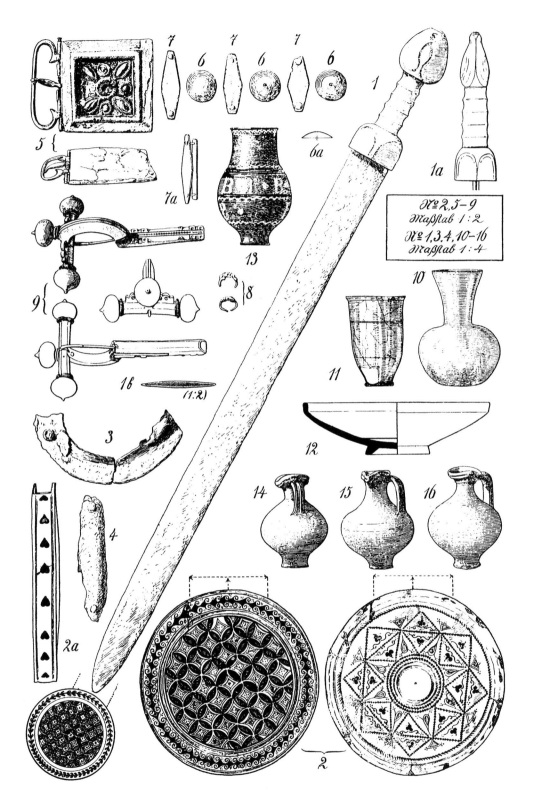

155 Tomb from Severinstor, Cologne, early fourth century (after G.Behrens, 1919)

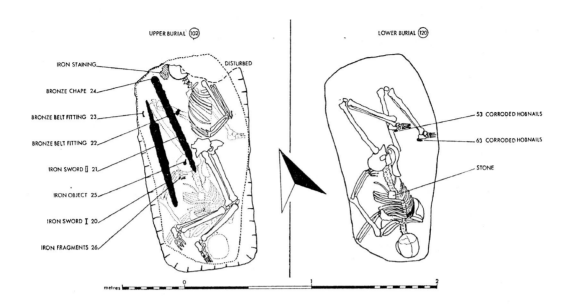

156 Murder at Canterbury. The grave with its two skeletons, the *spathae* with their chapes (after Ant. Journ. 1979)

the form of an inlay, marks were placed at the upper end of the blade, positioned so they could be read by the user. Some marks give the maker's name in the nominative case – *Cocillus, Aciro m(anu), Marci. m(anu), Natalis m(anu), ALF* . . . etc. – while other manufacturers limited themselves to symbols, one being a small rose of which there are several variants. A final group, proving the Roman origin of these weapons, draws on Greco-Roman traditions and shows Mars, Minerva, Victory and an eagle and crown, for instance, often in pairs, and one sword from Pontoux (Saône-et-Loire departement) appears to be stamped with a lion or other large feline, a type without a known parallel so far.

When excavating third-century levels, parts of handgrips and scabbards are much more frequently found than swords themselves, and we should now look at modifications introduced after the legionaries had adopted the *spatha*. The three-part grip found on *gladii* continues, but the handgrip changes from the deeply-grooved form characteristic of the *gladius* to longitudinal tubes of similar length, usually decorated with either a continuous motif, or a simple symbol repeated at random over its surface. Bone handgrips of this type are to be seen in many museums, and they were also made in wood, which explains the presence on the Lyon sword of the 'lacework' plate, which can only have been intended to serve as reinforcement. In the double tomb from Canterbury, the handgrips have completely disappeared, but desiccated fragments on the sword tangs clearly show that they were of wood; as at the start of the Empire, higher quality swords could have been fitted with ivory handgrips.

157 Funerary portrait of Tertiolus, Augsburg: his servant presenting him with a *spatha* and its baldrick. After J. Oldenstein, 1976

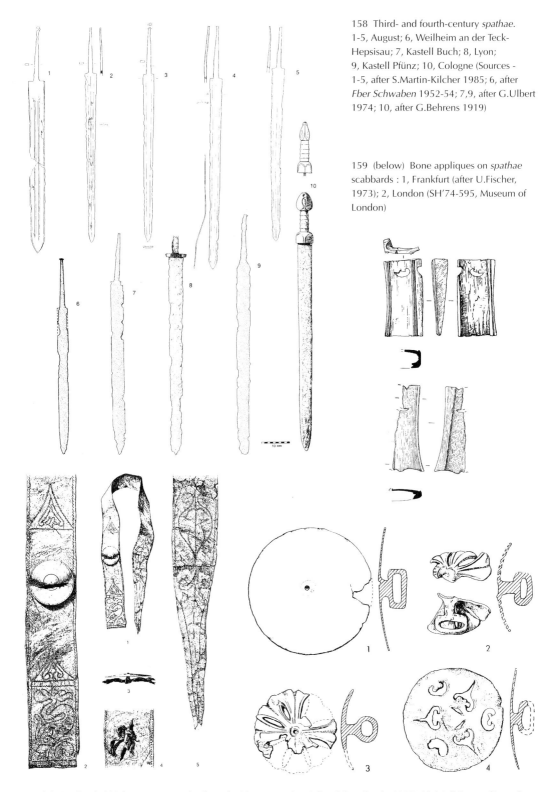

158 Third- and fourth-century *spathae*.
1-5, August; 6, Weilheim an der Teck-
Hepsisau; 7, Kastell Buch; 8, Lyon;
9, Kastell Pfünz; 10, Cologne (Sources -
1-5, after S.Martin-Kilcher 1985; 6, after
Fber Schwaben 1952-54; 7,9, after G.Ulbert
1974; 10, after G.Behrens 1919)

159 (below) Bone appliques on *spathae*
scabbards : 1, Frankfurt (after U.Fischer,
1973); 2, London (SH'74-595, Museum of
London)

160 (left) Leather baldrick to carry a *spatha*, from the Vimose peatbog (after C.Engelhardt, 1869); (right) fixing appliques for
spathae baldricks : 1-3, Saalburg; 4, Zugmantel, after B.Stjernquist, 1954)

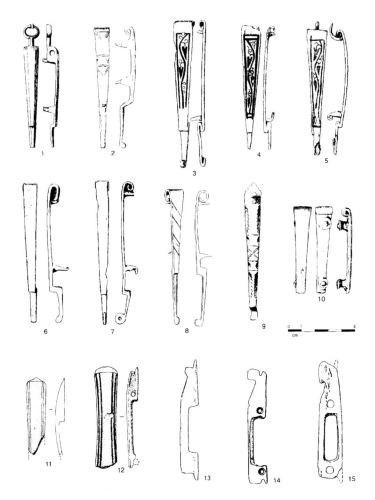

161 Suspension hooks from *spathae* scabbards. Bronze (1), iron (2-10), bone and antler (11-15) : 1,2,3,8,10, Vimose; 4,Osterburken; 5, Zauschwitz; 6,7, Saalburg; 9, Rimburg; 11, Escolives-Sainte-Camille; 12, London; 14, Cologne;15 RGZM Mainz (1-10 after H.J.Hundt, 1959-60; 11, after D.Prost, 1983; 12, from the original; 13-15, after J-C Béal and M.Feugère, 1987)

Spatha scabbards, fitted with the new suspension system, are very different from those of *gladii*. In every case they have a metal circlip fitted at the scabbard mouth to hold the two scabbard laths firmly together – we are talking here of the wooden scabbards as used in the first and second centuries. The suspension ring hangs vertically and has extended fixing plates, in some cases riveted. Known examples vary considerably one from another. A first series, in iron, seems to have come only from Germany and neighbouring regions, and an example was found *in situ* at the top of a scabbard found at Vimose. This type of suspension unit may be damascened, in styles reminiscent of box-shaped chapes ('Dosenortband') and ring pommels ('Ringknaufschwerter'), which are discussed further below. We therefore have an indication of origin for arms which were undisputedly made in the Upper Danube and Rhine regions from the third century onwards.

Known examples of bronze suspension hooks are still so few that no significant conclusions can be drawn about their distribution, but we have a large group of bone and deer-horn hooks. These have been found on all the northern frontiers of the Empire, from Britain to Dacia and beyond; but we lack the itemised precise information which would enable an accurate analysis of types to be undertaken.

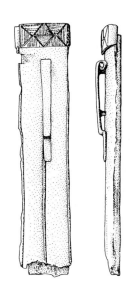

162 Top part of a wooden *spatha* scabbard, with its iron suspension loop: Vimose peatbog, third century (from a photo)

121

163 Bronze chape from Cologne, Bayental. Third century AD (photo Röm.-Germ. Museum, Cologne)

Scabbard chapes are equally numerous. The oldest type, as found on the Lyon *spatha* for example, is a simple round bronze ferrule, notched at the top and resembling a *pelta* shape. This type developed early in the third century into a closed-top form in which the *pelta* is suggested only by two symmetrical cut-outs, each *pelta*-shaped. This is the start of the box-shaped form ('Dosenortband'), whose size and decor developed spectacularly during the second half of the third century. In this same period, craftsmen were quick to make more complicated chapes, circular or trapezoidal, an example of which was found still in place on a *spatha* at Dura-Europos.

Other sword types

Other types of sword were used by the Roman army at the same time as those described above, particularly towards the end of the High Empire. Whilst some were just local variants, others belonged to relatively coherent cultural groups. This is the case with the 'Ringknaufschwerter', swords with a ring shape at the top of the grip; and the research started in the early 1900s by J. Déchelette and P. Couissin has recently come to fruition, thanks largely to finds collected in the German area by H. J Hundt, K. Raddatz and H. J. Kellner.

164 Equipment from a German tomb, including a ring-pommel sword ('Ringknaufschwert'): tomb 79 from Malente-Krummsee (after K. Raddatz, 1959-61)

A tomb at Wehringen has enabled the type to be dated to the middle of the second century AD, and a discovery at Geneva shows that it was in use around AD 180. Like other *spathae*, however, ring-pommel swords only became widely used at the end of the second century, and they are met much more frequently in later times. Identified by its most unusual grip,

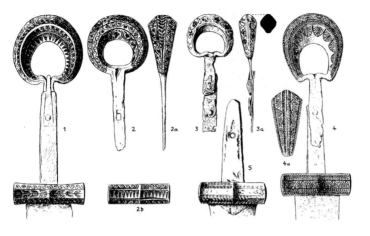

165 Examples of damascened decoration on the pommels and guards of 'Ringknaufschwerter': 1, Pocap; 2, Vimose; 3, Straubing; 4, 'Bodensee'; 5, Condren (after H.J. Hundt, 1952)

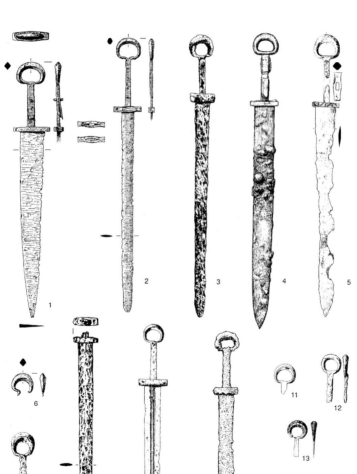

166 Ring-pommel swords ('Ringknaufschwerter') : 1. Denklingen; 2, 'Tyrol'; 3, Chalon-sur- Saône; 4, Hamfelde; 5, Malente-Krummsee; 6, Eining; 7, Ljubuski; 8, Wehringen; 9, Steinamanger; 10, Vertault; 15 and 13, Sisak; 12 and 14, Frankfurt-Heddernheim (1,2,6 and 8, after H.J.Kellner, 1966; 3 and 10, after J.Déchelette 1913; 4 and 5, after K.Raddatz, 1959-61; 7,9,11-14, after H.J.Hundt, 1955)

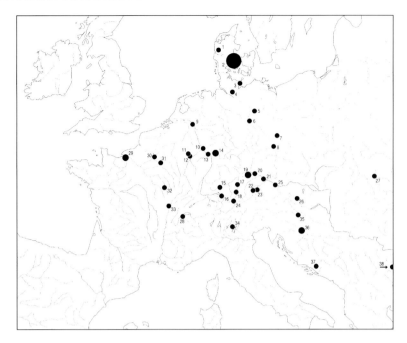

167 Distribution map of ring-pommel swords ('Ringknaufschwerter').
1. Brokjaer Mark; 2. Vimose; 3. Malente-Krummsee; 4. Hamfelde; 5. Töppel; 6. Hohenferchesar; 7. Litten; 8.Pocap;
9. Xanten; 10. Koblenz; 11. Ittel; 12. Welschbillig; 13. Mainz; 14. Frankfurt-Heddernheim; 15. Sigmaringen; 16. 'Bodensee';
17. Wehringen; 18. Denklingen; 19. Eining; 20. Straubing; 21. Künzing; 22. Mühlthal; 23. Tabing; 24. 'Tyrol'; 25. Linz a. d.
Donau; 26. Szombathely-Savaria; 27. Ardanovo-Aranhaza; 28. Genève; 29. Montfort-sur-Risle (Eure); 30. Chauny (Aisne);
31. Limé (Aisne); 32. Vertault (Côte-d'Or); 33. Chalon-sur-Saône (Saône-et-Loire); 34. Lovere; 35. Ptuj; 36. Sisak-Siscia.
37. Ljubuski; 38. Dranovets-Senowo

168 (left) *Parazonium*, grip detail; (right) bronze grip from another *parazonium*. Both in the National Museum of Naples
(photo Röm.-Germ. Zentralmuseum, Mainz)

ending in a vertical ring, sometimes profusely decorated, these swords circulated mainly in romanised Germany (Rhineland, Württemberg and Bavaria) and in free Germany, but were also in general use throughout the whole of Europe apart from the Mediterranean littoral, from Normandy in the West to the Carpathian basin in the East. J. Werner suggests that the design is of Sarmatian origin.

The decoration on ring-pommel swords has been compared with that on several models of the box-type forms on the scabbards of other designs of long sword. These iron scabbard chapes testify to the great skill of the craftsmen in the specialist techniques of damascening, particularly in the third century. It seems probable that this technique was a Romano-Germanic speciality and one which several centuries later was used in the decoration of the iron buckle-plates worn by peoples of Germanic origin.

To conclude this section we should mention some short swords, generally of third century date, which seem to weaken the case for the supremacy of the *spatha*. Some of these, from the Künzing and Mâcon finds (length 46cm), have converging cutting edges, rather resembling a very long stiletto. Elsewhere, at Augst and in the Künzing deposit, some short swords about 40cm long have parallel blade edges like the older *gladius*, but the ogival shape of the point shows that they were contemporary with the first *spathae*.

Apart from these entirely practical weapons, the Romans also revived the Greek idea of the sword as a symbol of power and authority to be carried by high ranking officers and the emperor himself. P. Couissin very appropriately calls this weapon a *parazonium*, drawing on the title of one of Martial's *Apophoreta* (XIV.32), a word used previously for a dagger. Such swords continued for many years without significant modification, as they were essentially symbolic objects, and were, like their name, Greek in origin. It was a short weapon, always shown in its sheath and worn on the left side, its major feature being a handgrip in the form of a bird of prey. One of the earliest appearances is on the Pergamum frieze, and the general on the 'Ahenobarbus Relief' is also wearing one. During both the High and Late Empire, these swords were strictly exclusive to generals (the bireme from Preneste), emperors (the Relief of the Tetrarchs, the surrender of Valerian on a Sassanian bas-relief) or deities (Mars, on horse armour from Straubing).

Until recently, actual objects which could be a *parazonium* have had a rarity in inverse proportion to their frequency of representation, to such an extent that one might have doubted whether they ever really existed; and the rare known examples, such as the eagle head pommel from Dalkingen, clearly come from statues. However, the National Museum of Naples has a complete example, with an iron blade (which proves that it is not part of a statue) and a bronze handgrip which shows an eagle's head on one side and victory on a globe, holding a *gorgoneion*, on the other; there is also a second, similar grip in the same collection. The *parazonium* did therefore actually exist, but considering its rarity, it is understandable that so few have come down to us.

169 Bronze *parazonium* from a statue, found at Murrhardt (photo Württembergisches Landesmuseum, Stuttgart)

THE DAGGER

170 Dagger detail from the memorial to Annaius Daverzus (photo Röm.-Germ. Zentralmuseum, Mainz)

Like the *gladius*, the Roman dagger was borrowed from the Iberians and then developed; it even had the 4-ring suspension system on the scabbard, characteristic of the *gladius*. It was not so extensively modified by the Romans as the sword, to the point that one cannot always be sure – with finds from Republican camps in Spain, for example – whether a dagger belonged to a Roman or an Iberian.

This lack of development in dagger design is the result of the Roman attitude to these weapons, which they regarded as prestige items rather than as part of their fighting equipment. From the early first century daggers, and particularly their sheaths, were very carefully made and decorated; some of them were true works of art. Like the *gladius*, daggers, hung from a *cingulum* but on the left side, and as the two belts of the *gladius* and the dagger crossed on the abdomen of the wearer, some representations on Rhineland memorials make one think of some ancient cowboy from the American West. However flippant this may seem, it is not entirely inappropriate, as the dagger was primarily the outward display of its wearer's power, though it remained an effective fighting weapon.

The Roman dagger, worn by legionaries and auxiliaries alike, was a cherished object to its owner. It had been thought that the former carried the more attractive examples, and the auxiliaries the less appealing, but memorials like the one to Annaius show that as with the *gladius*, the most attractive weapons were not the preserve of elite troops or the higher ranks. With the exception of an example examined by R. Forrer, which was decorated with mythological scenes, it appears that most dagger sheaths displayed geometrical patterns, differing from *gladii*, which at this time (Mainz Type) showed politico-religious or plant motifs, when they were not decorated with propagandist depictions of past or current military campaigns – though plain undecorated sheaths are also known, for example from London, Basel, Mainz and Carnuntum (Obmann, 2000).

Craftsman drew deeply on traditional first-century decorative motifs, but their treatment of this material produced some of the finest damascening and enamelling of their period. One, Caius Antonius, proudly signed his name on the handgrip of an early first-century dagger from Oberammergau. Sheath fronts are generally divided into panels, some by single lines, others by more complex rows of dots and hatchings, and the panels themselves are filled either with geometrical patterns or ornamental motifs – vine leaves on the Oberammergau sheath, temple facades on those from Velsen and Vindonissa and a palm tree on another from Vindonissa, for instance. A sheath found in the Rhine near Mainz has the inscription LEG (io) XXII / PRIMI(genia) worked into the design. Brass and niello inlays and overlays provided colour contrasts against the iron backing, which must have been specially darkened when silver was used, and some craftsmen achieved special colour effects by enamelling.

a

b

171 a. Dagger scabbard with encrusted decoration, from the
north of France (?) (photo Röm.-Germ. Zentralmuseum Mainz);
b. Dagger in its scabbard; the encrusted decoration in silver
mentions the XXIIIrd Legion Primi(genia) Mainz, first century
(photo Röm.-Germ. Zentralmuseum, Mainz); c. Dagger
scabbard decorated with scenes from mythology (after a
sketch by R. Forrer; d. Dagger in encrusted scabbard from
Leeuwen (after J.Ypey, 1960); e. Dagger from Buciumi,
Romania (after N.Gudea, 1972); f. Legionary dagger from
Allériot (Saône-et-Loire) (after L.Bonnamour and H.Fernoux)

c

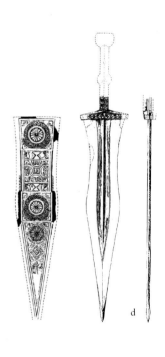

d

e

f

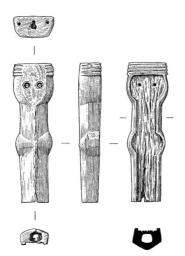

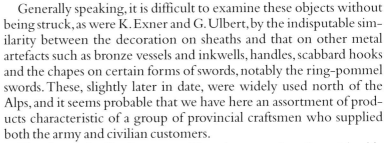

172 Dagger grip in ivory (Museum of London, PCD/ER-546).

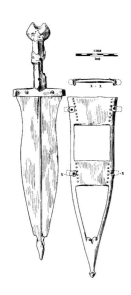

173 Legionary dagger and scabbard discovered in the heart of the City of London, at Copthall Court in 1951 (drawing Museum of London, inv. 59.94/1)

Generally speaking, it is difficult to examine these objects without being struck, as were K. Exner and G. Ulbert, by the indisputable similarity between the decoration on sheaths and that on other metal artefacts such as bronze vessels and inkwells, handles, scabbard hooks and the chapes on certain forms of swords, notably the ring-pommel swords. These, slightly later in date, were widely used north of the Alps, and it seems probable that we have here an assortment of products characteristic of a group of provincial craftsmen who supplied both the army and civilian customers.

The dagger itself, often up to 35cm long, can be of considerable length, but was not in such cases very functional (see examples from Nice-Cimiez, Köln etc). The leaf-shaped blade has a central dividing groove, which can also take the form of two shallow grooves alongside a centre spine; the point may be thickened, a feature frequently found on swords also. The handgrip, which covers the top of the blade, consists of two plates fastened together by rivets on each side of the tang. With the exception of some in bone or ivory, this grip is generally iron, decorated in the same style as the frame.

As a number of dagger finds, including some of the best examples, have came from rivers, it is not usually possible to date their manufacture, but specimens are also known from among the oldest German camps such as Oberaden and Dangstetten. The most splendid sheaths seem to date from the middle and third quarters of the first century; but an example from Corbridge comes from a level known to be later than AD 85. Although decreasing in numbers with the passage of time, daggers appear to have been still in use during the second century, as is evidenced by the Buciumi find and the memorial to *Castricius Victor* at Aquincum. The Künzing find, the stock of a military workshop which must have been buried during the third century, provided 59 dagger blades and 29 sheaths, from which it has been possible to obtain a good idea of the weapon's evolution during this period. The two-lobed pommel, already discernible on the Buciumi dagger, becomes the norm, and sheaths become much less complex, being just a simple sheath with two strengthening plates at the top and middle.

THE *PILUM*

The *pilum* in the time of the Principate developed directly from its Republican-period predecessor, showing only minor variations. In the early years AD, the Roman army was the only Western fighting force to use this type of weapon, and whilst it fell out of favour towards the end of the Empire, the idea of a throwing weapon with a long sharp iron point resurfaced during the Late Antiquity. Some writers see the Roman *pilum* as the forerunner of the Frankish *ango*, a weapon of major importance in the High Medieval period.

The High Empire *pilum* had a long thin iron head some 60-90 cm in length or more, and complete specimens are therefore rare finds. Design development was mostly in the way the head was fastened to the wooden shaft, of which the length is not easy to determine, even on reliefs. Continuing the Late Republican tradition, examples from the early Principate show two fixing methods, the tang and the socket. The Caesarian system of a tang with transverse holes at its base seems to have been rapidly discontinued, as no examples have come to light on sites on the Rhine-Danube *limes*. Embedded in the thickened end of the wooden shaft, the High Empire *pilum* tang was secured by cross-pinning, and a square-section ferrule prevented the end of the shaft from splitting.

The best preserved specimens of this type of *pilum* come from the Augustan camp of Oberaden, and among those found three still have the pyramid-shaped wooden block in which the tang is secured by three rivets, conserved by the damp conditions. Such discoveries are of course exceptional, but the pyramidal ferrule shape enables a fairly exact estimate of chronological evolution. Well known from German Augustan camps such as Dangstetten, similar finds have been made at Kalkriese, associated with the defeat of Varus in AD 9; the upper angles of the ferrule are lengthened into 'spurs', a feature which later disappears. The last datable specimens seem to be of the Claudian period (Hod Hill and Rheingönheim).

Socket fixing, well known from Alésia finds, was still in use at the start of the Principate (Augsburg-Oberhausen), though seemingly less common than the type described above. Judging from the best preserved examples, the heads of these *pila* are noticeably less tapered than earlier ones (Ouroux-sur-Saône, Waddon Hill). This model continued in service, which explains its resurgence in the third century, proven by several discoveries on the Rhineland *limes* and at Caerleon (Wales) which can be dated to shortly before AD 260. On a later *pitum* from Saalburg, the socket is not in an extension of the shaft not in a prominent bulge. This desire to strengthen the head/shaft fixing can also be seen in the Rhineland (Saalburg and Eining camps; in the Rhine at Mainz), where *pila* have deepened sockets, square in section; but such types do not seem to have been widely adopted.

These discoveries show that the *pilum*, contrary to what might have been deduced, did not disappear from legionary use after the second century. The rarity of depictions of this weapon on Rhineland memorials after the first/second centuries stems from the small number of memorials to legionaries in comparison to those of auxiliaries (see,

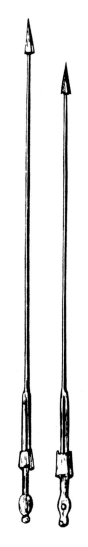

174 Two *pila* shafts from the Ljubljanica near Dolge njive (Slovenia) (after J. Horvat, 1990)

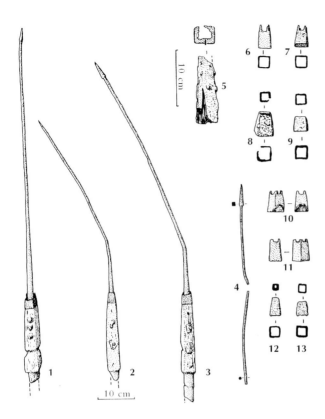

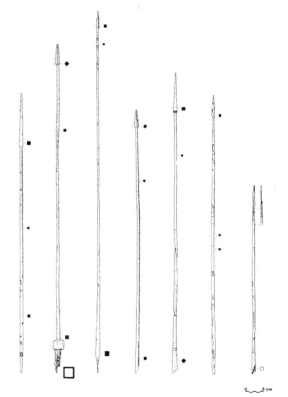

175 First century *pila* : 1-3, Oberarden;
4,6-9, Dangstetten; 5, (*pilum* ?), Lexden;
10-11, Kalkriese; 12-13, Hod Hill. Sources :
1-3 after S.Loeschcke and C.Albrecht, 1948;
4,6-9, after G.Fingerlin, 1986; 5, after J.Foster,
1986; 10-11, after W.Schlüter *et al.*, 1992;
12-53, after W.Mannig; 1985; Scale 10 cm

176 *Pilum* points found in the valley of the Saône
(after M.Feugère, 1990)

however, *C. Valerius Crispus* at Wiesbaden; *Petilius Secundus* at Bonn; *Flavoleius Cordus* (?) at Mainz). Also, the bulk of the written evidence mentioning the *pilum* dates from the early days of the Principate. In the third century, depictions of *pila* on memorials hardly appear outside Rome, where they are shown on memorials to pretorians; in a way, the *pilum* turned back in on itself, and it had in any event always seemed unusual to non-Romans.

Some illustrations of the *pilum* (the Chancellerie relief, the Adamklissi monument) show a spherical lump under the pyramid-shaped block fixing the head to the shaft, and this has been interpreted as a weight added to the weapon to enhance its penetration; some third-century memorials show *pila* fitted with two or even three such spherical lumps. Until now, no examples of these have been found – or at least identified – in excavations.

Writing in 52 BC, when Cicero was readying his camp to receive an imminent Gaulish attack, Caesar mentions the hasty preparation of a large number of *pila muralia*; what were these *pila*, and how did they differ from the infantryman's normal *pilum*? It has been suggested (L.A. Constans) that they derived from the 'heavy *pilum*' described by Polybius, which was heavier than a standard *pilum* and was therefore well suited for use by troops defending against attackers below. If this is the case, the massive *pilum* head from Koenigshofen (Strasbourg), at 30cm long, could be from one of these weapons.

THE LANCE

Several generations of archaeologists have attempted to classify Roman lances, but there are so many styles and regional variants, judging from the known specimens, that none has been able to produce a convincing analysis. One of the obstacles in the path so far is the fragmentary nature of the material found, usually nothing more than a few metal components. The length of the shaft, the weight of a complete lance, etc, must have conformed to some ancient standards, as is shown by written records which frequently use different terms when referring to these weapons; but these must have been so familiar to contemporary readers that there was no need for the writer to go into detail.

Moreover, this problem is not limited to Roman weapons, as ancient writers also use a variety of terms for the lances of their enemies, usually without any detailed description. The ancient reader knew the details of any named weapon, which regrettably we do not; what is the difference, for instance, between a *tragula* and a *verutum*, both of which are mentioned by Caesar in his *Gallic War* (V.35, 48)? Matters are further complicated by the fact that the same weapon could have been used both by natives and by Romans, and this may partially explain why ancient authors used these words so readily. This is certainly the case with the *tragula*, a type of lance particularly used by the Helvetii but also mentioned by Roman authors (Plautus, *Pseud.* I.4.14; *Cas.* 297; *Epid.* 690).

The term *gaesum*, which linguists tell us is of Celtic origin, appears for the first time when used by Caesar as he writes of the attack on

177 Lance point from Vindonissa (photo Th.Hartmann, Vindonissa-Museum, Brugg)

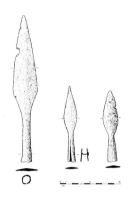

178 Lance points from Newstead (from the originals)

Galba's camp at Octoduros (Martigny) in 57 BC, so it must have been a weapon used against him by the local tribes. Based on this episode and a reference from Augustan times to the *alpina gaesa* (Virgil, *Aeneid* VIII.661), it is thought that this arm was characteristic of some Alpine peoples, an hypothesis which is supported by the reference on later inscriptions to Raeti *gaesati* (at Risingham and Great-Chesters in Britain); but in spite of the efforts of specialists, we still do not know the exact form of the ancient *gaesum*.

We must therefore resign ourselves to examining the archaeological evidence alone, without the support of ancient texts, and we can at least be sure – based on Rhineland memorials – that the lance was to the auxiliary what the *pilum* was to the legionary. Certainly, the cavalry used different types of lance, mostly short javelins during the Principate, and every soldier carried several of them. The form of the grip of his shield enabled him to hold them, as well as the reins, in his left hand; alternatively he may have entrusted them to a servant or put them into a form of quiver.

As far as the javelins themselves are concerned, the conclusions which we have been able to draw are not encouraging, as they seem to have come in a wide variety of shapes and sizes, and we do not know why. Head lengths can vary from 6-8cm up to nearly 40cm, the most common being shaped liked a willow tree leaf with a widened base. Some, however, are at their widest half way along their length, while others are triangular with almost straight edges. The iron heels are even more varied, cones from 7-13cm long forged from a single sheet, and there is no way to distinguish them from those used by the Gauls or the Germans.

There is, however, one particular series characteristic solely of the Romans. These have a conical or hemispherical button on the point, and have on occasion been confused with catapult bolts; they were perhaps fired from war machines, and were not used as lances or javelins.

7 THE CAVALRY

In the absence of any strong Italian traditions, cavalry grew to be a major force within the Roman army only as a result of contact with races with greater experience of this arm – Numidians, Iberians, Gauls, Thracians, Scythians and Persians. As a consequence, Roman cavalry arms, equipment and even tactics were largely borrowed from barbarians (*socii*, and later, auxiliaries). From the start of the Principate, however, the situation settled, and the Roman cavalry became a stable unified force in spite of its varied origins.

THE ORGANISATION OF THE ROMAN CAVALRY

Under the reforms of Augustus, the Roman legions regained the mounted contingents which they had lost a century before. These were small contingents, however, of about 120 men according to Flavius Josephus, compared to some 5000 infantry, and the major mounted force remained the cavalry auxiliaries, who were much better equipped. One should not perhaps attach too much weight to just one writer's simple statement, and the situation was clearly different from the third century (under Gallienus or even earlier, according to M. Speidel): Vegetius (*Mil.* 2.6) writes of a legion having 726 *equites*.

The auxiliary cavalry under the Principate was at first grouped into *alae* ('wings'), normally of 500 men (*ala quingenaria*), or more rarely, of 800-1000 men (*ala milliaria*) for certain elite units. Each wing was in turn divided into 16 *turmae* of 32 cavalrymen, each led by a decurion, the equivalent cavalry rank to an infantry centurion. Other mounted auxiliaries, of lower status, were to be found in the *cohortes equitatae*, units of diverse origins who actually comprised most of the basic troops.

It has been estimated that in the time of Augustus the Roman army had a total strength across the empire of some 300,000 men, of which around 30,000 were cavalry. By the start of the second century these figures had risen to approximately 385,000 and 65,000 respectively, and the cavalry continued to grow in tactical importance, justifying the in-depth studies which are now fortunately possible, thanks to a quantity of recent specific research in this field (general studies by K. Dixon, A. Hyland, A. K. Taylor-Lawson, M. C.

179 Old reconstruction of a Roman cavalryman (after L. Fontaine, 1883).

Bishop and E. Rabeisen for the harness, plus reconstructions by P. Connolly and M. Junkelmann).

SOURCES

Ancient depictions of cavalry are plentiful and well-detailed, and supported by abundant archaeological material, so although certain points remain obscure, we are better informed on the cavalry than the infantry.

Memorials, especially those found in the Rhineland, are an irreplaceable source of information. Those which show a soldier and his equipment fall into two categories. The first type is conventional, showing the mounted cavalryman charging right and a fallen barbarian; with variants, this type is known from Britain to Israel, as well as in Mauretania and Numidia. The second, well represented in Germany, shows the deceased in an upper panel, usually wearing a toga and celebrating, while a lower panel shows his servant leading his ownerless horse to the stable. On some particularly moving memorials, such as that to *Caius Julius Primus* from Trier (Bonn Museum), both horse and servant are running as they would in training. Such memorials are taken here in conjunction with archaeological evidence, which they often help to clarify; but we should not forget when considering this geographical and temporal concentration of information that the cavalry had played a major military role since its earliest days or that it continued to evolve throughout its long existence.

THE HARNESS

Much Roman military equipment retains traces of its ethnic origins, so we should not be surprised to find that the harness, saddlery and other related items were largely based on Gaulish originals. The Gauls in their turn borrowed heavily from the Central European Celts; this is the case, for instance, with spurs, which originated in Bohemia and neighbouring areas in the second century BC.

A passage from Caesar's *Gallic War* (IV.2), in which he compares the Gauls with the Germans, provides similar evidence in the case of the saddle: 'In the eyes of the Germans, using a saddle is a sign of weakness', showing that such items existed before the middle of the first century BC, but we know no more. The oldest representation of the 'saddle with horns' with which the cavalry of the Principate was equipped is slightly later, appearing on a frieze in the Julii mausoleum at *Glanum* (St Rémy-de-Provence) which shows a battle between Gauls and Romans in which, because the saddled horse is defeated, we can be sure that a Gaulish warrior was being portrayed.

Although all the known saddle components which have been found come from later sites and are clearly 'Romanised', this is no proof that the saddle, as a Gaulish invention, did not continue to be preferred by the Gaulish auxiliaries serving with the Roman cavalry for many years. At the beginning of the Augustan period, several vases bearing

---

An attack on the Britons

Using the tightly limited space as a rampart, the legionaries hurled their deadly arrows at the approaching enemy, then charged in a spearhead formation. Simultaneously, the enemy and the auxiliaries also charged, lances to the fore, and broke any last resistance.

Tacitus, Ann. XIV.36

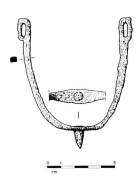

180 (above) Iron spur from Hod Hill (British Museum, inv. PRB 43.6.1-124.), now though to be of Carolingian date. (below) Horse in harness on memorial to Marcus Sacrius; Cologne, last quarter of first c. AD (photo Röm.-Germ. Zentralmuseum, Mainz)

181 Memorial to the cavalryman M. Aemilius Durises, found at Cologne. The deceased is portrayed in civilian clothing, reclining for a banquet, while his servant — note his Weiler-Guisborough type helmet — is seen on the lower panel leading his horse in full harness (photo Rheinisches Landesmuseum Bonn)

182 Memorial to the cavalryman T. Flavius Bassus who died at Cologne at the end of the first century (photo Röm.-Germ. Museum, Cologne)

the seal of an Aretine potter, T. Bargathus, show horses with these saddles, which can also be seen a little later on Gaulish terracotta statuettes and other monuments.

The Gaulish saddle has several interesting features brought to light by recent reconstructions, in particular those of P. Connolly. The main function of its wooden frame was to protect the horse's spine from shocks during a charge, and its design transfers the rider's weight to the animal's flanks as with asses, mules and other baggage train animals; its fore and aft 'horns' have the specific purpose in battle of enabling the rider to use his sword and shield freely, and to turn and lean in every direction without being thrown. This design of saddle was intended to meet the needs of the rider in battle, whereas until Caesar's time, saddles were constructed for general use by mounted soldiers moving rapidly from place to place.

This military saddle was therefore very different from what we define as a saddle today; indeed the word *sella* does not appear in Latin texts until the fourth century AD. Under the High Empire the 'horned' saddle was called a *scordiscus*, perhaps after the barbarians encountered by the Romans in Illyria and Pannonia, though the term drops out of the everyday vocabulary at the same time as the saddle itself after the Antiquity.

A horse with this design of saddle could be guided by the pressure of the rider's knees alone; stirrups were unknown in ancient times, an early mention of them being in the *Strategikon* of the Byzantine emperor Maurice (AD 582-602). The earliest known archaeologically found stirrups come from seventh-century Avar tombs in Dacia. As for spurs, these were of Gaulish origin like the saddle, and although reserved until the first century BC for the aristocratic cavalry, they spread through the Roman army, as is evidenced by the spectacular growth of finds from the first century AD, and particularly later, from the third and fourth centuries.

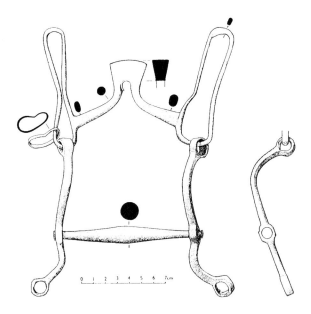

183 Bit from Newstead (drawing by P. Connolly after A.Hyland, 1990)

184 Memorial to the cavalryman T. Flavius Bassus (photo Röm.-Germ.
Museum, Cologne)

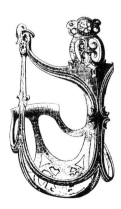

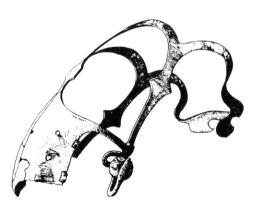

185 Horse muzzles : left,
Greek (?); right, example
from Lerida (after A.K.
Taylor, 1975)

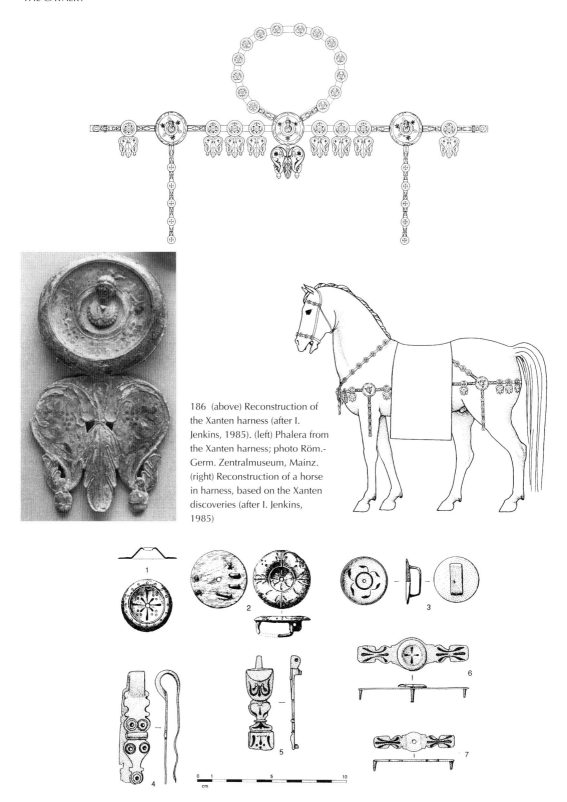

186 (above) Reconstruction of the Xanten harness (after I. Jenkins, 1985). (left) Phalera from the Xanten harness; photo Röm.-Germ. Zentralmuseum, Mainz. (right) Reconstruction of a horse in harness, based on the Xanten discoveries (after I. Jenkins, 1985)

187 Harness decorations. 1-2, Hod Hill; 3-4, Newstead; 5-7, Fremington Hag deposit (1 and 2, after Brailsford, 1962)

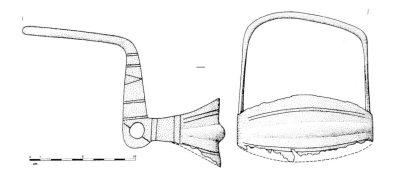

188 Bronze cavesson found
in the Saône in 1847 (Musée
Denon, Chalon-sur-Saône)

The head harness also exhibits the same mixture of Italian and Barbarian elements. The articulated bit, two rings joined by straight sections, and known to the Gauls from the Middle La Tène period onwards, remained in use until the Principate. From the second century BC, however, under oriental influence (Thracian?), the Italo-Greek world used different types of articulated bits, with lateral additions, and, notably, a rigid bar placed under the chin of the horse, making it much more responsive to the reins.

Another item of head harness, the cavesson, has a similar function. Various bronze 'muzzles' are known from several Mediterranean areas, and the lighter cavesson may have developed from these. The muzzles seem to have been more common in the East, but are also known in the pacified territories (Lerida, Saintes-Maries-de-la-Mer), as are cavessons (Chalon-sur-Saône, Saint-Saturnin, Saintes).

Much more frequent finds than these, on civil as well as military sites, are the decorative pendants and trinkets which adorned the leather harness straps and equipment from the beginning of the first century AD. Two types of pendant followed each other in the early Principate. In the Tiberian-Claudian period, the more common took the form of two 'winglets', and usually carried incised decoration; it was suspended from an open-ended hook – hence the frequent losses, no doubt – in the form of a dog's or a waterfowl's head. These pendants accurately reproduce, though we do not know why, the decoration on Late-Republican *simpula* which were made from the fourth to the first centuries BC in Etruria. Distributed widely throughout Gaul, the pendants could have been the products of a number of workshops, perhaps including Alésia, and their abundance in the Rhineland *limes* may reflect the importance of Gaulish recruitment into the auxiliaries at this time. From Nero onwards, this style of harness decoration was replaced by a new series, fastened to *phalerae* by hinges and decorated with more elaborate motifs based on plants. This second series, of more complex design and fabrication – silver inlays and niello work, for instance – has been found in volume in a civilian context at Alésia, which was renowned in Antiquity for its silver-plated and tinned bronzework.

Several archaeological finds of equipment, such as the harness at Xanten, supplement our knowledge from reliefs and have enabled Flavian harnesses to be reconstructed from their components – circular *phalerae*, suspension elements, strapends, elongated brackets, etc.

189 Harness trappings from civil sites in Southern Gaul: phalera from Caux, cavesson fragment from St-Saturnin, Hérault (photos L.Damelet, CDAR, Lattes)

With the help of these finds, specialists have been able to distinguish between 'ordinary' and 'parade' harnesses, the latter well illustrated on the memorial to T. Flavius Bassus. The purpose of these ornaments is, however, far from clear, and it is difficult to be certain of their specific military function. These harnesses do not seem to have been used in the *hippika gymnasia* (note, for instance, the total absence in tombs with sporting equipment, and see below also). They probably had a more everyday use in regions like Gaul.

THE CAVALRYMAN'S PROTECTION

The helmet

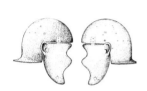

190 Iron protection of a cavalry Weiler-Guisborough type helmet, found at Xanten in 1987 (after F. Willer, 1988)

Although by the middle of the first century BC Caesar was already distinguishing between the cavalry helmet (*cassis*) and the infantryman's *galea*, archaeological evidence does not enable us to identify a particular type as being used by mounted troops before the start of the first century AD. The type of helmet later found in a tomb at Weiler in Belgium had been known for a long time from the evidence of carvings on first century memorials. These helmets, later grouped within the Weiler-Guisborough type, have a characteristic skullcap part, which resembles a human head with hairstyling, ears and sometimes even sideburns on the cheek-guards; they also feature a nape protector at right angles to the head. The finest example of this type, now in the Bonn Museum, was discovered in gravel workings near Xanten-Waardt.

This iron helmet, with its repoussé silver decorative layer, gilded in parts, is notable for the remarkable care in its manufacture. On top of the hairstyle is an olive branch wreath ending above the forehead in a prominent bust surrounded by weapons; on stylistic grounds, we may be seeing Caligula or Claudius, dating the helmet to the 40s AD. The owner of this work of art, evidently a cavalry officer of sufficiently high rank to have taken part in some official event of which this is a souvenir, had it made to measure to fit some skeleton deformities, but these had not prevented his attaining high military rank.

The eponymous helmet from Weiler near Arlon in Belgium is one of the simplest in the series. It is the type most easily recognised on funerary reliefs and on official sculptures such as the Arch at Orange (see p.36), so we know that this type was current in Tiberius' time,

---

Military cavalry equipment under Nero

The cavalry had on their right sides a large sword and held a long javelin in their right hand; a long shield was held obliquely against the horse's flank, and in a quiver were three or more javelins with flat blades, almost as long as lances. They all wore helmets and armour like the infantry. The weapons of the elite corps which surrounded the general were no different from those of normal cavalrymen.

Josephus, BJ III.96-7

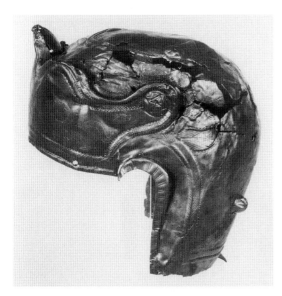

191 Eponymous Guisborough helmet used by the cavalry in the first century (photo Röm.-Germ.Zentralmuseum, Mainz)

192 Cavalry helmet from Chalon-sur-Saône (photo Röm.-Germ. Zentralmuseum, Mainz)

193 Cavalry helmet from Theilenhofen (photo Röm.-Germ. Zentralmuseum, Mainz)

194 Weiler-Guisborough type cavalry helmet from Nijmegen (photo Röm.-Germ. Zentralmuseum, Mainz)

The *cataphracti* in the first century

When they [the Sarmatians] charge in squadron order, hardly any formation of troops could withstand them. But today was a day of rain and thawing ground, and neither their lances nor their long swords which they swung with both hands were any use to them, because the horses slipped and the riders were weighed down by their cataphract armour. Worn by the chiefs and the nobles, made from very tough leather and iron strips, it was impervious to blows, but it made it impossible for any fallen warrior to regain his feet.

Tacitus, Hist. I.79

---

though the Weiler tomb itself dates back only to AD 40 to 50. At the other end of this series is the Theilenhofen helmet, a sort of 'over the top' cavalry helmet which was nevertheless actually used, as is proved by the marks of a succession of owners, all cavalry officers.

The Weiler-Guisborough type shows typological links with parade equipment (see below), which developed in parallel from the start of the first century AD; but reliefs show us that cavalry also used different types of helmets with smooth skullcaps. At the end of the 1800s, experts such as Lindenschmit attributed Niederbieber type helmets to the cavalry, and whilst we now know that this was not the case universally, we nevertheless accept that several types were adapted to cavalry use. Their principal features seem to be an authorised increase in both the lower-nape protectors and cheek-pieces, and the upper protection, with skullcap reinforcements and a frontal spine. Robinson sees these increases as tending to appear from the end of the first century and developing further through the second and third centuries. They are particularly visible on a – perhaps unfinished – helmet from Rainau-Buch in Germany, while another helmet, from Frankfurt-Heddernheim, even has lengthened cheek pieces to partly cover the neck.

Armour

The different types of armour worn by the Roman cavalry had their origins in the different ethnic origins of the auxiliaries. The Numidians, for instance, seem always to have fought as light cavalry, without helmet or armour, whereas the Gauls preferred to wear a chain mail coat for easy arm movement. During the course of the second century the idea took hold of reinforcing the light cavalry with better protected groups, the *cataphracti*, who are mentioned for the first time by Tacitus (*Hist.* I.79) in connection with an action during the war between Vitellius and Otho in AD 69. At that time, 9000 Sarmatian horsemen from the Roxolan tribe had just massacred two Roman cohorts and pillaged Moesia. After their defeat by the Third Legion, it was noticed with surprise that they wore highly developed armour, a combination of scales and plates which also protected the arms and legs, and the *cataphracti* were rapidly enrolled into the Roman army, Hadrian subsequently establishing a regular unit of them.

Even better protected, as both horse and rider were armoured, the *clibanarii* first became part of the Roman army during the third century AD; their bizarre appearance can be seen on a graffito from Dura-

195 Sarmatian *cataphracti* on Trajan's Column: the depiction of scales fitting closely against the horses' hooves probably results from hearsay, as actual examples of horse armour fall vertically to the ground from the animal's chest (photo D.A.I.Rome)

Europos which shows that beneath a conical helmet of vertical plates, probably lengthened by the addition of a chain mail nape protector, the *clibanarius* was totally encased in a tight-fitting 'suit'. A chain mail coat or a scale armour vest covered the upper body and the thighs, while large vertical plates were preferred for the lower trunk. Arms and legs were protected by articulated bands similar to those worn at the start of the Empire by gladiators – such protection can also be seen on the frontispiece showing *fabricae* in the *Notitia Dignitatum*. The horse is also armoured, in a garment of large plates, of which two remarkably well-preserved examples, conserved by the dry climate, have been excavated at Dura–Europos, complete with their leather backing.

Metal scale armour which covers both the horse and the rider goes back in fact to very early times in the East, and pieces of it have been found in South Russian tombs dating to the third and fourth centuries BC, the period when the Romans first encountered it, in their war against Antiochus III of Syria. The weight of the *clibanarii*, however, and their inability to manoeuvre in much other than a straight-line charge, did not seem to justify their inclusion into Roman forces until a much later date.

The armour most frequently worn by the Roman cavalry was scale armour plus a chain mail coat, these being, it seems, the cavalryman's traditional protection in both the Celtic and the Eastern cultures; and the auxiliaries appear to have had a marked preference for it, either because of their origins or because it was used by the units in which they served. Illustrations of cavalrymen supply us with information not only on how they looked, but also how the armour moved with its wearer.

196 Cavalryman depicted on the Arch of Galerius, dating AD 297-311, wearing a 'Spangenhelm' type helmet (after Robinson, 1975)

197 Graffito from Dura-Europos showing a Parthian *clibanarius*; second century or first half of third (after Robinson, 1975)

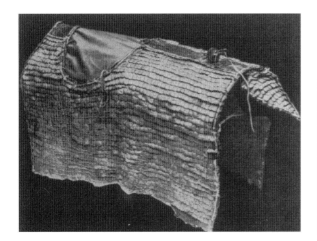

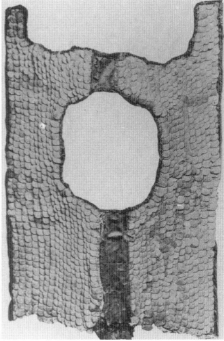

198 Equine scale armour from Dura-Europos, as found. Dating mid-third century (after Prelim. Report, Sixth Season, 1936)

The clibanarii in 357

And from both sides advanced two columns of armed men, with measured tread, shields, plumed helmets and splendid cuirasses sparkling in the sun. Among them rode the armoured cavalry which men call *clibanarii*, faces masked by their visors, chain mail coats on their chests, iron swordbelts at their waists, the whole ensemble making one think of Praxiteles' polished statues rather than mere men. Arms, legs and body were sheathed in fine chain mail, so that however they might move, their close-fitting armour followed their every action.

Ammianus Marcellinus XVI.8

One may wonder here whether the author is not in fact describing parade equipment; if the cavalrymen were wearing face armour, this could be the basis for the reference to statues and fine chain mail.

Although the armour described above seems no different from that worn by the infantry, the cavalry have been connected with a particular type which developed from the early Principate. This incorporates two articulated bronze plates, decorated with reliefs, at the neck of the wearer (see below, parade equipment). Although chain mail coats seem to have been the most common (see the Bertoldsheim discoveries), in at least one case – at Hrusiča in Slovenia – a type similar to that worn with scale armour was also worn at the neck. It appears that scale armour became more popular over the years than the traditional chain mail coat, but our information in this area is based on relatively late depictions; from the start of the third century the coat became longer, covering the rider's thighs, and gave better protection, notably against arrows. The Vimose coat, the only one so far to be unrolled completely, is in this style.

THE *HIPPIKA GYMNASIA*

The wish to develop equipment for specific purposes, already evident in the Weiler–Guisborough type helmets, is particularly noticeable in the cavalry. Those descriptions of triumphs, parades and military exercises which have come down to us never mention any body of troops as wearing anything other than standard equipment; for infantry parades it seems to have been sufficient just to polish the weapons, helmets and armour, and historians are naturally curious as to why the Romans wished to be so specific.

It is useful first to look at the phrase 'parade equipment', though one might prefer to say 'sports equipment'. Under the Principate, the cavalry gave special public displays on the open area in front of the camp gates; for the *hippika gymnasia*, they wore special highly decorated equipment which never seems to have been used in actual combat. Bound by strict rules, like their medieval successors, these ancient tournaments no doubt took pride in the meticulous execution of orders, the skill of the cavalry and generally in the warlike demeanour of man and horse as a united force.

Several contemporary references tell us in more detail about these events, one being an *adlocutio* delivered by Hadrian to the legionary cavalry:

> Military training has, if I may say so, its own rules, and if one adds or subtracts something to them, it becomes either boring or too difficult. The more you add complications, the more you detract from the interest of the exercise. But you have carried out that most difficult of manoeuvres, throwing the javelin while wearing full armour ... And further, I congratulate you on your *esprit de corps*.
> *CIL* VIII.2532

This text shows the individuality of the cavalry and its internal rules which set it apart as a corps. The complex division of the horse soldiers into *equites legionis*, *alae* and *cohortes equitatae*, *numeri*, *exploratores* and *cunei*, not to mention the *equites singulares Augusti*, clearly show its individuality.

Another frequently quoted source of information from the same period is a text from Arrian, Hadrian's friend, which gives a comprehensive description of the *hippika gymnasia* (*Tact.* 34-44). According to him, the display showed two opposed cavalry units performing, no doubt watched by senior officers and honoured guests. One of the units, led by two cavalrymen in special armour, made a charge, and the other tried to hit them with javelins while at the same time defending themselves against the general assault. The two units took turns at charging and defending, just as they would in actual combat, demonstrating that the most important attribute of a cavalryman was to be able to throw his weapons fast and accurately while at full gallop and simultaneously defending himself against enemy attacks.

Completing the technical training, building an *esprit de corps* and encouraging a competitive spirit were the declared aims of these games, and we can learn more about the cavalry mentality and its place at the heart of the Roman army by studying the equipment they used, particularly the highly developed decoration on items such as the helmet.

The *hippika gymnasia* at the start of the second century

Within a work on cavalry motivation, origins and equipment, Arrian includes the following lengthy passage, obviously based on his own experience. Having described the Greek infantry, he continues by describing cavalry exercises in detail.

(33) I am aware that understanding the terms will be difficult, even for Romans, as only a minority have Latin as their mother tongue; there are Celts from whom they have borrowed actual exercises in order to learn how to fight them, and Iberians also. And the Romans are to be praised because they have not overvalued what was their own at the expense of what was valuable among the foreigners. [This point is made again at (44)] We can thus see that they

have borrowed weapons [or equipment?] (which will be referred to from now on as Roman, because the Romans have made excellent use of them) as well as training exercises, senior officers' accommodation and their purple robes. They even honour foreigners' gods as if they were their own. It is said that their religious practices follow the Achaeans, or, generally, the Greeks and even the Phrygians. They venerate Rhea the Phrygian, who came from Pessinonte and they brought to Rome the Mourning of Attis of Phrygia, and the ritual bathing which marked the end of his mourning was prepared for Rhea in Phrygian fashion. We see also that most of the laws written on the Twelve Tables were of Athenian origin, and it would be a vast undertaking to study their origins and their travels. But now it is time to tell of the cavalry.

(34) For their exercise area, they are not satisfied with a simple level space, they have to prepare one specially. In the middle they mark out a square in front of the viewing stand and level it with care. Those who are of high rank or have special skill in horsemanship wear gilded bronze or iron helmets to single them out for the spectators, not the ordinary combat helmets which cover only the head and cheeks but helmets which cover the whole face like a mask, with eyeholes so that they can see while remaining protected. The helmets have brightly coloured plumes, not for any practical purpose, but for their appearance; in the charge, and if there is a breeze, these float out to make a pleasant sight. Their shields, too, are not the standard fighting type, but lighter and profusely decorated to add to the beauty of the display, and instead of armour they wear Cimmerian tunics, scarlet, purple or multicoloured. They wear trousers, not baggy like the Parthian or Armenian ones but fitting close to the leg. Their horses have protection in front, but not at their sides, as it would not be needed; the exercise javelins have no iron heads, so the horses' flanks, mostly covered by harness, do not need to be protected, although it is necessary to protect their eyes.

(35) The opening movement on the carefully-prepared display area is a charge starting from a point out of sight of the spectators, its many parts meticulously choreographed for beauty and visual impact. The riders hurl themselves forward to make the charge terrifyingly brilliant, their banners waving, not only Roman but Scythian as well, made of coloured cloth fastened to shafts, all designed to be as frightening as possible. At rest, all one sees are scraps of multicoloured fabric, but as the riders perform their evolutions these swirl in the air like snakes, even hissing in the wind when it is strong enough. And these banners are not merely attractive to the eye, they help the onlookers to follow the different manoeuvres in the charge and to separate one mounted unit from another. Of the bannermen, the most skilful, execute circles and patterns as they ride while the rest of the troop follows, and no matter how complicated these movements may be, every rider keeps his place precisely, for if one should make a false movement or collide with another, not only would he spoil the overall effect, he would diminish the whole purpose of the exercise.

(36) When their charge has come to its end, the riders are in serried ranks to the left of the platform, having turned their horses' heads to face the rear, their backs and those of their mounts protected by their shields. This manoeuvre, similar to the 'wall of shields' of the infantry, they call the 'tortoise'. Two riders move away from the line so that their fellows can advance to the right of the formation while they themselves receive the javelins of the attackers, with half the cavalry in place, lined up to throw.

199 Eagle and Victory on a *fibula* : Töging, Altötting (Oberbayern) (Prähist. Staatsammlung, Munich, inv. 1977-1980)

At the bugler's call, one half of the group charges, to throw as many javelins as possible as fast as possible, throwing in turn in order of seniority, the first, then the second, and so on. The beauty of the exercise is that every rider, charging in a straight line, throws as many javelins as possible at the shields of their two comrades, who have moved forward to the left of the 'tortoise'. After this straight line charge, the riders turn as if to form a circle, turning to the right, their javelin side, so that they are not impeded when throwing, and are protected by their shields.

(37) The cavalrymen must carry as many javelins as they can throw during their charge, the stream of projectiles and the continuous noise having a frightening effect. Also, other cavalry charge forward en masse between the right wing of the formation and the two men in front, throwing their javelins; as they are moving to their left, their shield side, they are not fully protected, so they must be excellent horsemen to throw their weapons while at the same time protecting their right sides with their shields. Throwing javelins at the enemy while turning to the right, a most difficult operation, is called 'petrinos' in Celtic – throwing as hard as they can above the horse's tail using only their own body strength, then swiftly putting their shields behind them to protect themselves.

(40) There follows what is called a 'cantabrian' charge; I think the name comes from the Spanish tribe, the Cantabrii, because it was from them that the Romans borrowed this manoeuvre, which follows this pattern: as before, the riders form up to the left of the platform, apart from two who throw their javelins at them. The charge is from the right, towards the right as before, but this time there is also a charge from the left of the platform, a charge which develops into a circling movement. These riders do not throw light javelins as before, but wooden lances without their iron heads; their weight makes them awkward to handle, and they can be dangerous to their targets. The throwers are ordered not to throw at the head or at the horse itself; instead, as the rider turns, exposing part of his side and his back, he throws the weapon as hard as he can directly at his adversary's shield.

(41) The cavalry prepare themselves as if for battle, with armour, helmets and iron shields (which this time are not the lightweight type). The teams urge their mounts into a charge, each carrying a lance … The second charge is made carrying two lances which they must throw as accurately as possible as they charge.

(43) They also display a wide variety of weaponry; light arrows, projectiles not fired from a bow but by war machines, stones thrown by hand or using a sling, at the target placed between the two others of which I have already spoken … They then draw their swords and try to land as many blows as possible on a fleeing 'enemy'. Under different conditions, they finish off a man on the ground, or hit one from the side, drawing themselves up to his height … The final demonstration is of jumping fully equipped onto a horse galloping at full speed, an act which some call 'the traveller's leap.

(44) These are the traditional exercises carried out for many years by Roman cavalrymen …

Arrian, *Tact.*, 32-5; original French translation by M. P. Villard of the University of Provence, Aix-en-Provence.

SPORTS EQUIPMENT

Our accurate knowledge of the correct equipment started with helmets, which were among the first items of military equipment to receive the attentions of scholars (O. Benndorf's study in 1878); but it was the sensational discovery at Straubing in 1950 of 22 helmets, all from the same period, which revived worldwide interest in them. The 1975 find of a further 18 examples east of the camp at Eining added very significantly to this attention, and J. Garbsch's publication of the whole group, at a major exhibition in Munich in 1978, has enabled us to acquire greater knowledge of their designs and symbolism.

Helmets
The typical sporting equipment helmet is a 'face-helmet', usually with the a highly decorated skull-cap and the cheekpieces replaced by a solid face mask with holes for the eyes, nose and mouth; the mask may be two parts, to make it easier to put on, and for the comfort of the wearer. The oldest known helmet of this type is one recently found on the Teutoburgerwald battle site, a chin to forehead mask of iron with bronze and silver inlays, fastened to the skull-cap through holes beneath the eyes. Dating to AD 9, this partial helmet precedes the eastern helmets from Plovdiv, Vize and Čatalka and the Tiberian period depictions on the Arch at Orange by some ten or twenty years.

This discovery rather casts doubt on the hypothesis that all such helmets had an Eastern origin, on the grounds that the examples cited above have an 'Eastern' face. In fact, the appearance of this type at the beginning of our era is certainly a development from earlier styles which are still unknown to us, and we shall have to wait for further finds to bridge the gap between ancient styles (such as the Negau helmet – fourth to second century BC – in the Vatican Museum with cheekpieces forming a human face, or the face helmet on the frieze on Temple of Pergamon, around 180 BC) and those of the High Empire.

200 Face helmet from Pfrondorf (photo Röm.-Germ. Zentralmuseum, Mainz)

201 Face helmet, J.-Paul Getty Museum, Malibu, USA (photo Röm.-Germ. Zentralmuseum, Mainz)

We have already emphasised the similarities between Weiler-Guisborough type helmets and face helmets; apart from one example from Worthing, which has characteristics of both, the face helmet follows a coherent pattern in its development. Stylistically, two distinctly different series can be identified, clearly linked to their provenances – one Greek, well represented by the helmets from Straubing, Ubbergen, Stockstadt, Hiršova and so on, and the other Eastern, of which the most typical examples are those from Tell Oum Hauran, Plovdiv and Homs. It is possible that these helmets were intended to represent the 'enemy' in the *hippika gymnasia*, but equally they could just be reflecting a style used in the workshops where they were made. The construction features of the helmets could be another basis for classification, as proposed by M. Kohlert:

Type I: hinges at forehead level
Type II: hinges in the middle of the skull (first century)
Type III: in three parts; the features – eyes, nose and mouth –
              brought together on an adjustable mask
Type IV: skull cap and mask as one unit (*unicum*: Kostol)
Type V: hinges in the middle of the skull (second to third cen-
              turies)
Type VI: female masks, characteristically upswept hair styling

The decorative elements come from the classic repertory of military equipment – Mars, Minerva, Victory, eagle and shield; Jupiter appears, however, on some items, associated variously with a bull, an ox or the she-wolf who suckled Romulus and Remus. Sports equipment was thus used, like *umbones* and sword scabbards, as part of Roman internal and external propaganda; some detailed scenes (the Newstead, Nikyup and Tell Oum Hauran helmets) show Romans fighting Parthians, cavalry and infantry, and Triumphs. This obvious imagery also includes real and mythical animals to symbolise abstract qualities, or even for magical purposes (bull, boar, ox and capricorn).

Armour

In Arrian's time, the cavalry did not wear armour when participating in the *hippika gymnasia*, replacing it with 'Cimmerian Tunics' decorated with highly coloured embroidery. On the other hand, we know from archaeological finds that in the third century decorated armour was worn – even if the javelins lacked iron heads, they could still inflict a painful injury! Tailored as shown here, the chain mail coats and scale armour (see below) only had one part decorated, a sort of bronze breast plaque secured with turnkeys.

The decoration on these plaques was necessarily limited as they were less than about 15cm wide, and their motifs were symmetrically repeated, frequently Minerva, an eagle, a shield, Mars and Victory. Legionary symbols also featured at the base; a capricorn at Carnuntum (or Brigetio – six legions had it as their emblem); a bull at Orgovany, accompanied by the inscription (*legio X*) *gem* (*ina*). This lack of originality is doubtless due to limitations of size which ruled out any complex scenes.

202 Front part of a face helmet from Echzell (Kr.Büdingen) (Saalburgmuseum, photo Röm.-Germ. Zentralmuseum, Mainz)

203 Cuirass plaque from sporting armour (Archaeological Museum, Nimes)

204 Breastplates making up the chest protection part of the armour, and their fixing method (after Robinson, 1975)

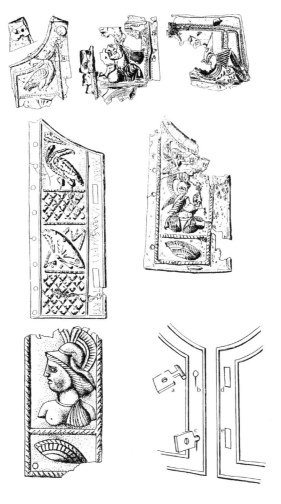

Shinguards

Although no strictly military shinguards have come down to us, we do have some thirty examples of sporting shinguards, thanks to the Straubing deposit and several individual finds. Remarkably carefully made (often with articulated knee joints) and decorated, their shape lends itself naturally to illustrations of standing figures; Mars is by far the most frequently shown (Straubing, Speyer, Slavonski Brod, Budapest) but Victory and Hercules are also featured, the latter being well–illustrated generally on sporting equipment.

Some shinguards with mythological illustrations are also known, for example, Aeneas carrying his father Anchises (Fort-Louis) and the abduction of Ganymede (Lauriacum), as well as religious or magic figures; as with helmets, snakes often form part of the design (Walsenburg, Brussels Museum). Water poured from a vase is an explicit Mithraic allusion (Regensburg). Decoration is most frequently in cut-out form as on the breastplates, in overlapping panels showing the usual themes – Minerva or Virtus, an eagle, a shield – and one often sees animals and sea monsters, those reminders of the fringes of the known world so common in Roman iconography.

205 Parade shinguard from Slavonski-Brod in Slavonia: Mars, second century (photo Röm.-Germ. Zentralmuseum, Mainz)

The Straubing Deposit

Discovered by building workers in 1950, the 'Straubing Deposit' contained not only iron tools and implements but also an impressive assemblage of cavalry parade items, some 116 in all. These pieces of armour, all in a large bronze cauldron, had been buried a few dozen metres from the *pars urbana* of a nearby villa, probably during the Alemannic invasions in the AD 230s. The number of helmets – at least seven – and the abundance of other parade equipment make it impossible for the deposit to have been the property of one individual, and this is confirmed by a study of the graffiti. Before they were buried, they were perhaps in the care of an armourer (*custodes armorum*) or an official connected with the games, as described by Arrian above.

Further reading: Keim, Klumbach, 1951; Garbsch 1978.

Medallions

Some 20 medallions, around 20-30cm in diameter, are also connected with the equipment used in the *hippika gymnasia*, though their precise function is uncertain; some authors see them as shield bosses, whilst others, including P. Connolly, think that they were decorative *phalerae* on horse's chests. Those with a flat back could have been mounted on shields, but the others may have had a different use. In any event, their decorative appeal was more important than their practical utility, a comment which can be applied to much of the equipment used in these displays.

The faces of most of these medallions are mostly taken up by a bust surrounded by different motifs, usually representing a female such as Minerva (Miltenberg, Tabris) or Ceres (Bonn), but there are also four examples portraying Ganymede being carried off by an eagle (Schwarzenacker, Lauriacum, Carnuntum, Machmud Bunar). On some other, rarer, medallions, a single head appears in a wreath, sometimes surrounded by vegetation (Blerick; Medusa head), and a final example, found in Asia Minor, carries a triangular bust of Virtus.

Though the feminine – or feminized – element predominates, nevertheless Hercules appears on one (or two) medallions as the central figure (Baly Bunar, Saalburg?) and on one example as a subsidiary motif (Szöny). The underlying theme of these medallions is markedly different from that of the cavalry's other personal equipment, being less unified and concentrating on tournaments in general and on the roles played by the opposing teams.

Chamfrons

Covered in elaborately decorated equipment themselves, cavalrymen could not neglect their horses' appearance and presentation either, and deposits and single finds have presented us with chamfrons which not only protected the animal but also enhanced its appearance. The Straubing deposit alone contained eight, each composed of three separate sections hinged together, with perforated convex cut-outs for the eyes in the side pieces. In several examples, motifs on the chamfron have pierced holes to give at least a little vision.

The central section of the three-piece construction lent itself very well, as with shin guards, to decoration based on a standing figure,

206 Sidepiece from a decorated *chamfron* from Eining (Kelheim, Bavaria; photo Prähist. Staatsammlung, Munich)

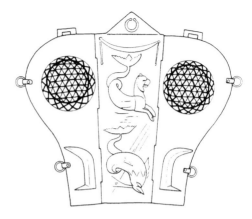

207 Composite bronze *chamfron* from Eining, assembled (after J.Garbsch, 1978)

208 Detail from an Eining *chamfron* :Hercules, with dot-punched inscription ELI VIRILIS (Prähist. Staatsammlung, Munich)

209 Central part of a bronze *chamfron* from Eining (Prähist. Staatsammlung, Munich)

210 Reconstruction of the leather *chamfron* from Newstead (photo Röm.-Germ. Zentralmuseum, Mainz)

Mars being the best represented, though Hercules with the eagle above appears on an example from Eining. One also finds motifs which appear as medallions, such as Ganymede and other popular themes – bust of Minerva, eagle, sea creatures (dolphins) and monsters as were mentioned above when describing shin guards.

It should be noted that these hinged units, with their complicated and probably fragile construction, are not the only types found under the Principate. Convex 'shells' to protect the horse's eyes have been found singly on several sites, such as Neuss and Carnuntum. These have pierced holes round their circumference to enable them to be attached to leather chamfrons like those found at Newstead and Vindolanda. Similar 'shells' with a system of buckles to hold them in place on the horse's head have also been found, at Pompeii and Mainz.

211 *Chamfron* in leather, with stamped dacoration and bronze appliques, from Vindolanda (after C. van Driel-Murray, 1989)

Miscellaneous

Roman and Scythian flags were also used in the *hippika gymnasia*, and the description of the Scythian type corresponds exactly with the Niederbieber *draco*, being a snake's head with a long tube of brightly coloured pieces of cloth attached, which waved in the air as the cavalry charged.

To close, we should recall the painted wooden shields found at Dura-Europos which have also been classed as sporting equipment. Their decoration is so elaborate that it would be out of place on a fighting shield and accords well with the decoration on items used in the displays. One of the Dura-Europos shields shows a map of Pont-Euxin, but the others carry religious and mythological scenes similar to the iconography of the metal equipment.

The most outstanding common denominator of sporting equipment iconography is its completely Roman basis, which may seem surprising at first; there is nothing which seems to reflect the fact that most auxiliary cavalry recruits were 'natives'. Was sporting equipment reserved exclusively for use by the legionary cavalry – the *equites legionis*? Definitely not: both find sites and graffiti showing ownership clearly show that the wearers were sometimes legionaries, sometimes auxiliaries. Also, the finding of graffiti of ownership on top of similar graffiti shows that sporting equipment was expensive; one chamfron from the Eining deposit shows that it had at least six successive owners, serving in different *turmae*.

So we must look again at the manufacturing workshops to explain this universality of iconography. Undoubtedly produced in military camps by the official *fabricae*, all these items were decorated to comply with an empire-wide directive which left little scope for individual local artistry. In only one single case – and that doubtful – a design may perhaps be influenced by Germanic mythology.

8 THE ARTILLERY

War machines represented one of the highest points in technical achievement in Antiquity, bringing together the skills of the engineer and the expert carpenter; a number of texts show that leading mathematicians of that period also took a serious interest in them and how they might be improved. Some of these engineers' writings have come down to us: the *Belopoica* (*Treatise on War Machines*) by Heron of Alexandria, published in the second half of the first century AD describes arbalests – *gastraphetes* – which we shall look at further, and two catapults which worked on the *tormenta* principle (see below); he is also credited, but in all likelihood wrongly, with a *chirobalista*. Vitruvius, himself an artillery commander we are told, sets out in Book X of his *De Architectura* the relative proportions of the parts of a catapult: these values, calculated from the size of the arrow to be fired, are certainly based on the highly advanced work of the Greek engineers. Several other works, which have not survived, can now only be studied in part, working from

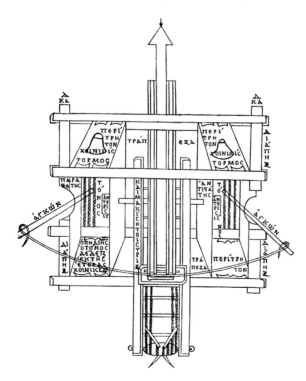

212 Medieval copy of an ancient illustration of Heron of Alexandria's *Belopoica*; how the catapult worked (after Wescher)

The role of the artillery

In attack: The taking of the fortress of Celenderis in Cilicia after the death of Germanicus:

Sentius then ordered the trumpets and bugles to sound, and the soldiers to advance to the rampart and position the scaling ladders; the bravest then mounted the assault while others fired arrows, stone balls and flaming torches from the war machines.

Tacitus, Ann., II.81

The taking of Volanda by Corbulo:

He divided his army into four parties: one formed the tortoise and advanced to undermine the walls by sapping; another was ordered to position the scaling ladders against the rampart, while a large group of the others hurled arrows and flaming torches; the fourth group, the slingers and 'hurlers', was placed where it could fire on the enemy from a distance.

Tacitus, Ann. XIII.39

The attack on Jotapata (Galilee) in AD 69:

Vespasian surrounded the place with his artillery, 160 war machines in all, and told them to fire at the men on the rampart. Then, at the same time as the catapult arrows were whistling through the air, the stone throwing machines opened fire, hurling one talent weight [36kg/70lb] rocks, this hail of fire making not only the wall but also the space inside untenable by the Jews. At the same time, the large contingent of Arabian archers, slingers and spear throwers gave supporting fire.

Josephus, BJ III.166-8

Roman texts and the examination of archaeological finds. This is particularly the case with Archimedes (who died aged 75 in 212 BC), and his treatise which was probably devoted to war machines.

Right from the start, artillery engineers designed their war machines around the basic 'torsion' system, whether they were intended to fire arrows – this style was called *doryboles* or *oxybeles* by some authors – or stone balls, when they were sometimes known as *lithoboles* or *petroboles*. The single-armed stone-throwing *balista* – formerly known as an *onager* – was called a '*scorpio*' in Late Antiquity descriptions (Ammianus Marcellinus).

In his account of the Siege of Syracuse in 214 BC, Polybius cannot disguise his admiration for the ingenuity and the ingenious war machines used by Archimedes on that occasion against the attackers. Two centuries later, Flavius Josephus found himself in a similar position as he repeatedly extolled the power and precision of the war machines used by Vespasian and Titus against the Jews. Intended to demonstrate the invincible character of the Roman army to his fellow citizens, Josephus' book is one of our most valuable sources on ancient artillery. There is hardly any doubt that in spite of having acquired most of their knowledge of it from Greek engineers, the Roman army was very proud of its artillery.

In the mid-1800s, a German artillery captain called Deimling attempted to reconstruct a number of war machines, following the publication of

213 E. Schramm's catapult reconstructions in the Saalburg museum (photo Saalburgmuseum)

214 Native auxiliaries at the start of the second century (after Trajan's Column) : Eastern archer, Balearic Islands slinger (illustration P.Connolly, photo Röm.-Germ. Zentralmuseum, Mainz)

'Griechischen Schriftsteller' in 1853-4, and these were on display at the Karlsruhe Museum until they were destroyed during the Second World War. Some 12 years after Deimling another artillery captain, this time a Frenchman, Verchère de Reffye, made models for Napoléon III of war machines like those thought to have been used by Julius Caesar at the siege of Alésia, and these can still be seen, some of them dismantled because of their size, in the Musée des Antiquités Nationales at Saint-Germain-en-Laye. The most advanced models of such machines, however, are those made by a German artillery major, E. Schramm, from 1903 onwards, and eight of his twelve models are still preserved in the Saalburg museum, where D. Baatz continued Schramm's work.

Before examining the advanced types of machines used by the Roman legions during the Empire, mention must be made of the 'little artillery' – the slingshots and the arrows used by special units. Relatively simple, these ancient weapons continued to be used long after ancient times.

215 Lead slingshot inscribed *feri Pomp(eium Strabonem)* (after E. Babelon and J-A. Blanchet, 1895)

THE SLING

If stones and other assorted hand-thrown projectiles were always among the weapons used in battles or sieges, it was the sling, with the power and accuracy imparted by its whirling strings, which led the field in this area. The slingers' shot, at first of stone or baked clay, were also sometimes cast in lead in Greece from the Bronze Age (lead slingshots were found at Cnossos, level LM III). Slingshots with inscriptions appeared in the sixth century BC and are widespread in the Classical and Hellenistic eras, being borrowed and used by the Romans until they fell out of use during the first century AD.

Antiquaries have always been attracted by slingshots bearing inscriptions, and many museums have assembled interesting collections. Inscriptions may be symbols – a thunderbolt on a slingshot from Alésia for instance – or a short phrase, usually only a few letters. Some of these may be an invocation to the slingshot itself (*feri Pomp(eium Strabonem)* on a slingshot from the siege at Ausculum, referring to Cn. Pompeius Strabo, consul in 89 BC), or invective aimed at the enemy: *avale*, 'swallow this', or again, 'death to the fugitives'. Other inscriptions, generally cut in by hand, in longhand writing, and not cast into the shot like the ones just mentioned, bear witness to the soldier's graveyard humour – *Fulviae (la)ndicam peto* on a shot slung by Caesar's troops at the siege of Perusia in 40 BC, for instance, evoked a matching response *peto Octavia(ni) culum* from the besieged forces of M. Antonius. These exceptional objects have naturally attracted the efforts of forgers, and the German archaeologist Zangmeister revealed hundreds of such fakes early last century.

More usually, and bearing in mind that only a very small proportion of slingshots carry any sort of message anyway – it is the name of a military campaign commander or a legion's senior officer which appears. Such inscriptions enable us to date the slingshots, and sometimes, if the find spot is known, to relate them to a particular event; thus a slingshot marked *L. Piso L. f. cos.* found at Enna in Sicily names the consul who led the war against the Sicilian slave uprising in the second century BC. A slingshot from Spain bears the inscription *Cn. Mag(nus) imp(erator)*, identifying Cnaeus, Pompey's son, who fought against Julius Caesar in the Civil War; another, found at Perusia, gives the number and title *L. XII Victrix* – one of the legions involved in the siege of 40 BC.

Slingshots with inscriptions are rarely found in Gaul, but some discoveries can be of great interest, as is the case with one found recently at the Mas d'Agenais site in southern France. Its letters MANL possibly recall the pro-praetor L. Manlius, governor of the Transalpine province in 77 BC. Rushed to Spain to give support to Q. Metellus who was fighting against Sertorius at that time, Manlius was defeated in battle by one of the rebel general's lieutenants and forced to retire precipitately to Gaul. Written records tell us that he was killed in an ambush set up by Aquitanian forces, perhaps at the Mas d'Agenais if one can rely on this discovery (Plutarch, *Vit. Sert.* XII.3; Frontin, *Str.* IV.5.19; Livy, *Per.* XC; Florus, II.10.6; Orose, V.23; Caesar, *B Civ.* III.20).

216 Lead slingshots from the Mas d'Agenais (Lot-et-Garonne, SW France) : the letters MANL(?) may refer to the ambush of the pro-praetor L. Manlius by Aquitaine forces in 77BC. Private collection

---

In defence: The attack on Caesar's camp in 52 BC:

A considerable force made the attack, with fresh troops replacing the tired ones in rotation as it progressed; our troops had to fight on continuously, however, due to the large size of the camp [built to hold six legions].
A storm of arrows and all sorts of missiles inflicted many casualties, but our war machines (tormenta) were a great help.

Julius Caesar, B Gall. VII.41

The control of a strategic path; Caesar deprives the inhabitants of Uxellodunum of water in 51 BC.

Having seen how difficult it was for the enemy [to get to the river], Caesar posted archers, slingers and even war machines on the gentler slopes, and so prevented the besieged citizens from drawing water from the river.

Julius Caesar, B Gall. VIII.40

The supporters of Otho and Vitellius form up at opposite ends of a pontoon bridge over the River Po.

Access to the bridge was blocked by a tower which had been pushed from the river bank onto the boat nearest to it; catapult and ballista fire from this tower drove the enemy back. On their side of the river the Othonians had built on the bank, from which they fired stones and flaming torches.

Tacitus, Hist. II.34

Although used by the Romans throughout the Republican period and the early Principate, the Gauls do not seem ever to have adopted lead slingshots, except of course when they were fighting as Roman army auxiliaries; but they sometimes made ingenious use of other materials. The Nervii, for example, attacked Cicero's camp during the Civil war with 'flaming balls', probably a mixture of clay and grass (Caesar, *B Gall.* V.43).

THE LONGBOW

Another traditional weapon, the longbow was probably used by most races from the Mesolithic period onwards, and its long history explains the high degree of development which it reached among the Romans, who drew particularly on Eastern sources. It was actually the Scythians, Parthians and other Eastern peoples who developed the bow and arrow to its highest level, and then passed their archery techniques on to the Romans, although a large number of other barbarians also used the weapon, doubtless more frequently for hunting than for war. The adoption of the bow by the Romans was largely in response to enemy pressures, notably that of Scipio Africanus who incorporated a number of *sagittarii* into every '*centuria*' of his army in Spain. Although Livy writes that there were archers in the Roman

217 Memorial to the archer Monimus, from Mainz (after L.Lindenschmidt, 1882)

army as early as 207 BC, they were fully integrated into the Roman military system very slowly; Caesar himself had to arrange the inclusion of troops of archers into his forces, and he notes with surprise the large number of bowmen in Vercingetorix's army (*B Civ.* VII.31). Set up as wings and cohorts under the Principate, archery units became more important in the Later Empire.

The Roman bow, with its Eastern origin, was of 'composite' construction, its components of different materials held together by adhesives and bindings. The central part, supple hardwood, had antler reinforcements at its tips which increased its power; examples have been found on many military sites, particularly those of the first century after the reign of Augustus. When not needed, bows were unstrung to preserve their natural curvature, which was placed under a high degree of stress during use. To string the bow, the archer bent it under his leg, an action which can be seen on a number of Scythian depictions.

Judging by a Greek example, the arrowheads used by Roman archers from Republican times were of triangular cross-section (see the Numantia finds) which made them more accurate as well as more deadly. Made from bronze in the early days, they were later made from iron, with the exception of those from the Porolissum site in Dacia, where more than 200 bone arrowheads of this design were found. The distribution of arrowheads in the *limes*, together with bow-tips, shows

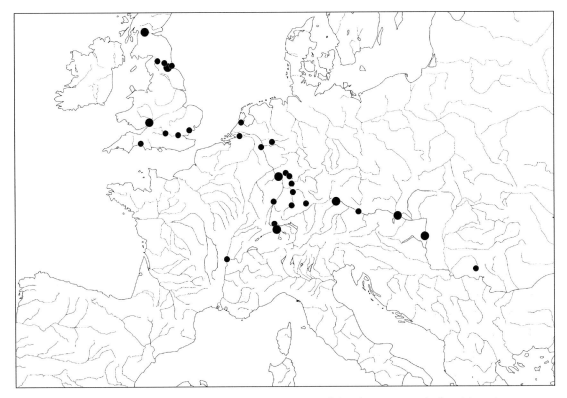

218 Distribution of Roman antler bowtips (mod. From W.Zanier, 1988. Small dots show 1-5 examples found; large dots, more than 5)

Fire arrows in AD 363

Malleoli are special incendiary projectiles based on reeds, made in the following way. A reed is careful-ly hollowed out, and slots are cut between the arrow head and the arrow shaft, rather as women spin-ning linen thread prepare a distaff; lighted material together with something to burn is then inserted. The arrow should be fired gently from a half-drawn bow – discharging at full power would blow out the flame – and it will continue to burn as it sticks into its target; putting water on it will only enhance its burning, and the only way to extinguish such arrows is to stifle them with dust.

Ammianus Marcellinus, XXIII.IV.14

A little later in his writings (XXIII.VI.37) the author reveals the secret of these arrows' flammability, a substance which he calls 'Oil of Medea' in which the *malleoli* are coated. A mention of naphtha in the same work could imply a military use for this highly inflammable substance.

the importance of the *sagittarii* under the Principate, especially in Britain and on the Rhine-Danube frontier. The abundance of such finds in these regions where archaeological research is so advanced is supported by epigraphical references to *sagittarii*, particularly well-evidenced along the Danube (Pannonia, Dacia and Moesia) as well as in the East (Syria, Cappadocia). While on this point, there is a written mention of nine corps of *sagittarii* in North Africa, though so far there is no actual archaeological evidence of bowmen in Mauretania, Numidia or Proconsular Africa.

Several finds appear to support the use of other types of arrowheads by the Roman army; this is the case with hollowpoint arrowheads, a specimen of which was found among other types at the Tiberian camp at Aulnay-de-Saintonge. It is possible that such traditionally native arrowheads were used only occasionally, and by some auxiliary corps, but their primary application in the civilian (and military?) context seems to have been for hunting.

Fire arrows are known to us from some ancient texts – the best known being that of Ammianus Marcellinus in AD 363 – and from some archaeological finds; they consist of a sharpened core which supports a sort of small cage to hold incendiary material. Fairly rare discoveries (their nature has only recently been identified), such heads could have been fitted to arrows (examples from Wroxeter, Bar Hill and Nauportus) or catapult projectiles (the point from Dura-Europos). Other incendiary projectiles, perhaps made entirely from organic material, were evidently thrown by hand.

THE CROSSBOW

We are touching here on the territory of Greco-Roman engineers, the area of war machines. A true 'mechanical bow', the crossbow can actually be included among the most advanced of such machines, to such an extent that it was thought for many years that such bows were unknown in Antiquity. At present, the Roman period crossbow as we understand it is known only from two funer-

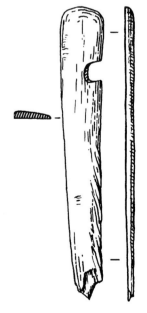

219 Bone bowtip from a composite bow found at Frankfurt (after U.Fischer, 1973)

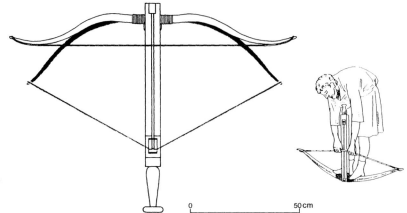

220 Roman crossbow: reconstruction from the Haute Loire reliefs; probable method of spanning bow (after D.Baatz, 1991)

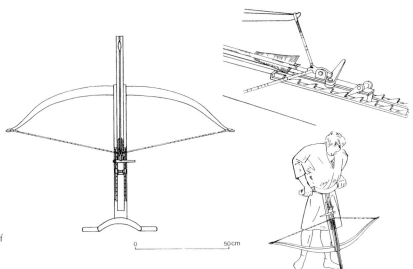

221 *Gastraphetes*: reconstruction and firing mechanism, after Heron of Alexandria; method of spanning

ary reliefs in the Haute-Loire (Espaly and Solignac-sur-Loire). Although we do not at present know all its applications, it seems to have been limited to hunting use.

However, we shall not stop here, at this technical curiosity, because the basic idea behind this ancient development was to be expressed much more significantly in much larger machines.

TORSION POWERED WAR MACHINES

In studying Republican artillery we have seen that the principle of the *tormentum*, the bundle of cords at the heart of the war machine's power, came into use shortly after the Greeks invented artillery. High

Empire artillery continued to be based on the same principle, in spite of the vulnerability of the bundle, which was one of the weak points of these machines; a well-aimed projectile or a brave enemy soldier could cut it, disabling the catapult completely. Tacitus relates an incident at Cremona in the Civil war between Galba and Vitellius (AD 69) in which the latter's forces were destroying their enemy with projectiles from an enormous *balista*; two of Galba's soldiers succeeded in infiltrating Vitellius' lines and putting it out of action by cutting the cords.

To overcome this weakness, the small catapult which developed at the end of the first century AD, and was first used by Trajan against the Dacians, was fitted with an easily changed cord bundle, and this new system enabled a damaged coil to be replaced by a reserve bundle, even in battle; this 'campaign catapult' is illustrated as a new development on Trajan's Column. In previous military campaigns it had been necessary to disassemble war machines and transport them on pack animals, along with their projectiles (Josephus, *BJ* II.546).

The late Republican catapult, with its wooden frame (see the examples from Ampurias and Teruel) was really a heavy and clumsy machine. Replacing the trusses with a set of metal rods reduced the weight considerably, and at the same time increased the weapon's stability, as well as making it easier to repair when necessary. An example

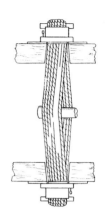

222 Operating principle of a torsion war machine (*tormentum*) (after D. Baatz, 1985)

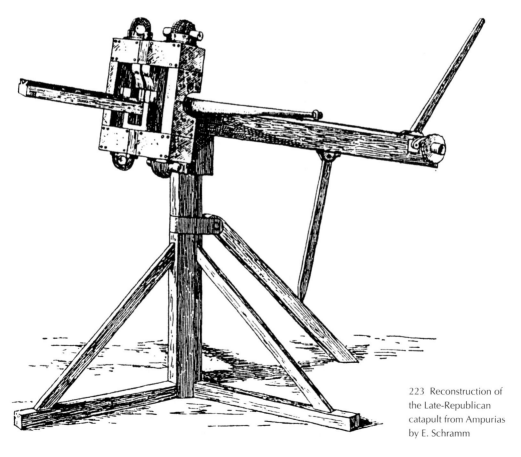

223 Reconstruction of the Late-Republican catapult from Ampurias by E. Schramm

The power and accuracy of the artillery

At the siege of Bourges (Avaricum) in 52 BC:

There was a Gaul in front of a gate who was throwing at the burning tower balls of fat and pitch which his comrades were passing to him from hand to hand; a bolt from a *scorpio* hit him on his right side, and he fell unconscious. One of his comrades, stepping over his body, replaced him in his task; he too fell, hit in his turn by a shot from the *scorpio*; a third followed, and a fourth, and their post continued to be manned until the fire was extinguished all along the battlefront and the fighting ceased.

Julius Caesar, *B Gall*. VII.26

At the siege of Jotapata in AD 67:

The violent power of the *oxybeles* and the catapults could transfix several men with one bolt, and the stones from the roaring war machines carried away the battlements and broke the corner walls of the towers. In fact, there was no file of troops which could withstand being bowled over to the last man by the weight and force of one of the stones. One can obtain an idea of the power of this machine from what happened that night. A soldier standing on the rampart near to Joseph was hit by one of its stones, which ripped off his head and threw it, as if thrown by a sling, three stades distance [about 530m]. As day broke, a pregnant woman was hit in the belly just after she had left her house, the stone sending her unborn child a half stade distance [nearly 90m]. Such was the power of this stone-thrower. Even more frightening than the machines themselves was their grinding noise, and more frightening than that, the noise the stones made when striking their targets.

Josephus, BJ, III.243-7

Emphasising Roman power and the invincible nature of its army is one of Josephus' continuing themes throughout his 'Jewish War', and although he frequently exaggerates, the power of the Roman war machines remained unsurpassed in Antiquity.

At the siege of Amida (Mesopotamia) in AD 359:

The king of the Chionites Grumbates advanced towards the ramparts . . . however, realising that the king had just moved into range, a nimble gunner fired his balista and hit his son, a mere youth who never left his father's side; the bolt transfixed the prince's armour and chest, and knocked from his horse this young man whose physique and beauty had made him pre-eminent among his companions.

Ammianus Marcellinus XIX.1

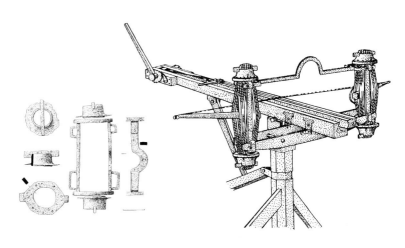

224 (left) *Kambestrion* and *modioli* from the catapult from Lyon (after D. Baatz and M. Feugère, 1981).
(right) Reconstruction of the Lyon catapult, without the sheetmetal pieces to protect the cord bundles (after D. Baatz and M. Feugère, 1981)

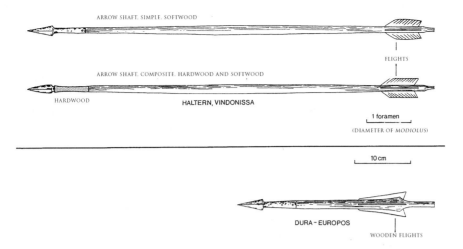

ARROW SHAFT, SIMPLE, SOFTWOOD

FLIGHTS

ARROW SHAFT, COMPOSITE, HARDWOOD AND SOFTWOOD

HARDWOOD   HALTERN, VINDONISSA

1 foramen

(DIAMETER OF *MODIOLUS*)

10 cm

DURA - EUROPOS

WOODEN FLIGHTS

225   Reconstructions of catapult arrows from the first to the third centuries (D.Baatz)

of this new catapult, with a *kambestrion* and two *modioli,* has been found at Lyon, making it possible to examine the characteristics of this type of machine in detail.

In the *chiroballistra*, the various components have been simplified as far as possible: two cord bundles (*kambestria*) with their cylindrical end bushes and transverse cotter pins are fastened together by a shaped brace (*kamarion*) and a cross piece. Two bars for spanning the bundles, which were missing from the Lyon example, have been found together with a *kambestrion* on a find from Orşova, a late fortress on the Danubian frontier in Moesia. This find has enabled measurements to be taken to check the accuracy of the illustrations in Heron's treatise, later copied and recopied by medieval draughtsmen ; and, allowing for differences in techniques in perspective, the ancient drawings were found to be accurate.

Ancient war machine artillery was never organised into independent units as were the archers and slingers; instead, every legion was equipped with several machines. The auxiliary units had no such artillery, as they lacked both the qualified 'gunners' to use them and the support workshop facilities essential for maintenance and repair. There is just one known reference to artillery used by an auxiliary unit, and this is exceptional in both its date and its area of operation. Two third-century inscriptions have been found at High Rochester, well north of Hadrian's Wall, commemorating the erection of a *ballistarium* by *Cohors I fida Vardulorum millaria*; this isolated event can probably be explained by its location on one of the Empire s furthest frontiers.

Under the Principate the artillery was used to fire not only arrows but also, particularly in siege warfare, stone balls which were equally devastating against both buildings and troops in ranks. Such stone balls, proving the use of war machines, have been found in the oldest levels of many excavations, particularly on sites in southern Gaul (notably the *oppida* inland from Marseille which were attacked by the legions of *C. Sextius Calvinus* in 124 BC). As D. Baatz has rightly said, however,

The Romans under fire from their own artillery

Simon . . . sited his artillery on the ramparts, both the weapons seized from Cestius [three years earlier, in August 66] and those he had captured when he defeated the garrison at Antonia [in November 66], but most of them could not be brought into action, as his troops did not know how to use them, and the few that were fired, under the guidance of deserters, were clumsily handled.
Flavius Josephus, BJ,V, 267-68.

The Jews were now fully trained in the handling of war machines, daily practice having little by little developed their skill. They therefore had at their disposal 300 *oxybeles* and 40 stone throwers, with which they made the building of earthworks difficult for the Romans.
Flavius Josephus, BJ,V,359

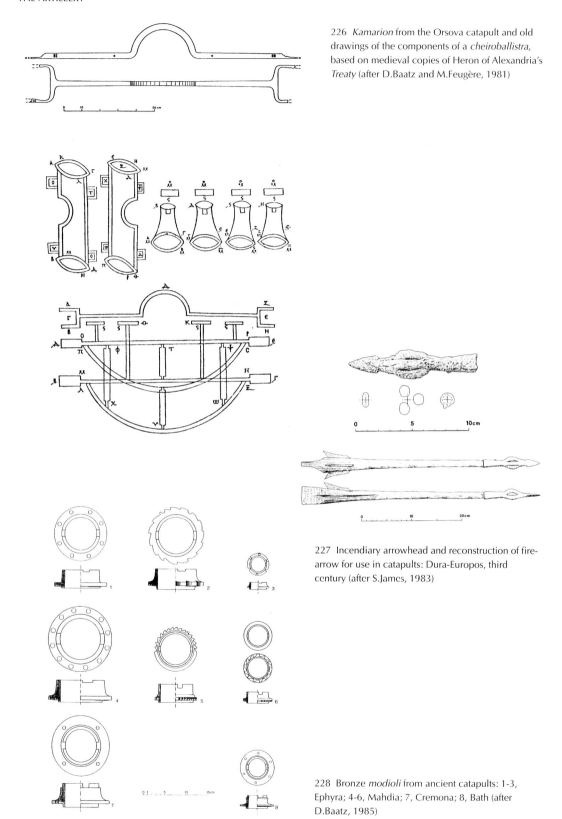

226 *Kamarion* from the Orsova catapult and old drawings of the components of a *cheiroballistra*, based on medieval copies of Heron of Alexandria's *Treaty* (after D.Baatz and M.Feugère, 1981)

227 Incendiary arrowhead and reconstruction of fire-arrow for use in catapults: Dura-Europos, third century (after S.James, 1983)

228 Bronze *modioli* from ancient catapults: 1-3, Ephyra; 4-6, Mahdia; 7, Cremona; 8, Bath (after D.Baatz, 1985)

not all the stone balls found on Roman period sites had necessarily been fired by war machines; small balls could have been thrown by hand, and larger ones may have been dropped from battlements and towers, some perhaps even being aimed in a rudimentary fashion by rails or chutes.

The interpretation of ancient stone balls is difficult in the absence of precise measurements, but it can justifiably be reasoned that each machine fired stones whose weight best suited it. Also, a machine capable of throwing heavy stones could not operate in a small confined space and needed the support of a rampart, or at least a solid firing platform. R. Forrer has studied a number of balls found in different parts of the city of Strasbourg, and four ancient specimens weighed respectively 410, 820, 1220 and 1385g, suggesting a basic modular weight of about 405/410g for the first three, which leads us to ascribe a late date to them.

The conversion of various actions (motive power, tensioning, firing) from human to mechanical opened the door from ancient times onwards to the development of machines of a power vastly beyond human capability; interestingly, though, it seems that the ancients never thought of indirect fire, that is, firing at a target beyond their immediate range of vision. Also, some of the writings on machines describe models which were a theoretical or propaganda exercise and were never actually constructed. In his 'Treatise on Artillery', Philon brings to the readers' attention machines capable of throwing 78kg stones, but this must have been a theoretical exercise – such a machine would, for instance, have had to be more than nine metres high. Vitruvius pursues this idea still further, and gives the dimensions of a machine to hurl 162kg boulders! The weight of projectiles in general use seems in fact to have been within a fairly impressive range of 3-26 kilos.

A 'mini' catapult – though C. Baatz's reconstruction suggests that it was about 2.6m in height – was found in the ruins of a rampart tower in the town of Hatra in Mesopotamia, which was captured by the Sassanids in the middle of the third century. Judging from its dimen-

229 *Ballista* balls from the late-Roman levels at Strasbourg (photo Musées de Strasbourg)

The *balistas* of the Tenth Legion at Jerusalem, AD 69

Although the war machines of every legion were excellent, those of the Tenth Legion were outstanding; their *oxybeles* were more powerful and their stone-throwers bigger, enabling their gunners to hit not only groups attempting a sortie but also the defenders on the rampart. The stones they threw weighed about 36kg (one talent in Attic measurements), and the machines had a range of more than 350m (more than two stades). Their striking force destroyed not only those first hit, but often those behind them as well. At first, it is true, the Jews could avoid such stones, which were white, when they heard them rushing through the air and their first impact. Watchers posted on the towers shouted warnings when they saw the machine being loaded and the stone fired, shouting 'Baby on the way!' in their native tongue. Those who were in the line of fire could scatter and lie down so that the stone landed harmlessly. To remedy this situation, the Romans blackened the stones, and being no longer visible, they hit their targets, causing many deaths.

Josephus, BJ V.269-73

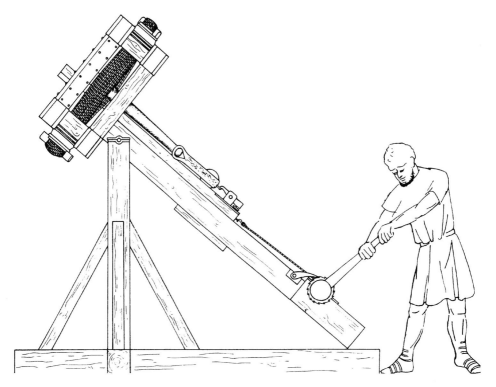

230 Torsion-powered war machine (stone-thrower) from Hatra (after D.Baatz, 1978)

231 Reconstruction of an *onager* by E.Schramm (photo Saalburgmuseum)

232 Reconstruction of the Ampurias catapult (second century BC) by E.Schramm (photo Saalburgmuseum)

sions (it is possible that it was not an entirely Roman machine), it seems probable that it fired stones weighing around 10 Roman pounds (3.27kg) at the attackers.

Generally speaking, Roman artillery shows a high level of technical ability combined with a remarkable appreciation of how it should be employed. Some Roman machinery, such as the famous crane shown on the Haterii monument in the Latran museum, was intended more for show than for practical use, but this is certainly not the case with the Roman army's artillery. Although the auxiliaries did not have war machines, doubtless for technical reasons as we have seen, each legion did have its own artillery section; and two pieces of direct evidence enable us to assess the resources usually assigned. Describing the siege of Jotapata in the first century AD, Josephus counted 160 war machines in Vespasian's three legions, or 50–5 machines per legion. In the fourth century, Vegetius says that every century had a mobile catapult (*carroballista*), whilst assigning an onager to every cohort; this would make 10 onagers and 55 catapults to every legion, each with an 11-man team (*Mil.* II.25). One may therefore be surprised at the relative rarity of archaeological discoveries of identified catapult components from Roman times (only about a score of sites), though this apparent scarcity may be unrealistic, as researchers regularly discover such components in collections of finds which have not been recognised. The recent discovery of fragments of the moulds for bronze *modioli* on the Auerberg site in Bavaria (G. Ulbert) shows that further research in this area can add to our knowledge of ancient artillery.

9 INFANTRY EQUIPMENT

We come now to other items which could be considered as military equipment; as well as his weapons, the soldier had special clothing and other objects which were part of his way of life without being essentially of direct military application. Considerable progress has been made in this area in recent years, but the increased volume of published information raises a number of problems of interpretation. One might even go so far as to ask if there was a specific standard military outfit in Roman times, or whether just wearing a sword (for instance) defined a man as a soldier.

These questions are particularly relevant to first-century finds, where the *gladius*, usually found with its *cingulum*, is the only proven military object. This is the case with the soldier's remains found on the beach at Herculaneum in 1983, who by all appearances was a *miles classis* – a 'sea-soldier'. He was wearing only a *gladius* in a scabbard, hanging from a bronze *cingulum*, and a purse of coins which surprisingly included a gold *aureus* of Nero. The several monuments to soldiers of the fleet which have come down to us show little support for this 'minimal' equipment. Because of this, we shall have to look again at the weapons found on commercial ships of the period; swords are well represented (Comacchio, la Chrétienne H, Porto-Novo), but helmets are even more frequently found (Albenga, Giens, Dramont A, Gruissan, Cabrera). Does the presence of these items imply that the owners were necessarily soldiers? Or could travellers take weapons on board to protect themselves, especially against pirates?

MILITARY EQUIPMENT?

In recent years a large number of writers have argued that the idea of a uniform – nowadays inseparable from the definition of military personnel – did not exist in the Roman army. Even so, the legionary, and even the auxiliary, did not have complete freedom of choice, and there is general agreement that there were both limits, and some form of 'basic equipment', although it is not always possible to be precise about how much of this was centrally issued or subject to explicit regulations.

For the infantry, this basic equipment seems to have comprised a sword, one or more spears (*pilum* or lance), a shield, a helmet and body

233 Memorial of Annaius Daverzus (photo Röm.-Germ. Zentralmuseum, Mainz)

armour. As we have seen, the type of shield varied from unit to unit, but was the same throughout an individual corps, especially when it played a part in collective drills and manoeuvres. The dagger seems to have been optional, perhaps in relation to the soldier s personal means rather than in accordance with a general regulation. We know from a papyrus record that a certain L. Caecilius Secundus, an auxiliary cavalryman, borrowed a sum of money from one of his companions in AD 27, giving as part of the security for the loan a dagger sheath of silver with ivory inlays, obviously a very special object.

Whatever the facts, the helmet and shield were carried by soldiers only when in combat, or when travelling in hostile territory, as is shown clearly on Trajan's Column. In peacetime the soldier must have been satisfied just with his sword hanging from its special belt, which is why archaeologists can identify by 'military equipment' most of the items found in conjunction with such a belt (*cingulum*). This belt was an everyday object, identifying the soldier's profession as clearly as the weapon it was designed to carry, and was a valued possession which received its owner's care and attention. It should be emphasised here that the sword and its *cingulum*, and even more so the dagger and its *cingulum*, were regarded as a single item. When a soldier did not wish to carry his sword, he took it off complete with its *cingulum* : a number of third century reliefs (Pula relief; memorial to S*everius Acceptus*) show the two items together.

The High Empire *cingulum*, at first just a simple leather belt, usually bore a series of metal plaques whose function was basically decorative. With the exception of the Vachères soldier, whose belt was decorated with small round studs in a zigzag pattern, such plaques are usually rectangular, with their height equal to the belt's width. The simplest plaques, usually tinned, carried a circular motif round the edge, but not every plaque on a *cingulum* followed the same design (see an anonymous monument from Bonn). In the same way

234 Memorial of an unknown legionary (photo Rheinisches Landesmuseum, Bonn.)

235 (top) *Cingulum* from Rheingönheim; Speyer Museum. (bottom) *Cingulum* from Chassenard (Musée des Antiquités Nationales)

236 Applique and fixing method on *spatha* baldrick inscribed *optime maxime con (sera) / numerum omnium / militantium* from the camp at Zugmantel (photo Röm.-Germ. Zentralmuseum, Mainz)

that dagger sheaths usually had carefully executed decoration, so did dagger belts, in both cases more than the sword *cingulum*. The most common decoration was a niello-inlaid motif, particularly common at Vindonissa. A number of *cingulum* plaques are decorated with scenes or personages, some for propaganda – an imperial bust on two *cornucopiae* – some with everyday yet symbolic scenes such as hunting. These are mostly from the Western empire (the Rhine-Danube *limes* and Britain), and matrix for stamping a hunting scene has been found at Colchester.

Such decorated plaques were accompanied by particularly careful-ly-made buckles; the remains of three rectangular repoussé plaques showing a bust (Tiberius?) above *cornucopiae* were found in a tomb at Chassenard (department of Allier) dating from the AD 40s; and with them was a buckle also decorated with embossed motifs. As such funerary deposits are rare, it is not easy to determine how many plaques would be found on a *cingulum* of this period. The most com-plete assemblies, from Cesena and Rheingönheim, each have six, and in the latter case one of them was hinged to the belt buckle. On some memorials, such as that of the auxiliary *Annaius*, the whole belt appears to be covered with plaques edge to edge (at least their rear edges), which is not the case on the relief from Pula.

Some discoveries, obviously fewer in number, have unearthed silver belts, and the most recent, from a shipwreck at Porto-Novo in Corsica, has a buckle and a plaque which carry the same design. Currently being cleaned and conserved, one can nevertheless make out two captives, one each side of a standing figure (perhaps an Imperial personage), who is leaning on a lance. The scene can be linked to the propaganda designs of which several examples have been found on first-century sword scabbards. The plaques and buckles recovered from rural sites destroyed by the eruption of Vesuvius in AD 79 carry mythologically-inspired motifs which appear to be exceptional on military equipment. We have here dropped the themes usually found on such objects in favour of those common to Roman silverware in general – the evocation of more or less obscure mytho-logical episodes which were an 'in joke' among members of the same social class.

Between them, the sword and the dagger as depicted on Rhineland funerary memorials usually show a collection of hanging straps covered with small round studs and generally overloaded with pendants. This 'apron', the word used by archaeologists seems to have had no function but to add to the jangling noise already made by the armour, belt and hobnailed footwear which heralded the approach of the Roman soldier. It is one of the benefits of modern reconstruc-tions that we are now aware that the impression of power created by a cohort in marching order was not based solely on the appearance of the individual infantrymen, but also on the noise made by the sol-diers *en masse*.

It is also possible that these straps were important only because of the buttons or studs fixed to them. The number of straps varies on different depictions (the proudest, such as Annaius, have up to eight of them) and their studs possibly carried a motif, though these would be too small to

237 A third-century march past. Bronze medallion (badge of an officer, Aurelius Cervianus ?) found in France; vexillationes of the XXth Legio Valeria Victrix and the IInd Legio Augusta (after J.Casey, 1991)

238 (right) *Cingulum* buckle in silver, from Pompeii : Neptune and Minerva, olive tree between them (after E.Künzl, 1977). (below right) First century *cingulum* plaque from Oberstimm : the wolf suckling Romulus and Remus (photo Prähist. Staatssammlung, Munich). (below left) Roma and Victory on a silver *cingulum* plaque from Pompeii or Herculaneum (after E.Künzl, 1977)

reproduce on a memorial sculpture. Stamped sheet metal buttons, particularity in evidence along the western *limes*, have been identified as *cingulum* decorations, and there appears to have been a manufacturer at Besançon. They often show a head accompanied by palms or clubs – symbols of authority?, commemorations of particular feats of arms, such as a naval or other victory? Perhaps these buttons were issued to troops on special occasions to mark memorable campaigns or events? In this case it would be natural for soldiers to wear these mementoes with pride, as 'lapel badges' worn only by the participants.

THE SOLDIER'S 'CIVIL' EQUIPMENT

As well as their weapons, soldiers obviously had a wide range of 'domestic' accessories, some of them specifically made for military users – leather bags for personal effects and ground sheets, for instance. Writing at the end of the fourth century AD, Vegetius sets out an impressive list of all that a legion took on campaign to meet any eventuality (trench digging, crossing rivers, etc), including a force of fully-equipped labourers. Other items were also obtained on the civilian market, such as the bronze vessels produced in large numbers first in Etruria, and subsequently in Campania from the Augustan period onwards. A specifically military design for these does not seem to have been produced, in spite of the enormous market which the army represented (250,000-300,000 men on campaign in the first century for example), and the fact that it would have been easy to produce models to suit a soldier's way of life. In this instance the Roman army merely contributed to the prosperity of Italian industry and assisted in distributing its products across the Roman Empire. To supply such items, the army probably relied on the traders and merchants who travelled with the troops and could meet the thousand different needs of the soldiers, especially when they were in their semi-permanent winter camps. That there were such civilians, both men and women, encamped close to the army units is well known, and many prominent Roman settlements grew out of a *vicus* originally established to meet the 'civilian' needs of the soldiers for craftsmen, shopkeepers, barkeepers and concubines.

As troops obviously could not depend on these people when on service in enemy territory, they called on them only for comfort items, such as tableware for example; for goods to meet essential needs it was the army which was responsible for their manufacture and maintenance. This is the case, for instance, with shield covers, which were made by military craftsmen, as is shown by the excavations at Valkenburg, and particularly clearly by the *fabrica* at Bonner Berg. *Caligae,* the nailed footwear with finely cut straps, were hard-

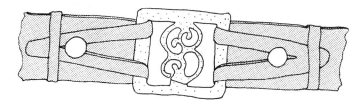

239 Third century buckle type and fixing method using two buttons (after J.Oldenstein, 1976)

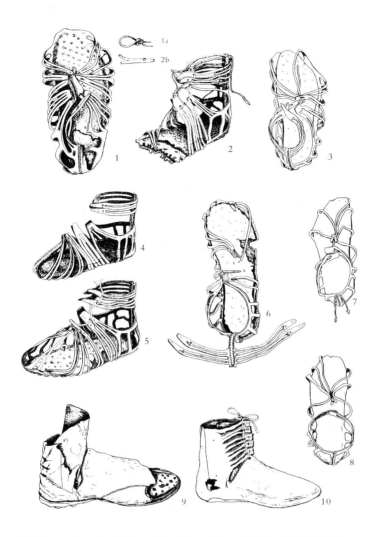

240 Roman shoes from Mainz : 1-8, *caligae*; 9-10, *calcei* (after J.Göpfrich, *J.B. Saalburg* 42, 1986)

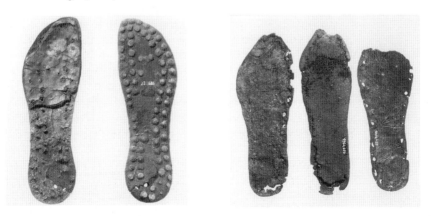

241 (left) Hobnailed sole of a *caliga* from Vindonissa (photo Th.Hartmann, Vindonissa-Museum, Brugg.) (right) Sole of a leather shoe from Dambach (Prähist. Staatsammlung, Munich, inv. 1966-442)

wearing, supple and permitted the feet to breathe; they were obviously locally made, as were the campaign tents; the workshops attached to every unit undertook the repair and maintenance of animal harnesses, carts and similar equipment, doing all that was necessary to ensure the smooth running of the military machine. The amount of work needed to supply and look after this vast range of complex military equipment, some of it fragile, inevitably led to the development of higher technical skills and standards than those found in the civilian sector. The 'turf cutter', for example, and the *dolabra* (a special type of pickaxe) were tools specifically developed for digging trenches and ditches in northern regions, and such tools are found only in military contexts, proving that there must have been 'soldier-blacksmiths' in special workshops whose importance has often been underestimated.

The advanced techniques in use by the military manifest themselves in many important details. In civilian society, metal objects were marked in two different ways, inscriptions composed of pinpoint dots and those cut with a graving tool. M. Martin has clearly shown that in the case of silverware the dotted inscriptions were the work of the manufacturer, who had the tools and special skills required for such work, whereas the owner made do with a graver. In the army, however, because the owner and the craftsman were so close together, a large number of marks of ownership are of the pinpoint type.

It seems clear that under the Principate the soldier led a privileged existence when it came to technology and its benefits, which perhaps enables us to answer, at least in part, the question which we posed at the start of this chapter. Too often, people have sought a link between a soldier's equipment and his military rank, whereas examination of funerary monuments shows that the wearer's sophisticated equipment, and the care taken in the monument's construction, in reality reflect the level of the soldier's own savings or a payment either by his heirs and executors or by his comrades. Without doubt, such expenditure was directly related to the soldier's own means, but whatever his rank, he occupied a privileged position in his contemporary society. With a regular basic income and stable living costs, he could also expect monetary windfalls during his service, either as a result of campaigns or his personal conduct. To put it simply, the Roman soldier equipped himself in accordance with his means rather than his military rank – plaques on his *cingulum*, buckles or *fibulae*, in bronze,

242 Leather strap still with its endpiece and decorative bronze studs; Vindolanda, *c.* AD 105-115 (Vindolanda Trust)

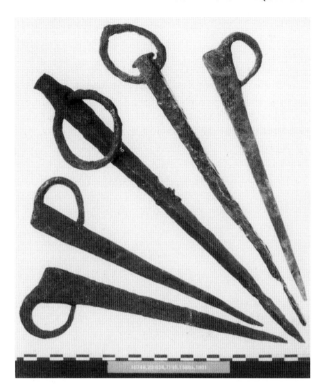

243 Tent pegs from Vindonissa (photo T. Hartmann, Vindonissa-Museum, Brugg)

244 Tools used by Vindonissa legionaries (photo T. Hartmann, Vindonissa-Museum, Brugg)

silver or even gold. The range of financial benefits seems to have increased over the years, either as direct pay or in the form of imperial largesse. Thus a mid-third century cremation burial at Bruiu in Dacia has a silver *fibula* as well as bronze belt accessories. A richly furnished tomb from Durostorum yielded the remains of a silver-decorated *cingulum* plus a gold ring and *fibula*, and an early fourth century officer's tomb at Carsium contained silver belt-fittings and a gold *fibula*.

Here, as in other areas, developments in the situation between the start of the Principate and the Late Empire force us to consider the latter separately. Pressure from the Germans on the Rhine-Danube *limes* and the Persians on the Eastern front from the period AD 250-70 had disrupted the empire; a more settled situation was restored around AD 300 by the establishment of imperial *fabricae* to ensure stable supplies for the troops. Because of this change, military items, and not only weapons, were distributed from the fourth century onwards in a radically different way.

10 THE LATE EMPIRE

The military equipment of the Late Empire is much less well known than that of the early Principate. The abandonment of many camps on the Rhine-Danube *limes* – the excavation of these has yielded examples of most of the items used in the earlier period – certainly played a major part in the disruption of written records in the West. The scarcity of official reliefs and funerary memorials has also deterred researchers into this period, long known for its sparsity of written evidence. It is only in about the last four decades that archaeologists have specialised in this period; the technical and cultural heritage of the Classical age was only saved for the Middle Ages by information preserved through the Late Empire. It is therefore essential to look at this period with an unbiased eye when investigating how military equipment and weapons evolved and developed – a query we shall try to answer here, concentrating principally on the fourth and fifth centuries.

THE NEW EQUIPMENT – INVENTIONS, BORROWINGS OR REJECTS?

Only a few new items came onto the scene in the Late Empire, but some proved to be very popular, such as the barbed and socketted spearhead, the predecessor of the *ango* used by the Franks in the sixth century. It has sometimes been said that this was a version of the *gaesum,* a weapon so distinctive that it identified certain army units, such as the *Raeti Gaesati.* The latter, however, are mentioned from the second century by Polybius (II.34), and the weapon seems to have had its origins in North Eastern areas; barbed and socketted examples, admittedly somewhat smaller, have been found in some first century Polish tombs. Their use in the West and in the South spread westwards: a Scandinavian site from around 100 BC contained examples, and hundreds more, dating from the third and fourth centuries, have been recovered from peat bog deposits, notably at Nydam and Ejsbøl.

Widely used throughout the Germanic regions, this characteristic weapon spread from the fourth century onwards, and it is possible that Vegetius (*Mil.* I.20) is referring to it when he mentions the native weapon called a *bebra*. It is a weapon of this type that the Vandal *Stilicho* is seen holding proudly on the Monza diptych. Finally, specimens have been found in Bavaria, Burgundy (between

245 (left) Barbed and socketted point found in Burgundy (after M.Feugère, 1990).
(right) Barbed and socketted points 1. Lorch; 2,7 and 9. Nydam; 3, Ihringen; 4. Messkirch; 5. Vindonissa; 6. Moosberg; 8. Münchhof-Hornberg; 10. Sargans (after S. von Schnurbein, 1974)

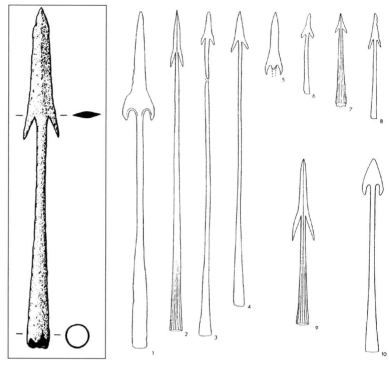

246 *Plumbata* from Vindonissa (photo Th.Hartmann, Vindonissa-Museum, Brugg).

247 *Plumbata* from Vrhnika (Slovenia) (after J.Horvat, 1990)

Saunières and Pontoux, Allériot, Gergy) and Britain (Carvoran, South Shields).

A variation on this weapon, the *plumbata,* also described by Vegetius, has a characteristic cigar-shaped lead bulb cast onto the iron spearhead shank at its base, designed to increase its penetration. A number of fourth- and fifth-century Western sites have yielded specimens (Wroxeter, Strasbourg, Carnuntum, Sisak, Nauportus), but a somewhat later sixth-century specimen has also been found, east of the Black Sea. By its size and the shape of its barbs this powerfully effective weapon is clearly linked to the spearheads described above, but it may be that the addition of a lead weight was to adapt it to a different fighting technique, perhaps Mediterranean in origin. The *plumbata* must also be considered in conjunction with the *pila* of the High Empire which had a weight at the head end of the shaft (the Chancellerie Relief). More common during the Late Empire than they had been earlier, these powerful arms remained no less so, it seems, during the fourth and fifth centuries. A late variant, which Vegetius calls *martiobarbulus,* was thrown by hand.

Although the dagger seems to have fallen into disuse from the end of the third century, the sword remained the main weapon used in close combat. The slender blades characteristic of the Nydam-Straubing type seem also to have been abandoned before the fourth century: wider blades were preferred under the Tetrarchy. Generally speaking, the archaeological evidence from the fourth and fifth centuries is very different from that of the second to third centuries; with the advent of the imperial *fabricae*, for instance, the circulation of

---

An exceptionally effective new weapon: Vegetius' 'Heavy dart'

It is good for soldiers to throw the lead-weighted darts called *martiobarbuli*. In previous times, two Illyrian legions, each of 3000 men, could throw them with such force and skill that they acquired the honorary title of *martiobarbuli* themselves . . . They always carried five of these darts inside their shields. Throwing them at the right time turned soldiers armed only with shield and spear into archers as well, able to wound men and horses beyond arrow range and before the hand-to-hand fighting began.

Vegetius, Mil. I.17.

---

weapons could not continue as it had previously, and only the Germans, for instance, continued their traditional practice of placing swords in the tombs of their dead.

THE LATE EMPIRE *FABRICAE*

Although there was a large number of small or medium sized workshops in operation from the beginning of the Principate, in many, if not all, permanent military camps, State workshops were set up towards the end of the third century right across the empire. The scale of operation of such veritable arsenals was probably greater than that of the older local workshops, as they had to cater for the needs of huge sectors of the empire; some of them specialised, which no doubt enabled them to supply large quantities of equipment when the need arose. Actually, it is on the authority of only one Latin writer, a contemporary of Diocletian, Lactantius, whose text was without doubt copied in the sixth century by the Byzantine chronicler Malalas, that these new facilities were introduced by this emperor. Certain arsenals may have been in operation in earlier times, growing in size since the second half of the third century; unlike the others, the *fabricae* at Aquincum, Carnuntum and Lauriacum do not seem to have been started from scratch but to have developed out of the existing workshops in legionary camps at different sites, and they were very likely 'official arsenals' from the second half of the third century onwards. The creation of new workshops, however, and their organisation into a subtle compromise between regional requirements, local traditions and the administration of dioceses (the administrative areas created under the Tetrarchy) probably goes back to the late third/early fourth century period.

Our best documentary source on the new system is an official text describing the economic and administrative organisation of the late empire, the *Notitia Dignitatum*. Modified throughout the fourth century and compiled early in the fifth and even later, Chapter XI (the East) and Chapter IX (the West) list some forty *fabricae* and, almost always, what they produced. If we add to this information gleaned from other sources (minor texts, inscriptions), we arrive at the following list:

Equipment	*fabrica*
Shields	Trier, Augustodunum, Aquincum, Carnuntum, Lauriacum, Cremona, Horreum Margi (in Illyria)
Shields, swords	Ambianum
Shields, saddle covers and various weapons	Sirmium
Shields and other arms	Antioch, Damas, Edessa, Nicomedia, Sardis (in Lydia), Hadrianopolis Marcianopolis, Verona
Armour – *loricariae*	Mantua
Armour – *clibanariae*	Augustodunum, Antioch, Caesarea in Cappadocia, Nicomedia
Swords	Luca and Reims
Lances	Irenopolis in Cilicia
Bows	Ticinum (Pavia)
Arrows	Concordia, Matisco
Artillery	Trier, Augustodunum (Autun)
Various weapons	Thessalonica, Naissus, Ratiaria, Salona, Argentomagus (Argenton-sur-Creuse, Suessiones, Ravenna (?), Constantinople (from the time of Justinian)

The locations of these *fabricae* were carefully chosen. It can be shown that several of them occupied sites which were already known for their local raw material resources and their trained labour (Argenton, Autun, in Gaul) and which could also provide backup in the form of security and good communications. Other *fabricae* doubtless took advantage of the workshops already established in a legion while continuing to rely on the troops for their production – the Danubian *fabricae* are a case in point. The main question, however, remains: what was the reason behind this reorganisation? Why was a semi-autonomous organisation (assuming every legion had been able to source its weapons either from its own workshops or from local civilian craftsmen) replaced by a vast empire-wide production network?

Various strands must be drawn together to give the answer. The historians were surprised at first that the State needed to set up workshops when an apparently efficient system had been working until the mid-third century. Bringing into operation nearly 300 new *fabricae* must reflect a need both to regain control over an organisation which had been badly disrupted by recent events, and to meet the new demands created by Diocletian's massive recruitment drives. The reason may be, as S. James suggests, that the whole of third century provincial society had been disorganised and that a change was essential; many craftsmen, in both civil and military workshops, lost their jobs in this reorganisation. Along the Rhine and the Danube, and also on the Euphrates in the East, there were many camps of auxiliaries which could no longer guarantee production and the maintenance of equipment, or even the safety of stores which could not be allowed

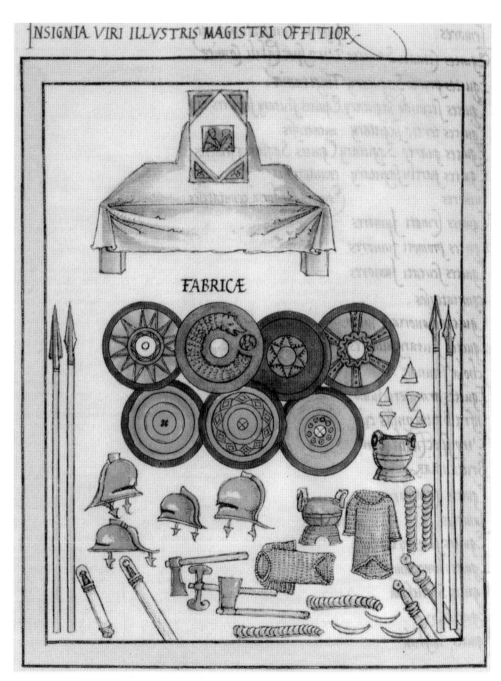

248 Illustration from the *Notitia dignitatum* : *insignia viri illustris magistri officiorum*. Control of the State workshops was included in the functions of the *magister officiorum*. The colour illustration shows, under a table with a picture of two emperors, a selection of officially approved products. Copy made in 1551 from an early fifth century MS (Munich, Bayer. Staatsbibliothek)

to fall into enemy hands. Furthermore, the collapse of the monetary system through successive devaluations made private investment impossible even in areas well away from the combat zones. In brief, the needs of the army had to be met, and only the State could step into the breach. It is possible that Diocletian's nationalisation of the major arsenals was only the formal recognition of a state of affairs brought about by the urgency of the situation in the provinces.

249 Iron helmet from Dunapentele (?) fourth century (photo Röm.-Germ. Zentralmuseum, Mainz)

Although in the fourth century the Imperial weaving mills and the mints were staffed by slave workers, the workers in the *fabricae* enjoyed a privileged status. Freemen, they were taken on as *milites*, and the years they spent working in the *fabricae* counted as years of military service; there is no doubt that many of these workers were simply transferred from legionary to Imperial workshops. In spite of their workers' protected status, however, the nationalised workshops could not maintain the high standards of earlier centuries when it came to the manufacture of often complex and sometimes fragile and finely decorated items – helmets are a particularly apt example. Whilst mid-third century specimens still show the highly skilled craftsmanship which went into their production, overcoming difficulties of assembly and making a major feature of ornamentation, early fourth-century helmets had to be quick to make and strictly functional. Previous helmets had a one-piece forged skullcap; the new skullcaps were two half-caps riveted to a central spine, and these half-caps were themselves sometimes only three triangular plates held together by riveted bands. It seems certain that these new helmets (examples of which are known from Intercisa, Worms, Augst) reflect new production methods and could be made more rapidly and in greater numbers than previous models, using less skilled labour. The sudden increase in troops under Diocletian had made such a development inevitable.

Still on the subject of helmets, several examples of high quality workmanship have nevertheless come to light. Whilst still retaining the same structure as the 'new' types described above – two-part skullcap, inserted nape protector – some, surprisingly, are profusely decorated; the helmet discovered in 1910 at Deurne (North Brabant) is a good example. Made from iron plates covered with gilded silver sheet, it has stamped decoration and silver rivets which give an impression of luxury and good taste, and it carries two dry-point inscriptions, one of which mentions a certain *M. Titius Lunamis*, followed by a weight: we may be seeing the name of the quality controller responsible for checking the amount of silver used in the helmet's construction. Did such a helmet come from a *fabrica*? The other graffito, STABLESIA.VI., is connected with a *vexillatio comitatensis stablesiana VI* mentioned in the *Notitia Dignitatum*. Other items, equality splendid, or even more so (Berkasovo, Budapest), present the problem of how military production was organised in this period; it is hard to be certain that highly skilled craftsmen had not continued to work for the army in the fourth century even though the bulk of the production would in future stem from the *fabricae*. In Gaul, the *fabricae* system probably did not survive the general collapse of the administrative and military systems which

250 Fourth century soldier equipped with chainmail coat (?) with long sleeves, crested helmet, round shield, lance, and *spatha* hanging from a baldrick. Linz memorial, Austria (after J.C.N.Coulston, 1990)

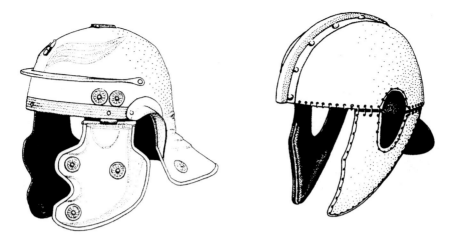

251 Comparison between first century helmet made by an independent craftsman (?) and a fourth-century specimen from a State *fabrica* (after S.James, 1988)

252 The Deurne helmet, fourth century (photo Rijksmuseum van Oudheiden, Leiden)

253 Chainmail coats with protective hoods: Nisus and Euryalus before the council, painting from manuscript, *Vergilius Vaticanus* (Cod.Lat 3225), fourth century (?) (after J.C.N. Coulston, 1990)

occurred after the end of the fourth century, but in the East (and also in Italy in a changed form), a number of different legal sources prove that the state arsenals not only continued to exist but also expanded until the sixth century at least.

Apart from helmets, it is not easy to see the effect of the new system on different weapons; besides, not all weapon production was carried out in *fabricae*. Bows and arrows, for instance, had thousands of years of traditional manufacture behind them and the only manufacturer of bows listed in the *Notitia Dignitatum* was at Ticinum in northern Italy, whilst arrows are shown as being made at Mâcon and Concordia. It is obvious that the needs of Dacian, Persian and Numidian bowmen were met by local suppliers, ensuring that these native archers had no need of a State *fabrica*.

Body armour seems to have been much less used in the fourth century, and Vegetius complains about the risks run by infantrymen unprotected against arrows and opponents' blows. However, he is reiterating a literary cliché popular at that time, as writers frequently looked back with nostalgia to the bravery, skill and advanced training of the ancient armies. Despite such writings and the increasing rarity of weapons in illustrations, it is hard to accept that there was a complete abandonment of such equipment as the fourth century progressed. Several archaeological discoveries show that the chain mail coat in particular was still in use in the fourth century; its reappearance at the start of the Middle Ages shows clearly enough that it had not entirely disappeared from the military tradition, even if its use in the Late Empire was certainly not as widespread as it had been in the early Principate.

The fourth-century shield, Vegetius tells us (II.18), resembled its predecessors in continuing to display different cohort motifs. Attempts have been made to identify military units from illustrations in the *Notitia*, but close study has shown that the copyist, although creatively inclined at the start, became tired as the work progressed, and his vignettes cannot be used to establish how Late Empire shields really looked (although an overall impression can be gained). As to its physical characteristics, the fourth-century shield, even for the infantry, was larger than previous versions, and oval or even circular in shape, to judge from contemporary memorials and paintings.

Turning to swords, some 20 burials in northern Gaul have yielded specimens of the *spatha* characteristic of this period. Partly stemming from the Lauriacum type, these are 70-90cm long, with blades wider (at 5-6cm) than their forerunners. The design is thus approaching that of the Merovingian sword which was to follow it, which sometimes raises problems of identification with finds from undated sites, such as isolated single specimens or river finds. Damascening is present on some swords from the late fourth century onwards, feature which enhanced the reputation of High Middle Ages weapons. The handgrips, well preserved on Scandinavian bog site examples, could be of wood, bone or ivory and always consist of three parts threaded onto the tang: an almost cylindrical centre section (often grooved transversely) flanked by the guard and the pommel, both usually just a simple oval plate.

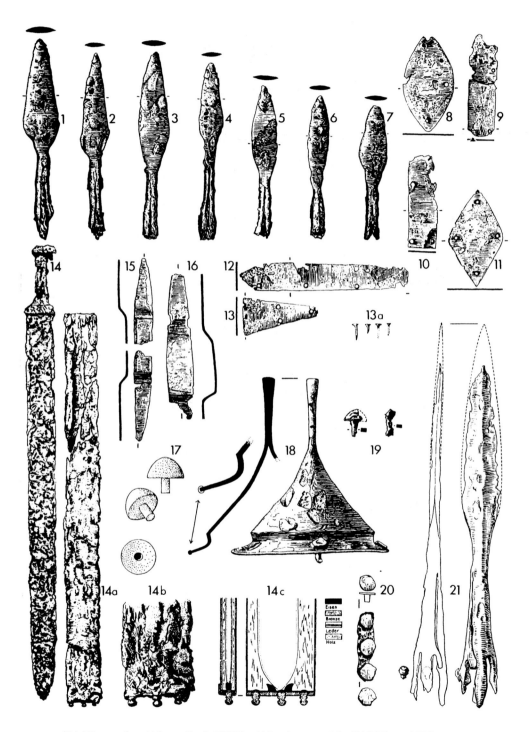

254 Weapons from Liebenau Tomb 1/1957, mid-fourth century (after H.W.Böhme, 1974)

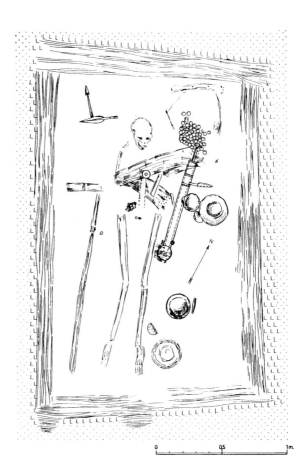

255 A fourth-century grave with weapons: *spatha* with its baldrick, two lances, shield: Tomb 2 from Simris (Skane, Denmark) (after B.Stjernquist, 1954)

A new type of sword shape appears alongside the Germanic rounded type, and is clearly shown on sculptures (the Tetrachic Relief at Venice; gravestone of Lepontius at Strasbourg). The rectangular end of the scabbard is simply encased in a tube protected by three bronze studs at its end (Gundremmingen type). A tomb at Liebenau in Germany enables us to see how far this new system simplifies scabbard manufacture: it may have been an innovation by the *fabricae*. Equally, one may note that the suspension hooks of the scabbards, whilst inspired from the older arrangement, have a simplified design.

Lance points, now more frequently larger in size, are more difficult to categorise than previous styles, with the exception of a new type, the 'Saufeder', a model with a winged point which was to develop spectacularly at the start of the Middle Ages. First appearing in Gaul from the second century as a hunting weapon, it had been adopted by the military by the end of the fourth. An example from Augst, interpreted as early by its stratigraphical position, shows that the two wings were at first riveted to the socketed head, then forged integrally with it in later versions.

Artillery developed slowly after the innovations at the time of the Dacian Wars, and Heron's *cheiroballista* was still being manufactured in the fourth century, along with a small war machine which Vegetius names as *manuballista*. Another type, the *arcuballista*, may have been a sort of arbalest or crossbow. There seems to have been a tendency towards greater ease of handling, if we are to attach importance to three very small *kambestria* recovered from the late period fortress at Gornea in Romania, which are respectively 13.3, 13.7 and 14.4cm high (end of fourth century). On the neighbouring site of Orsova a larger *kambestrion* (36cm high) was found in conjunction with two rarely preserved components, the spacers needed to keep the cord bundles apart. These discoveries show that the *balistaria* at Autun, where these machines probably originated, had continued to build the same weapons as it had manufactured under the Principate. We are here seeing one of the rare occasions – of limited significance admittedly, because of the specialised nature of these weapons, which could have been built only by very highly skilled artisans – where a *fabrica* did not attempt to alter a weapon's design in order to increase output.

MILITARY EQUIPMENT AS A SOCIAL IDENTIFIER

Although military equipment in the Late Empire generally speaking suffered a drop in quality due to the manufacturing standards in nationalised arsenals, its significance socially increased; let us take an example from the post-Constantinian period, the Vandal *Stilicho* as he is shown on the Monza diptych which dates from around AD 395. Formally dressed, he wears neither helmet nor armour, just a simple tunic with a splendidly decorated *paludamentum* pinned to the shoulder; at his left side as in earlier centuries is a long sword hanging from a belt, not from a baldrick as it would have done in previous times. He leans on a lance held in his right hand, its head with its two winglets typically Germanic, and the shield lying on the ground before him has the conical *umbo* equally Germanic in origin.

In this relief *Stilicho* is clearly stating his Gothic lineage. The prestige attaching to his station – he was probably *comes domesticorum*, chief of the emperor's bodyguard, as well as *magister militum*, army chief of a whole province – is shown only through the superior nature of his clothing and no doubt of his weapons also, as his sword scabbard and shield are richly decorated, the latter bearing an imperial medallion.

Similarly, Theodosius' bodyguards (*protectores*) shown on the Monza *missorium* seem to be armed only with a lance and a shield with a circular *umbo*. In contrast to these depictions, where high status does not seem to require the wearing of full equipment, is a series of illustrations of lower ranking personnel who have retained their traditional attributes right through the fourth century. The *signifer* (?) Lepontius from Strasbourg has the same style of crested helmet as that found on a memorial from Linz, and the soldiers on the Museo Chiaramonti relief in the Vatican are wearing carefully carved scale armour and chain mail coats. These apparently contradictory images only serve to emphasise the widening gap between the military-administrative cadre and the common people, and typical of this distinctive division is the development of the *cingulum*, which became the insignia and symbol of a public functionary.

256 The Theodosius *missorium* found in 1847 near Merida and now in the Archaeological Museum, Madrid. Surrounded by four bodyguards armed with lance and oval shield, the Emperor is enthroned between his co-regents Arcadius and Valentinian II in front of a temple or a decorated screen; the inscription dates this work of art to AD 388 (photo DAI, Madrid)

257 (above) Buckle and belt fittings from Wessling, fifth century (photo Prähist. Staatsammlung, Munich)
(below) Buckle and belt fittings from Wessling, towards AD 400 (photo Prähist. Staatsammlung, Munich)

THE BELT

At the beginning of the Principate, as we have seen, the *cingulum* was both a practical item of equipment and the chosen backing for decoration; in the third century the *balteus* or baldrick, which was to the sword what the swordbelt had been to the *gladius* and the dagger, took on the same role. Belt buckles were very simple, and circular, as can be seen from monuments and funerary deposits. In the fourth century the swordbelt was still not used with the sword, and reverted to being a backing for decorations as well as rapidly acquiring other attributes. The buckle assembly – buckle, buckle plate and counterplate – was in three to five parts, frequently with additional mounts and assorted buttons; the belt strap itself, narrowed down, was fitted with a metal strap end which was larger and more decorative than the third century type.

258 Buckle and appliques from a military belt found at Altenstadt, beginning of fifth century (photo Prähist. Staatsammlung, Munich)

In short, the swordbelt became a complex object, the study of which, notably in northern Gaul, has enabled various groups to be defined on stylistic and cultural grounds attributed to *foederati* or *Læti*, German warriors settled in the Rhineland and northern Gaul, according to the *Notitia Dignitatum*.

From the start of the fourth century, the number of military recruits declined, and the authorities had to call on natives to make up the shortfall in Roman recruits; the Germans played an essential part in this development, becoming increasingly involved, at least in the west, as recruited troops and particularly as officers. It is thought that by the second half of the fourth century the Roman army was largely 'Germanic', and that this shift in ethnic emphasis was one of the major factors in the *partitio* of the Empire on the death of the Emperor Julian II in AD 363.

Considered from an archaeological standpoint, however, there is a tendency for all decorated or engraved ('Kerbschnittgarnituren') belt fittings - very abundant in the Rhineland and northern Gaul, an area where Late Roman archaeological studies are highly developed – to be interpreted as Germanic. It is nevertheless rather dangerous to confuse objects found in graves and labelled 'Germanic' with the intrinsic nature of the objects themselves, which may have been in wider use at this time than purely funerary finds would lead us to believe; although naturally in smaller numbers, similar objects are also found in other very different areas.

Taking into account the apparently exceptional nature of finds of Germanic style items well away from their places of origin, such objects are often interpreted as evidence of a particular event. Thus the discovery of a complete belt with an unusual buckle (Ehrenburg-Ostrach type) at Mazan, Vaucluse, was linked by H. W. Böhme to confrontations between supporters of Constantine III and Jovinus in the Valence / Arles region between AD 408-13. However, such hypotheses are best left in abeyance until relevant items found outside northern Gaul and the Rhineland have been studied and catalogued.

In southern Gaul and Spain a fair number of discoveries have been made, some of items similar to northern types, some original; a rural location in the Languedoc even turned up a (defective) example of a dolphin buckle ('Delphinschnalle') of a type well known in Britain at the end of the fourth century. This example, of which several variants have been found in the same area, had been rejected in manufacture because of a fissure in the mould. Buckles of this type – of German inspiration? – were thus being made and used widely in this region during the fourth and fifth centuries AD.

The late belts developed from the much simpler models of the third century, and a discovery from Cologne, unfortunately not accurately datable, is perhaps the missing link between the old and new types.

259 Germanic style belt pendants from Southern Gaul: 1, Versols-et-Lapeyre, Notre-Dame du Cayla (Aveyron); 2, Eyguières (Bouches-du-Rhône)

260 (left) Gilded silver belt decorations found at Cologne, third century; photo Röm.-Germ. Museum, Cologne. (below) Gold buckle from the Ténès hoard, Algeria: end of fourth century? (after J.Heurgon, 1958)

261 Gilded silver buckle from the Ortiz collection, found in Asia Minor; towards AD 400

Whilst retaining the original form of a central piece with two free end pieces, this belt has two openwork mounts and an openwork pendant which on stylistic grounds appear to date to the end of the third century. Helical decorative mounts appeared during the first half of the fourth century, preceding the wider belts (10-12cm) associated with cut-out decorative plates ('Kerbschnitt') and buckles with zoomorphic motives, which were the most commonly used models at the end of the fourth and during the first half of the fifth centuries.

Very beautiful buckles in precious metals have been found on the Empire's frontiers, the most spectacular being those from a discovery made in 1936 at Tenes in Algeria. In this hoard of jewellery and clothing accessories, buried during the fifth century, were two exceptional carved buckle plates together with five belt components and three gold *fibulae*, as well as other valuable jewels. The plates are delicately cut in the *opus interrasile* style (a sort of metal lacework), and one of the buckles has two facing swans' heads. Another decorated buckle plate was in the hoard found at Thetford (eastern England) in 1979, thought to have been buried at the end of the fourth or the start of the fifth centuries. The buckle is formed by two facing horses' heads, and a walking fawn in a pearl border is engraved as a small separate picture.

Such material has recently been enriched by the discovery in Asia Minor, along with some silver vessels, of an outstanding gilded silver buckle adorned with three narrative panels. The centre panel shows a rarely featured mythological depiction of Daphne turning into a laurel bush to escape the unwelcome attentions of Apollo. Taken in conjunction by its owner, M. G. Ortiz, with the Thetford hoard, this buckle can be dated to around AD 400.

Can these prestigious luxury buckles be interpreted as the symbols of authority of high functionaries close to the Court, perhaps on a mission to the frontiers of the Empire? This is possible, but the implications of such a hypothesis show how much work remains to be done on the identification of regional groups and the workshops in which they were produced.

To sum up, the evolution of arms and military equipment in the Late Empire can be seen as falling into roughly two parts:

1 The State takeover of the manufacture, and thus the distribution, of weapons from the late third century onwards, with a resulting decline in quality generally, although high-quality items continued to be produced, the reasons for this remaining unclear at present;
2 Military recruitment of Romans became more difficult, resulting in a growing number of native troops using 'ethnic' equipment and weapons.

Although it is difficult to identify a particular break-point in the technical and cultural progress towards the early Middle Ages, there is one which should be noted as we close this section, which is that Rome's abandonment of a Greco-Italian pre-eminence in arms and tactics shows that she is no longer the centre of the world. Instead of Rome sharing her empire only with the Byzantines, the world has now become wide open, and other cultures, until now on the sidelines, start to move into the limelight.

11 THE ARMY
AND ROMAN SOCIETY

THE HONOUR OF ROME

The primary purpose of the army was to defend Roman interests even
when such defence became attack; first and foremost, the army was
the mailed fist of the State's policies. At a less conscious level perhaps,
the army was also the defender of Rome's honour, and severe defeats
could not go unavenged, nor were insults forgotten. The Gaulish capture of Rome in 337 BC, the defeat at Cannae in 215 BC, and above all
the massacre of the three legions in the Teutoburgerwald by Arminius'
German forces at the end of Augustus' reign in AD 9 : so much shame
to be washed away with blood. Rome, however, took careful note of
such disastrous setbacks, and remembrance of them led to a less aggres-

262 Germanicus on the battlefield where Varus' legions perished; mid-nineteenth century German engraving

263 The eagle, symbol of the power of Rome, seen here on the Theilenhofen helmet (photo Röm.-Germ. Zentralmuseum, Mainz)

sive policy from Augustus' time, followed by a static and finally a defensive policy from the third century onwards.

Whatever the result, it was the possession of a permanent army which enabled Rome to defeat new enemies as they arose in response to Rome's expansionist policies. The Jewish turncoat historian Josephus made the point at the end of the first century when, writing from the Roman viewpoint, he said that the Romans alone of all the world's peoples maintained such an army, which trained continually, even in times of peace.

Historical research has shown us that alongside its primary function, the Roman army also played a by no means insignificant economic, social and cultural role as well. It is not our intention here to justify an army which could impose a foreign rule by force of arms on whole races; it is simply that to appreciate all the ins and outs, we must look at all the aspects and implications of a permanent military presence in a society.

THE MILITARY CAREER

Throughout its history, the Roman army always stressed the career opportunities and financial benefits it offered to its soldiers; in economic terms a soldier was always better off than his civilian contemporaries. His guaranteed wage offered greater security than most civilian occupations could provide, especially at the lower social levels, and, particularly in Republican times, he could share in the spoils taken from a defeated enemy. One must obviously take into account an individual's situation when he joined the army; recruits differed in their resources and possessions, and there were social and economic differences in the military just as there were in civilian life. Had the soldier whose silver saucepan finished up in the Ruffieu hoard earned enough in the army to acquire such a luxury item? It is hard to say, but this example seems to indicate a large economic disparity between the troops, and it is certain that at the start of the Principate such disparities showed in a soldier's personal possessions. An auxiliary or a legionary who could afford to do so would certainly have spent more on a high quality *gladius* or a dagger with a carefully decorated scabbard. In this area, the army of the first or second century reinforces, or even exacerbates, social differences, more than it was to reduce them to a common level, as it seems to have done in the fourth century.

264 Hand to hand fighting, portrayed on Trajan's Column: although outnumbered, the legionaries are putting up a heroic resistance to protect the baggage train (photo D.A.I., Rome)

Soldiers who survived 25 years of campaigning, however, seem to have received relatively equitable rewards; a veteran's gratuity, the *missio*, as far as we know, seems to have been based on his rank, and although this might be related to his social position, a soldier's financial situation on retirement was largely based on how his career had progressed. Up to the end of the first century AD, retiring veterans could receive a monetary payment or land; from Hadrian onwards, the gratuity was monetary, but it increased noticeably over the years. The sum paid to every veteran by the *aerarium militare* in Rome rose to 3000 *denarii* under Augustus, to 5000 under Caligula, and to 8250 at the start of the third century (AD 212). At the same time, the regular compulsory contributions which he had made to the treasury kept in the regimental temple were returned to him, so a retired soldier could find himself with a very useful capital sum. It was moreover an experienced man who rejoined civilian society, one who was able to choose his role in rural or urban society.

However, the real reward for a military career was not monetary. The army gave every recruit the chance of social and cultural advancement and the opportunity of acquiring a professional skill which would assist him on his return to civilian life, such as metalworking or carpentry, depending on where his talents lay. Furthermore, as he became proficient in military skills he could expect advancement in rank, even to relatively senior level.

265 Symbols of *felicitas* on a
gladius scabbard from
Vrhnika-Nauportus, Slovenia
(photo Röm.-Germ.
Zentralmuseum, Mainz)

THE CULTURAL SIDE OF ARMY LIFE

It is easy to forget that the Roman army, in addition to its purely military functions, had cultural and administrative aspects as well. Vegetius
insisted that at least a certain proportion of soldiers should be able to
read, write and count. A considerable number of archaeological finds
from military sites bear this out, such as writing implements – the sty-
lus – and seal boxes, showing that there must have been considerable
correspondence and communication, not only within the army but
also with the 'outside world'. Where the conditions have been
favourable, such as humid peat or dry desert sands, readable writing
tablets have been recovered which shed direct light on everyday life in
a Roman camp. Typical sites are Vindolanda on Hadrian's wall, Bu
Njem, Dura-Europos, and of course, Egypt.

Not only were items of military equipment such as shields and helmets
marked with their owners' names, but a large part of military life in general
used written documents – duty rotas for guards, postings, goods received
and despatched, etc, of which examples have been found. Certain responsible posts, such as standard-bearer, who acted also as the legion's treasurer,
required someone who could handle figures. Knowing how to read, write
and calculate were among the cultural skills which many soldiers were able
to acquire during their service, skills which would be useful when they
retired and which they could pass on to others.

Finally, decorated objects and painted or carved pictures were probably
among the soldier's possessions when he retired. As we have seen, military
equipment was used for propaganda, whether to illustrate mythological
scenes and spread knowledge of Greco-Roman culture in general or
politico-religious, generally more specific and often personalised.

266 Letter on a wooden
tablet from Vindolanda,
probably addressed to one
Cerialis, mentioning the
ability of Vocontius –
Voconce – to load a hundred
chariots in a day (photo
Univ. of Newcastle-upon-
Tyne, with the kind
permission of E. Birley)

267 *Cingulum* with stamped
decoration from Risstissen
(photo Württembergisches
Landesmuseum, Stuttgart)

MILITARY EQUIPMENT
AND ROMAN PROPAGANDA

The Roman way life, and particularly its political and religious aspects, was broadcast to the provinces through both carved images and the coinage. It should be emphasised that these two media had full support and approval at the highest governmental levels, and it is probable that the master illustration, the *imago*, for coin portraits and statues had to be expressly approved by the emperor himself.

It is also significant that the scenes and motifs appearing on weapons and military equipment directly reflect government propaganda. Some is military-focussed, not surprisingly showing an eagle or the goddess Victoria, or suitable references to them, such as a palm frond or a laurel wreath. The barbarian prisoners and trophies of captured weapons shown on triumphal monuments frequently relate to specific events, though these are not often identified, the underlying purpose of the illustrations being to reinforce Roman power worldwide.

From the start of the Principate, and particularly during the reigns of Augustus and Tiberius, there is a marked tendency towards an Imperial 'cult of personality'; as E. Künzl rightly points out, Augustus was the first to use politico-religious symbols whose very presence was sufficient to evoke his authority. Thus the capricorn (or more precisely, the sea–goat) appears not only on coins struck in his name but also as the symbol adopted by several legions, such as I Adiutrix, II Augusta, III Augusta and XIII Gemina. After Augustus, the capricorn features widely on military equipment and also on other items such as *fibulae*, seal boxes, etc, though it is not always possible to say whether this is a deliberate allusion to the ruler or merely a motif in common general use.

In fact, after the change from BC to AD, there is an increased penetration of Roman propaganda themes into all areas of production, whether of luxury goods such as silverware or everyday objects. Weapons and items of military equipment, objects intended to enforce the Roman will on barbarians, are obviously part of this development, both within the army as symbols for the troops and among the civilian population through official channels. We therefore need to look closely, as we have done on occasion in previous pages, at what the demobilised soldier could really take with him when he retired.

268 Portrait of Drusus on a
glass *phalera* from
Vindonissa (photo
Th.Hartmann, Vindonissa-
Museum, Brugg)

269 Propaganda motifs on *gladius* scabbards from Vindonissa (a-c), Baden (d) and Ptuj (e): Victory presenting wreath to Roma: two cherubs placing shield with portrait on back of eagle, captive between two trophies (photo Röm.-Germ. Zentralmuseum, Mainz)

270 Tip of *gladius* scabbard from Vindonissa, Tiberian period, showing a cavalryman striking down a barbarian, and a trophy (photo Röm.-Germ. Zentralmuseum, Mainz)

THE OWNERSHIP OF ROMAN ARMS AND MILITARY EQUIPMENT

Archaeologists and historians have long debated whether the Roman State, which issued its legionaries with increasingly standardised equipment, continued to own it after a soldier was demobilised. The question is particularly relevant for weapons, as the State must have wished to control the amount of arms held by the general public. The current theory is that during the Principate, soldiers had to carry the costs of their weapons in the same way that they had to pay for their food, and the State would only intervene if a soldier did not have sufficient personal funds to buy his essential equipment. The natural corollary was that it was forbidden, on pain of severe punishment, to sell official weapons, though soldiers with sufficient funds to buy their own could sell them also. The *custodes armorum* in each camp would be responsible for the safekeeping of 'army' weapons as well as those which were privately owned.

This theory is based, however, on texts whose interpretation is debatable, and it must be noted that in such a situation there would be no control at all over privately owned weapons. Archaeological evidence can hardly distinguish between these and 'army' weapons, and it is only in the case of grave goods that one can be sure that it was a personal weapon which was buried. A passage from Tacitus' *Histories*, for example (III.80), illustrates the ambiguity of the generally cited texts. The text in question concerns an insurrection at Rome in AD 69, shortly before the death of the emperor Vitellius: 'the people took up arms. Few had army shields, and most of them took up any weapons that were to hand and echoed the war cries'. It can be clearly seen from this passage that the 'arms' are not necessarily official regular army weapons; only the reference to shields suggests the presence of military equipment in a civil situation, but even so, were these really official or privately owned? Is one entitled to deduce from the absence of any mention of offensive weapons – swords or lances, for example – that the army kept such arms under tight control?

Whenever there are new archaeological finds this question arises, but a distinction must be made between several different types of discovery. It has been noticed that under the Principate, tombs containing Roman arms are to be found mainly among the Treveri and Nervii, areas which in the fourth and fifth centuries were to receive a large influx of Germans. It is precisely in the German areas that weapon burial takes on a ritual character, so one could ascribe the presence of weapons in tombs in Northern Gaul to an early German population or to a strong Germanic influence.

The oldest example of Roman military equipment in a burial in this area is actually very typical. Tomb 3 from Trier-Olewig yielded, along with a large (112.5cm long) Celtic sword and a native lance point, a cast bronze Mannheim type helmet which clearly indicates the status of its owner: a Gaul who served with the Caesarian army. Dating from the middle of the first century BC, it is thus possible under certain circumstances that a Roman soldier of Treveran origin

271 Inscriptions on a bronze helmet from Mainz giving the owner's name, L.Lucretius Celeris of the First Legion. Germ.Nat.Museum, Nurnberg (photo Röm.-Germ. Zentralmuseum, Mainz)

272 Cremation burial including a face-helmet; from Hellange (Musée du Grand-Duché du Luxembourg)

could have been cremated with all his military equipment, including its Roman elements. One can combine this occurrence with the weapons found in tombs in military zones, for example a *gladius* scabbard slide from the cemetery at Tietz, near Strasbourg.

Examples from outside this region are very rare, and always seem to concern unusual cases. The helmet, armour and sword from Chassenard (department of Allier) buried around AD 40 belonged to someone highly privileged, who combined an aristocratic native background with a good career in the Roman administration (coin dies); in the East Central region, the Testament of Lingon stipulated that the deceased should be buried with his sword and lances, but here again we are seeing a favoured individual whose last wishes show, behind a romanised facade, a desire for a sumptuous display very much akin to native practices. The same mixture of tradition and romanisation occurs at Charnay-lès-Chalon (Saône-et-Loire), where the *gladius* included in the cremation had been bent to follow a funerary practice already several centuries old.

Less certain in its interpretation, as it was an ancient find with no useful documentation, is the iron dagger from the tomb at Curel, near Die, which may also have belonged to a Gaul recruited into the Roman army. Apart from these isolated cases, no Roman arms have been found in tombs in the *Narbonensis*; such arms are not unknown, however, from dwelling sites in this region, so perhaps the practice was either socially unacceptable or forbidden by the authorities.

A discovery in the cremation cemetery at L'Hospitalet-du-Larzac, south of Millau, has enlightened us on the situation concerning arms and the civilian sector; two *gladii* found in first-century tombs had been carefully reworked into saws, then placed in the tomb as tools! It was probably therefore not impossible to obtain a Roman sword in Southern Gaul during the first century AD, but the practice of depositing arms in tombs, very popular in the valley of the Lower Rhône in the decades following the conquest of Gaul, had been abandoned in the South from the middle of the first century BC.

In the *Gallia comata* it is more difficult to interpret finds of military arms and equipment from a civilian setting. An analysis carried out some years ago in what is now the department of the Loire showed that only a small proportion of military finds could be classed as weapons, the rest being basically harness and related items. Finds seem to be more common in Burgundy; several weapons – a short *gladius*, two lance or javelin points, a *pilum* point and five arrowheads – were found on the villa site of Tuillières at Selongey (Côte-d'Or) in contexts datable to between the end of the second century and the middle of the third. Some of these items could have been used in hunting, but the *pilum* and *gladius* were strictly for military use, as was the fragment of chain mail also found on this site. Are we to see in this relatively abundant find an example of the special relationship which Rome had maintained with the Aedui since Caesar's time, and which is borne out by continuing military recruitment in this region throughout the first century?

A number of shipwrecks in the Western Mediterranean which have yielded arms and military equipment paint a somewhat different pic-

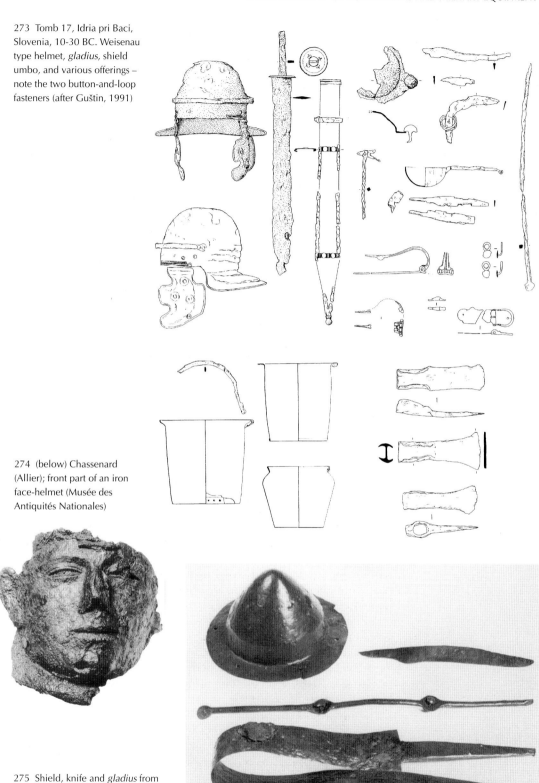

273 Tomb 17, Idria pri Baci, Slovenia, 10-30 BC. Weisenau type helmet, *gladius*, shield umbo, and various offerings – note the two button-and-loop fasteners (after Guštin, 1991)

274 (below) Chassenard (Allier); front part of an iron face-helmet (Musée des Antiquités Nationales)

275 Shield, knife and *gladius* from Tomb 1 at Verdun, Slovenia (after D.Breščak, 1989)

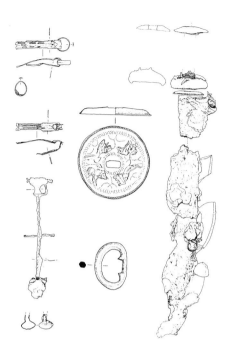

276 Augustan-period *gladius*, scabbard parts and suspension components from the shipwreck at Comacchio (after F.Berti *et al.*, 1990)

ture. Although several isolated examples from the third to the sixth century BC are known (see table), there was a marked increase in the mid-second century BC followed by a sharp decline before the end of the first century AD.

Analysing the finds, helmets are the most numerous (especially in the first to second centuries BC), but *gladii* are equally well represented in the first century AD; the example from the Porto-Novo wreck was found together with its *cingulum*. This was a highly remarkable find – the sword was still in its scabbard, which had retained all its mounts and its accompanying silver *cingulum*, a very valuable outfit. As we have seen, it is dangerous to assume that a valuable weapon must have been the property of an officer; in this particular case, however, the discovery of a gold *aureus* of Tiberius could suggest the presence of an important person on board, one who would have had an armed escort.

It seems to me more plausible to consider most of the weapons found in wrecked vessels as indicative of the presence on board of official military personnel, guards and messengers for instance, rather than as providers of personal protection – somewhat illusory it must be admitted – for the passengers against pirates, as has been thought. If the weapons found on shipwrecks were to meet this need, would the owner of the *gladius* on the Porto-Novo boat have risked wearing a belt which would itself have been an attractive prize? One should rather envisage, on some ships, a group of soldiers whose function was to take care of important passengers and their belongings, rather than a wide distribution of weapons among civilians; such escort parties, responsible for the safety of official emissaries, took part as a matter of course in Roman army missions.

Period	Wreck	Weapon	Dating	Bibliography
Sixth to third century BC	Bon-Porté	lance point	550–500BC	Joncheray 1976
	Marseillan	bronze helmet	550–400BC	Feugère, Freises 1994–5
	El Sec	lead sling shot	375–350BC	Pallares 1972
	Terrasini	2 iron swords	300–200BC	Purpura 1974
Second to first century BC	Chrétienne C	1(+?) swordpoint?	c.150BC	Joncheray 1975, 98
	Giannutri	1 sword	c.140BC	Lamboglia 1964
	Spargi	1 fgt bronze helmet	c.100BC	Lamboglia 1971
	Albenga	7 fgts bronze helmets	c.90–70BC	Gianfrotta 1981 *cit.*, 236
	Giens	2 bronze helmets	c.70BC	Gianfrotta 1981 *cit.*, 236
	Capo Testa	bronze helmet	c.100–50BC	Gianfrotta 1981 *cit.*, 237
	Dramont A	1 fgt bronze helmet	c.50BC	Fiori 1973
	L'Estérel	1 bronze helmet	first century BC	Carrazé 1972
	Rade d'Hyères	1 bronze helmet	first century BC	Feugère 1996
	Comacchio	1 *gladius*	c.10–1BC	Berti 1990
First to second century AD	Porto–Novo	1 *gladius*	c.AD 30	Bernard *et al.* 1998
	Gruissan	1 bronze helmet	c.AD 1–50	*Gallia* 31, 1973, 477
	Chrétienne H	1 *gladius*	c.AD 50	Unpublished
	Ses Salines	1 sword + 1 iron helmet	c.AD 50–100	Parker 1974
	Moro Boti	2 iron helmets	c.AD 50–100	Veny 1979
	Saint Jordi	1 iron helmet	High Empire?	Mascaró 1968

Arms found on ancient shipwrecks in the western Mediterranean

MILITARY EQUIPMENT AND ROMAN HISTORY: THE ROMAN TRUMP CARDS

Since ancient times the uniquely Roman knack of borrowing equipment and habits from others whenever it seemed like a good idea to do so has been widely recognised. Polybius wrote in the second century BC (VI.25) 'If one race has the ability to change its habits and imitate good examples, it is certainly the Romans'. In practice, military archaeology confirms much of this idea of acquisition; the *pilum* has a long Italian pedigree, but the *gladius* grew out of the *gladius hispaniensis*, the chain mail coat was borrowed from the Celts, scale armour from the East and most harness equipment probably had a Gaulish origin. However, one should also recognise that it was the Romans themselves who made the Augustan period *gladius* the supremely successful weapon it became when used by Roman troops, and that segmental armour was a great Roman innovation, unique to the Roman army.

Despite this, a large part of Roman military successes rests less on the arms or equipment of the respective opposed armies (in this area, the barbarians had numerous 'trump cards' which the Romans appropriated after their victories) but rather on Rome's experience in military tactics. Caesar was aware of this, and emphasises on several occasions – not without a certain smugness – the astonishment of the Gauls when they saw engineering skills, earthworks and war machines employed against their towns. Such technical superiority was often to force a surrender, but it could also bounce back against the Romans, as it did for example when the Nervii assaulted a Roman camp and used the same techniques which they had more or less perfectly assimilated (*B Gall.* V.42). Similarly, in the Jewish War, the Jews used captured artillery against the Romans, causing them heavy losses when they learned how to use it. Generally speaking, though, the barbarians had neither the technical skill nor the organisational ability to use Roman methods of warfare.

In the last resort, it comes down to the rigorous administrative system which was the heart of the Roman army. Recruitment, transportation, equipment and meeting the needs of gigantic numbers of troops – up to half a million by some estimates – are only feasible under a highly technical system of production, communication and the division of duties. This system emerged under the Republic from ideological bases founded on the expansionist policies about which we already know. However, as it became more complex, so the whole structure became more vulnerable, and every external shock to it shook the whole edifice. According to the latest generally accepted hypothesis, it was to be the monetary devaluations of the third century which, in ruining the normal payment systems for manufacturers and suppliers, led the State to install the system of *fabricae* manned by functionaries as rapidly as possible.

A parallel can thus be drawn between the growing number of fighting troops and the simplification of arms and equipment, a situation which did not, however, prevent certain workshops from producing high-quality weapons. It is also certain, nevertheless, that in the fourth century there was a growing gap between the mass-produced equipment for the rank and file and the artistic creations supplied – as they

277 Right from his recruitment, the Roman soldier shows a legionary's arrogance. Ermine Street Guard, Loupian, 1992

278 This relief from Trajan's Column, showing legionaries erecting stonework, is a good illustration of the Roman army's efficiency in technical matters, with each man playing his part in a collective enterprise (photo D. A. I., Rome)

have been in every age – to senior officers. Once its situation had crumbled to a certain point, the Roman army could no longer hold back the countless enemies on its frontiers, enemies more highly motivated and as well equipped – if not better equipped – than itself.

Military arms and equipment were throughout the long history of Rome never more than the accessories of a state of mind and policies which sought the most effective ways of dominating stubborn races. Skill with a sword, as cynical Roman authors put it, was in itself characteristic of this state of mind – one good push with the point was more certain to wound than the swinging blows of a barbarian. If warfare gained in efficiency what it lost in glory, the Roman army knew how to instil a system of internal values which would encourage the troops, and as long as Rome was able to devote the necessary resources to her army, she could preserve an empire in the same mould round her.

SIGNIFICANT EVENTS AND DATES

Entries in CAPITALS indicate Imperial reigns

BC		27BC to AD 14	AUGUSTUS
753	Traditional date for the founding of Rome	15	Drusus' campaign on the Upper Danube
509	Fall of the monarchy	9	Death of Drusus
387	Rome sacked by the Gauls	8-6	Tiberius' campaign in Germany
343-1	First Samnite War	**AD**	
326-04	Second Samnite War	4-6	Further campaign by Tiberius in Germany
298-0	Third Samnite War		
293	Samnite defeat at Aquilonia	6-9	Tiberius' campaign in Illyria
264-41	First Punic War	14-37	TIBERIUS
225	Gaulish defeat at Telamona	34-6	War against the Parthians
218-01	Second Punic War	37-41	CALIGULA
202	Punic defeat at Zama	41-54	CLAUDIUS
183	Death of Hannibal	41-2	Mauretanian War
181-79	First War against the Celtiberians	43	Conquest of Britain
153-1	Second War against the Celtiberians	54-68	NERO
		66-70	Judean War
		68-192	Flavian and Antonine dynasties
149-6	Third Punic War	69	GALBA, OTHO, VITELLIUS
146	Carthage captured and destroyed by Scipio Aemilius	69-79	VESPASIAN
		73-4	Roman campaign in Germany
143-33	Third War against the Celtiberians	79	Eruption of Vesuvius, burying Pompeii and Herculaneum
133	Fall of Numance	79-81	TITUS
133-01	War against the Cimbrii and the Teutons	81-96	DOMITIAN
		96-98	NERVA
105	Victory of the Cimbrii and Teutons at Orange	97-98	War in Germany against the Suebii
107-0	Consulates of Marius	98-117	TRAJAN
91-88	Social Wars	101-2	First Dacian War
59-1	Caesar's conquest of Gaul	105-6	Second Dacian War
52	Siege of Alésia	112-13	Trajan's Column erected
49-6	Civil War	114-17	Parthian War
44	Death of Caesar	117-38	HADRIAN
31	Naval victory of Agrippa over Antony at Actium	132-5	Judean War after revolt of Bar-Kochba
27	Octavian becomes Augustus	138-61	ANTONINUS PIUS
27BC to AD 68	Julio-Claudian emperors	161-80	MARCUS AURELIUS

161-9	LUCIUS VERUS co-emperor	293-305	CONSTANTIUS Caesar
166-75	War against the Marcomani, Quadrati and Sarmatians	305-6	Second Tetrarchy
		305-6	CONSTANTIUS Augustus
175-80	COMMODUS co-emperor	305-6	SEVERUS Caesar
176	Erection of the Aurelian Column	306-7	SEVERUS Augustus
		306-8	CONSTANTINUS Caesar
178-80	Second war against the Germani	306-12	MAXENTIUS, usurper
		308-37	CONSTANTINUS Augustus
180	Death of Marcus Aurelius and end of the war	324-37 ruler	CONSTANTINUS I, sole
180-92	COMMODUS	337-40	CONSTANTINUS II
193-211	SEPTIMIUS SEVERUS	340-50	CONSTANS
193-235	Severan dynasty	353-61	CONSTANTIUS II, sole ruler
211-17	CARACALLA	355-61	JULIAN Caesar
217-18	MACRINUS	361-3	JULIAN
218-22	ELAGABALUS	363-4	JOVIAN
222-35	SEVERUS ALEXANDER	364-75	VALENTINIAN I
235-8	MAXIMINUS of Thrace	375-83	GRATIAN
238	GORDIAN I and GORDIAN II	375-92	VALENTINIAN II
		379-95	THEODOSIUS I, in the East
238	BALBINUS and PUPIENUS	392-4	EUGENIUS, usurper
238-44	GORDIAN III	395-423	HONORIUS
244-9	PHILIP of Arabia	395-408	ARCADIUS, in the East
249-51	TRAJAN DECIUS	408-50	THEODOSIUS II, in the East
251-3	TREBONIANUS GALLUS	421	CONSTANTIUS III
253	AEMILIAN	423-5	JOHANNES, usurper
253-60	VALERIAN and GALLIENUS	425-55	VALENTINIAN III
253-68	GALLIENUS	425	PETRONIUS MAXIMUS
268-70	CLAUDIUS GOTHICUS	455-56	AVITUS
270-5	AURELIAN	457-61	MAJORIAN
275-6	TACITUS	461-5	SEVERUS III
276-82	PROBUS	467-72	ANTHEMIUS
282-3	CARUS	472	OLYBRIUS
283-4	CARUS and NUMERIAN	473	GLYCERIUS
284-305	DIOCLETIAN; the First Tetrarchy	473-5	JULIUS NEPOS
		475-6	ROMULUS AUGUSTULUS
285-305	MAXIMIANUS AUGUSTUS		

GLOSSARY

ala   Wing of auxiliary cavalry

Alésia   Last stronghold of the Gallic forces in the Gallic War, where they were defeated by Julius Caesar in 52 BC; their leader, Vercingetorix, was subsequently executed by the Romans. Alésia is now definitely known to be the modern Alise-Sainte-Reine in the Côte-d'Or departement, following excavations initiated by Napoléon III in 1861-5. The objects recovered are now in the Musée des Antiquités Nationales at Saint-Germain-en-Laye. The excavations also brought to light large defensive fortifications.

Avars   Originating in Central Asia, the Avars spread across Europe in the Early Middle Ages until they were stopped by Charlemagne in the eight century AD.

ballista   Torsion war machine or catapult.

balteus   Transverse suspension strap passing over the shoulder and carrying the *spatha*; it replaced the *cingulum* from the end of the second century AD.

Buggenum   Dutch site where the bronze helmet which became a type series was found; Buggenum helmets were developed from the Italian type, and date from the second half of the first century BC; they feature a button on top and an ogival profile.

Cáceres el Viejo (*Castra Caecilia*) Spain. Legionary camp in Estremadura attributed to Caecilius Metellus and dated to between 90-79 BC (Ulbert 1984).

caliga   Military sandal with a web of thin straps which cover the foot, combining strength with suppleness; the sole, composed of three layers of thick leather, was hobnailed.

cataphractus   Name used from the first century AD onwards to describe an armoured cavalryman of Eastern origin (Tacitus, *Hist.* I.79).

catapult   Very powerful torsion war machine used to fire arrows.

century   Basic legionary unit, commanded by a centurion and comprising about 80 men in the Principate.

chamfron   Shaped metal or leather protector for the upper part of a cavalry horse's head.

chape   Reinforced tip of a sword or dagger scabbard, usually metal or bone, *bouterolle* in French, *Ortband* in German.

cingulum   Leather belt covered with metallic decorations, from which hung the *gladius* in the first and second centuries AD; it became a badge of office in the fourth century.

Clibanarius   Name given in late antiquity to the Oriental cavalrymen who wore heavy armour which protected the horse as well as the rider.

cohort   A division within a legion, comprising six 'centuries' (some 400 men), with the exception of the first cohort in each legion which had 800 men in its five cohorts. Also the name used for auxiliary troop units, both infantry and cavalry.

Coolus   Commune in the Marne area of France where the first example of this bronze type-helmet with a plain undecorated skullcap was discovered in the early 1900s. First thought to be Gallic, it was later attributed to Caesar's forces by U. Schaaf;. H. Russel Robinson (1975), who subdivided the type into nine groups, widened the type-name to apply also to helmets

Corbridge derived from the primitive form in the second half of the first century AD.

Corbridge Known also by its Latin name of *Corstopitum*, this site 4km to the south of Hadrian's Wall was occupied from Flavian times (?AD 79) until the fifth century. Originally a wood and earth camp used by both infantry and cavalry, it was rebuilt and reoccupied on a 2.5 hectare site several times during the second century after having been destroyed by fire around AD 105. It is particularly known for its deposit of metalwork, a chest buried between AD 122-38 containing many pieces of segmental armour on which the most accurate reconstructions (Allason-Jones 1986) are based.

cuirass (*lorica*) Various types, including: *lorica hamata* – chain mail in English, *Kettenpanzer* in German, *cotte de mailles* in French – a chain mail shirt invented by the Gauls; *lorica squamata* : scale armour, of Oriental origin and worn, though not exclusively, by the cavalry; *lorica segmentata*, developed by the Roman army in the first half of the first century AD; *lorica plumata* which may have been a combination of chain mail and scale armour.

decurion The non-commissioned officer in charge of a *turma*, a division of a cavalry wing.

Dura-Europos Dura, on the Euphrates in Syria, called Europos by its Greek founders, was initially a Seleucid stronghold, then Parthian, and finally a Roman town from 165 BC. It was destroyed again by the Sassanids, in AD 256, and never reoccupied. See *Syria* 63, 1986; 65, 1988; 69, 1992.

episeme In Greek, a personal identification mark on a shield.

eponymous Typically applied to a site or an object whose name is used to denote a series or class.

gaesum: Type of lance used primarily by the *Raetii*; precise morphology unknown.

Gallia Comata: That part of Gaul not romanised before the time of Julius Caesar, as opposed to the *Provincia*, the *Gallia Togata* or *Narbonensis* as it became known from the time of Augustus.

gladius Basic sword of the Roman infantryman, a short weapon during the Principate, though its predecessor, the *gladius hispaniensis*, could be up to 80cm in length. Pointed for thrusting, it also had parallel or slightly concave cutting edges, so it could also be used for slashing. Worn on the right side, its scabbard was suspended from four rings fixed to two transverse sliders, a system adopted from the Iberians.

Haguenau The helmet now in the Haguenau (France, Dept of Bas-Rhin) Museum, actually found at Drusenheim, was chosen as a series-type by P. Couissin in 1926. Bronze, with or without a button on top, these helmets are notable for their frontal reinforcement and a right-angled nape protector; several variants (about 40 to date) appeared as these helmets evolved between the end of the reign of Augustus and that of Vespasian.

Haltern An area of Westphalia in Germany where two early camps were established during the Augustan period; a 36 ha marching camp suitable for two legions, then a 20 ha permanent camp intended for one legion, and occupied for some years. The Roman occupation of Haltern occurred in the years after the death of Drusus in 9 BC and the military reorganisation following the Varus disaster of AD 9.

hoplite Heavily armed (*oplon*) Greek infantryman – helmet, armour, shin guards, round shield, long pike, sword.

greave also shinguard. Metal protection for the exposed right leg of the infantryman and for both legs of officers : *jambière* in French, *Beinschiene* in German.

legion The Roman army's basic corps. Comprising 30 maniples in the Republican era, legionary strengths varied at different times and under changing circumstances, from 6000 men just after Marius' reforms to hardly more than 1000 at the end of the fourth century AD, though strengths did increase by the end of the ancient period. Under the Principate, an average legionary strength was about 5000 men.

limes, plural *limites*　The Roman name for the 'frontier' between regions under Roman authority and those outside it. The Roman army eventually erected barrier lines along these frontiers, plus towers and camps at selected points, and a road system.

lithobole　Greek name for a stone-throwing torsion war machine.

maniple　Tactical unit of a legion, comprising two centuries; divided after Marius' time into ten cohorts and commanded by a senior centurion.

Mannheim　Germany. Area around Mainz where a bronze helmet with a simple skullcap was found in the bed of the Rhine; later a series-type, it was a heavy version of the Coolus-type helmet, and both types can be linked to Caesar's troop movements. German writers, however, group both light and heavy types under the 'Mannheim-Type' heading.

manubalista　According to Vegetius (*Mil.* IV.22) this was the new name from the end of the fourth century AD for the war machine previously known as a '*scorpio*'.

metope　The square space between triglyphs in Doric friezes, thus by extension similar enclosed spaces in a linear decoration.

Montefortino Italy　Cemetary site from the second Iron Age chosen as the eponym for the type of helmet most popular in Italy from the third to the first centuries BC; it featured an ogival profile and a button on top. Known in England as a 'jockey-cap' or 'knob' helmet and in Germany as a 'Helm mit Scheitelknauf'. H. Russell Robinson (1975) extended this type-name, divided into five variants, to include Republican helmets from the first half of the first century AD.

Newstead (*Trimontium*)　Scotland. Excavated early last century (1905-10) and again in 1947, the fort at Newstead can be shown to have four successive occupation periods. The first, built around AD 80 under Agricola, covered 4.14 hectares and was succeeded by the second, with an area of 5.7 hectares, at the end of the 80s; it was violently destroyed around AD 100. The third camp was not built until around AD 140, and was shortly followed by a late-Antonine version which was abandoned during the third century (Curle, 1911).

Niederbieber　Roman camp on the German Rhineland *limes*, destroyed by the Germans in AD 259-60, in which was found the helmet adopted in 1926 by P. Couissin as a series-type for a group which is actually very varied. General type features are a prominent nape protector and openings for the ears. G. Waunick (1988) identified three variants: 1. undecorated helmets with a reinforced skullcap; 2. helmets with a decorated bow shape; 3. profusely decorated helmets. Niederbieber-type helmets of bronze and of iron date from the end of the second century AD into the third.

Numantia　Spain. This Celtiberian centre of the *Arevaci* found itself in the early second century BC at the centre of an increasingly serious revolt against Roman ill-treatment in the surrounding region. From 153 BC this revolt developed into an armed conflict in which Scipio Æmilianus emerged as the undisputed victor and burned the town in the summer of 133 BC. Some five miles away are the Republican-period camps at Renieblas, in some cases overlapping one another, and attributed to successive attackers – Cato in 195, 193 and 181BC; Nobilior in 153 BC; Mancinus followed by Scipio in 137 BC; a final occupation dates from the struggle between Pompey and Sertorius in 75-4 BC. To the south, the camp at Penarredonda is thought to be that of Marcellus, and other Roman remains have been found a little further north on the Castillejo, and to the east at Valdeborrón (Schulten 1914-31)

onager　'Wild ass', the name given in the late Empire (Ammianus Marcellinus XXIII.IV.1-7; Vegetius, *Mil.* IV.22) to a torsion stone-throwing war machine with a violent recoil or kick, hence its name

Oberaden　One of the oldest camps in Germany to be excavated, occupied from about

oxybelus An alternative name for a catapult which fired wooden-shafted arrows.

paragnathide (buccula) Helmet cheekpiece, rigid or hinged, to protect the sides of the face.

peltast Greek soldier who carried a *pelta*, a light, crescent-shaped shield.

phalanx A unit of hoplites in the Macedonian army, drawn up in battle in eight ranks to present a solid impenetrable barrier to the enemy. Its members were armed with a long lance, the *sarissa*, up to 5.5m long, held in both hands, and had a round shield for protection. The lance points of the front rank made an impressive display, but the formation was vulnerable to attack from the flank. The early Republican army initially used a tactic based on the hoplite phalanx, but later developed its own formations.

pilum Typically Roman throwing spear, comprising a long iron thin shank tipped with a sharpened pyramid-shaped head, fastened to a wooden shaft. The slender shank was designed to bend on impact to prevent its being used against its thrower.

Principate The period during which the Roman empire was ruled by an emperor (*princeps*).

scabbard Leather, wood or metal sheath for an edged weapon, usually fitted with rings for suspension and a chape to protect the point: *fourreau* in French, *Scheide* in German.

spina The vertical reinforcing rib on a shield.

tragula A heavy Gaulish lance with a particularly resistant head, according to ancient writers; it may have been barbed, but its exact form is unknown.

umbo The projecting boss of a shield, generally with a concave inner face to accept a handgrip for its user (*manipula*).

velites infanterymen forming one of the divisions in a Republican legion, composed of 1200-1500 young men who paid the lowest level of taxes; this category of soldier was discontinued after Marius' reforms.

verutum A throwing weapon of Italic origin, perhaps a form of *pilum* under the Republic; it may be the same weapon named by the Celtiberians as *soliferrum*. The word reappears in writings about fourth century equipment, and may in this case also refer to a late version of the *pilum*.

Vindonissa (Windisch) Switzerland. A legionary camp established on the left bank of the Rhine, probably around AD 16-17 to accept the legion XIII Gemina after its departure from Augsburg-Oberhausen; the finds at Vindonissa also do not rule out the possibility of there being an earlier, Augustan, camp on this site at the end of the first century BC. During the period AD 46-69 the legion XXI Rapax took the place of the XIII Gemina, accompanied by two cohorts of auxiliaries, one of them cavalry, and this force was in its turn replaced in AD 70 by the legion XI Claudia which leaves the site in AD 101. Despite having lost its strategic importance after the *limes* was moved northwards, the camp remained available until around the middle of the second century, when it was superseded by a simple *vicus*. The excavation of a rubbish dump used by legionaries from about AD 30-100, sited outside the north wall, produced a spectacular array of military equipment, including a particularly impressive assortment of organic items in wood, leather, etc.

Weisenau Germany. Site in the outskirts of Mainz where the Roman iron helmet was found which P. Couissin (1926) took as a series-type. Derived from the Celtic late La Tène iron helmet, Weisenau-type helmets are characterised by a well-developed, usually sloping, nape protector, apertures for the ears and a frontal reinforcement. The dates of the 40 known examples range from the end of Augustus' reign to the early decades of the second century.

BIBLIOGRAPHY

Listed below is a brief selection, omitting for the most part general works and histories, which can be found in the bibliographies available through specialist study groups. There are many works not cited here on history and on military organisation, such as the reports of the 'Limeskongresse' or the 'Mavors Roman Army Researches' published in Amsterdam since 1984, and more recently in Stuttgart. References to arms and equipment are usually relegated to appendices and brief overviews, but in the following pages, the reader will find more specific information on the particular subjects treated in the book. Similarly, the ancient source-works detailed below are those to which reference has been most frequently made.

Special note should be taken of the proceedings of meetings convened to discuss military equipment, first published in *BAR* (with the exception of the first volume) and later in *JRMES*:

Bishop M.C. (ed), *Roman Military Equipment*, Sheffield 1983.
Bishop M.C. (ed), *The production and distribution of Roman Military Equipment. (Proceedings of the Second Military Equipment Research Seminar)* (BAR S-275), Oxford, 1985.
Dawson, M, (ed), *Roman Military Equipment. The Accoutrements of War. (Proceedings of the third Military Equipment Research Seminar)* (BAR S-336), Oxford, 1987.
Coulston, J.C. (ed), *Military Equipment and the Identity of Roman Soldiers. (Proceedings of the fourth Military Equipment Conference)* (BAR S-394), Oxford, 1988.
van Driel-Murray, C. (ed.), *Roman Military Equipinent: the Sources of Evidence (Proceedings of the Fifth Roman Military Equipment Conference)* (BAR S 336), Oxford 1989.

ABBREVIATIONS

AJA   *American Journal of Archaeology*
ArchKorr   *Archäologisches Korrespondenzblatt*
Ber. RGK   *Bericht der Römisch-Germanischen Kommission*
JbRGZM   *Jahrbuch des Römisch-Germanischen Zentralmuseums zu Mainz*
JRMES   *Journal of Roman Military Equipment Studies*
MEFRA   *Mélanges de l'Ecole Française de Rome et d'Athènes*

SOURCES

Ammianus Marcellinus, *History*, trans. J.C. Rolfe, 3 vols (Loeb, 1935-40; repr. 1956-8).
Arrian, *Tactica*, trans. P.A. Brunt, (Loeb, 1976-83).
Julius Caesar, *Bellum Civile*, trans. S.A. Handford as *The Civil War*, revd ed. J.F. Gardner, (Penguin Classics, 1982).
Julius Caesar, *Bellum Gallicum*, trans. J.F. Gardner as *The Conquest of Gaul*, (Penguin Classics, 1982).
Josephus, *Bellum Judaicum*, trans. as *The Jewish War*, H. St J. Thackeray, R. Marcus, A. Wikgren & L.H. Feldman, (Loeb, 1926-65).
Polybius, *Histories*, trans. W.R. Paton (Loeb, 1922-7, with Eng. translation of text based upon Buttner-Wobst, 1889-1904, 1905).
Suetonius, *Lives of the Caesars*, trans. R. Graves, revd ed. M. Grant (Penguin Classics, 1976).
Tacitus, *Annales*, trans. M. Grant as *The Annals of Imperial Rome*, (Penguin Classics, 1973).
Tacitus, *Historiae*, trans. K. Wellesley as *The Histories*, (Penguin Classics, 1975).
Livy, Books IV-X trans. B. Radice as *Rome and Italy*, (Penguin Classics, 1982); XXI-XXX trans. A. de Selincourt, ed. B. Radice as *The War with Hannibal*, (Penguin Classics, 1974); XXXI-XLV trans. H. Betterson as *Rome and the Mediterranean*, (Penguin Classics, 1978).
Vegetius, *De re militari*, trans. N.P. Milner as *Epitome of Military Science*, (Liverpool University Press, 1993).

GENERAL WORKS

Bishop, M.C., Coulston, J.C.N., *Roman Military Equipment*, Aylesbury, 1989.

Bishop, M.C., Coulston, J.C.N., *Roman Military Equipment*, London, 1993.

Connolly, P., *Greece and Rome at War*, London, 1981.

Couissin, P., *Les armes romaines. Essai sur les origines et l'évolution des armes individuelles du légionnaire romain*, Paris, 1926.

Groller, M. von, 'Römische Waffen', *RLÖ* 2, Wien 1911, 85-132.

Hoffiller, V., *Oprema Rimskoga Vojnika u prvo doba Carstva*, Zagreb, 1911-12.

Le Bohec, Y., *L'armée romaine*, Paris, 1989.

Lindenschmidt, L., *Tracht und Bewaffnung des römischen Heeres während der Kaiserzeit, mit besonderer Berücksichtigung der Rheinischen Denkmale und Fundstücke*, Braunschweig, 1882.

Reddé, M., (ed.), *L'armée romaine en Gaule*, Paris, 1996.

Robinson, H.R., *The Armour of Imperial Rome*, London, 1975.

Ubl, H.J., 'Waffen und Uniform des römischen Heeres der Prinzipatsepoche nach den Grabreliefs Noricums und Pannoniens', unpubd PhD, 2 vol., Klosterneuburg, 1969.

Ulbert, G., *Römische Waffen des 1. Jahrhunderts n. Chr.* (Limesmus. Aalen, Kleine Schriften), Stuttgart, 1968.

Ulbert, G., Garbsch, J., Raddatz, K., 'Bewaffnung', in *Reallexikon der Germanische Altertumskunde*, 2 (4/5), 416-21 (G.U.), 421-3 (J.G.) and 423-37 (K.R.)

Warry, J., *Warfare in the Classical World*, London, 1980.

Watson, R., *The Roman Soldier*, New-York 1969.

Webster, G., *The Roman Imperial Army of the first and second centuries A.D.*, London 1969.

1 MILITARY THINKING AMONG THE ANCIENTS

Brunaux, J-L., Lambot, B., *Guerre et armement chez les Gaulois (450-52 av. J.-C.)*, Paris, 1987.

Connolly, P., *The Greek armies*, London 1977.

Connolly, P., *Hannibal and the enemies of Rome*, London 1978.

Connolly, P., *Greece and Rome at War*, London 1981.

Deschler-Erb, E., Ad arma! *Römisches Militär des 1. Jahrhunderts n. Chr. in Augusta Raurica* (Forsch. in Augst 28), Augst 1999.

Ducrey, P., *Guerre et guerriers dans la Grèce antique*, Fribourg-Paris, 1985.

Rapin, A., Brunaux, J-L., *Gournay II. Boucliers, lances. Dépôts et trophées* (Rev. Arch. Picardie), Paris, 1988.

Snodgrass, A., *Early Greek armour and weapons, from the end of the Bronze Age to 600 BC*, Edinburgh, 1964.

Stary, P.F., *Zur eisenzeitlichen Bewaffnung und Kampfweise in Mittelitalien* (Marburger Studien zur Vor- und Frühgeschichte, 3), Mainz, 1981.

2 THE ROMAN SOLDIER FROM EARLIEST TIMES

Allason-Jones, L., Miket, R., *The Catalogue of small finds from South Shields Roman Fort*, Newcastle-upon-Tyne, 1984.

Allason-Jones, L., Bishop, M.C., *Excavations at Roman Corbridge. The Hoard*, London, 1988.

Cichorius, C., *Die Reliefs des Traianssäule, herausgegeben und historisch erklärt von Conrad Cichorius*, Berlin, 1896-1900.

Crummy, N., *The Roman small finds fron excavations at Colchester 1971-79* (Colchester Arch. Report, 2), Colchester 1981.

Curle, J., *A Roman Frontier Post and its People. The Fort of Newstead in the Parish of Melrose*, Glasgow 1911.

Driel-Murray, C. van, 'A Roman tent: Vindolanda tent 1', in V.A. Maxfield & M.J. Dobson (eds.), *Roman Frontier Studies 1989. Proceedings of the XVth International Congress of Roman Frontier Studies*, Exeter 1991, 367-372.

Feugére, M., 'L'équipement militaire et l'armement romains: recherches et travaux récents en Grande-Bretagne', *Cah. Arch. Loire* 2, 1982, 79-85.

Fischer, U., *Grabungen im römischen Steinkastell von Heddernheim 1957-1959* (Schriften des Frankfurter Museums fur Vor- und Frühgeschichte, II), Frankfurt 1973.

Florescu, F.B., *Das Siegesdenkmal von Adamklissi, Tropaeum Trajani*, Bucarest, 1965.

Fontaine, L., *L'armée romaine*, Paris, 1883.

Garbsch, J., 'The oldest military diploma from the province of Dacia', in V.A. Maxfield & M.J. Dobson (eds.), *Roman Frontier Studies 1989. Proceedings of the XVth International Congress of Roman Frontier Sludies*, Exeter 1991, 281-4.

Junkelmann, M., *Die Legionen des Augustus. Der römische Soldat im archäologischen Experiment*, Mainz 1986.

Le Bohec, Y., *Militaires romains en Gaule civile (Actes de la table-ronde de mai 1991)*, Lyon, 1993.

Lepper, F., Frere, S., *Trajan's column. A new edition of the Cichorius plates*, London, 1988.

Oldenstein, J., 'Les armes des soldats romains', *Doss. Arch.* 86, août-sept. 1984, 35-49.

Richmond, L., *Trajan's Army on Trajan's Column*, London, 1982.

Santrot, J., 'La 'sépulture' d'un légionnaire romain : pièces d'armement antique à Jard', in *150 années de découvertes archéologiques en Vendée. La mort et le sacré*, Thonon-les-B., 1990, 188-191.

Settis, S. (ed.), *La Colonna Traiana*, Torino 1988.

Stemmer, K., *Untersuchungen zur Typologie, Chronologie und Ikonographie der Panzerstatuen*, 1978.

Waurick, G., 'Untersuchungen zur historisierenden Rüstung in der römischien Kunst', *Jb. RGZM* 30, 1983, 265-301.

3 THE STRUCTURE OF THE ARMY

Beeser, J., '*Pilum murale*? Kritisches zum 75. Jubiläum eines Meinungsstreites', *Fundber. ans Baden-Württemberg* 4, 1979, 133-42.

Behn, F., 'Die Musik im römischen Heere', *Mainzer Zeitschr.* 7, 1912, 36-47.

Cagnat, R., *L'armée romaine d'Afrique et l'occupation militaire de l'Afrique sous les empereurs*, Paris, 1913 (2cnd ed.).

Cheesman, G.L., *The auxilia of the Roman Imperial Army*, 1914, new ed. Hildesheim/New York, 1971.

Connolly, P., *Tiberius Claudius Maximus, the Legionary*, Oxford, 1988.

Coulston, J.C.N., 'The 'draco' standard', *JRMES* 2, 1991, 101-114.

Dieu, L., 'La musique romaine', *Musique ancienne (CAEL)* 19, 1985.

Domaszewski, A. von, *Die Fahnen nu römischen Heere*, Wien, 1885.

Feugère, M., 'Phalères romaines en calcédoine', *Misc. di Studi Archeol. e di Ant. (Modena)*, 3, 1989, 31-51.

Fuentes, N., 'The mule of a soldier', *JRMES* 2, 1991, 65-99.

Grant, M., *The army of the Caesars*, London, 1974.

Guillermand, J. et al., *Histoire de la médecine aux armées, 1. De l'Antiquité à la Révolution*, Paris, 1982.

Holder, P., *The Roman Army in Britain*, London 1985.

Isaac, B., *The limits of Empire, The Roman Army in the East*, Oxford, 1990.

Jahn, O., *Die Lauersforter Phalerae*, Bonn 1860.

Keppie, L., *The making of the Roman army, from Republic to Empire*, London, 1984.

Le Bohec, Y., *L'armée romaine*, Paris, 1989.

Le Bohec, Y., *La troisième légion Auguste*, Paris, 1989.

Le Bohec, Y., *Les unités auxiliaires de l'armée romaine en Afrique Proconsulaire et en Numidie sous le Haut-Empire*, Paris, 1989.

Le Bohec, Y., *La Sardaigne et l'armée romaine*, Paris, 1990.

Le Roux, L., *L'armée romaine de Bretagne*, Paris, 1911.

Le Roux, P., *L'armée romaine et l'organisation des provinces ibériques d'Auguste à l'invasion de 409* (Publ. du Centre Pierre Paris, 8), Paris 1982.

Lesquier, J., *L'armée romaine d'Egypte, d'Auguste à Dioclétien*, Le Caire 1918.

MacMullen, R., 'Inscriptions on armor and the supply of arms in the Roman Empire', *AJA* 64, 1960, 23-40.

Maxfield, V.A., *The military decorations of the Roman army*, London, 1981.

Reddé, M., 'Les ouvrages militaires romains en Gaule sous le Haut-Empire; vers un bilan des recherches récentes', *JbRGZM* 34, 1987 (2), 343-68.

Reinach, A.J., '*signa militaria*', in Ch. Daremberg & E. Saglio (eds.), *Dictionnaire des Antiquités grecques et romaines*, Paris, 1911.

Ritterling, E., '*legio*', in *Paulys Realencyclopädie* XII, 1 & XII, 2, 1924-5.

Rostovtzeff, M., 'Vexillum and victory', *Journal of Roman Studies* XXXII, 1942, 92-106.

Saddington, D.B., 'The development of the Roman auxiliary forces from Augustus to Trajan', *Aufstieg und Niedergang der römischen Welt*, 11.3, 176-201.

Speidel, M.P., 'Eagle-Bearer and Trumpeter. The Eagle-Bearer and Trumpets of the Legions, Illustrated by Three Tombstones Recently found at Byzantium', *Bonner Jahrb.* 176, 1976, 123-63 (*Roman Army Studies* 1, Amsterdam, 1984, 3-43).

Speidel, M.P., 'The rise of ethnic units in the Roman imperial army', *Aufstieg und Niedergang der römischen Welt* II, 3, 202-231.

4 REPUBLICAN ARMS AND EQUIPMENT

Brouquier-Reddé, V., 'L'équipement militaire d'Alésia d'après les nouvelles recherches (prospections et fouilles)', in M. Feugère (ed.), '*L'équipement militaire et l'armement de la République (IVe-Ier s. avant J.-C.)*', *Journal of Roman Military Equip. St.* 8, 1997 [1999], 277-88.

Couissin, P., *Les armes romaines. Essai sur les origines et l'évolution des armes individuelles du légionnaire romain*, Paris, 1926.

Duval, A., 'Les armes d'Alésia au Musée des Antiquités Nationales', *Rev. Hist. des Armées* 2, 1987, 56-62.

Feugére, M., 'L'équipement militaire républicain en Gaule', in C. van Driel-Murray (ed.), *Military Equipment in context* (Proceedings of the ninth international Roman Military Equipment conference, Leiden 1994) (*JRMES* 5), 1994, 3-23.

Feugére, M. (ed.), 'L'équipement militaire et l'armement de la République (IVe-Ier s. avant J.-C.)', *JRMES* 8, 1997 [1999].

Harmond, J, *L'armée et le soldat à Rome, de 107 à 50 avant notre ère*, Paris 1967.

Jaeckel, P., 'Pergamenische Waffenreliefs', *Waffen und Kostümkunde, Zeitschrift Ges.f. Hist.Waffen- und Kostümkunde* 1965 (2), 93-122.

Keppie, L., *The making of the Roman army, from Republic to Empire*, London, 1984.

Keppie, L., 'A centurion of legio Martia at Padova?', *JRMES* 2, 1991, 115-21.

Kimmig, W., 'Ein Keltenschild aus Ägypten', *Germania* 24, 1940, 106-11.

Quicherat, L., 'Examen des armes trouvées à Alise', *Rev.Arch.*, 1865, 1, 81 sqq.

Quicherat, L., 'Le pilum de l'infanterie romaine', *Mém. Soc. Nat.Antiq. de Fr.*, 1866, 245 sqq.

Reinach, A., 'L'origine du pilum', *Rev.Arch.* 1907, 1, 243, 425; 11, 125, 226.

Schaaff, U., 'Etruskisch-römische Helme', in *Antike Helme. Handbuch mit Katalog*, Mainz 1988, 318-26.

Schulten, A., *Numantia. Die Ergebnisse der Ausgrabungen 1905-1912*, Munich 1914-1931. *Bd. 1, Die Keltiberer and Ihre Kriege mit Rom*, 1914; *Bd. 11, Die Stadt Nuniantia*, 1931; *Bd. 111, Die Lager des Scipio*, 1927; *Bd. IV, Die Lager bei Renieblas*, 1929.

Sievers, S., 'Alesia und Osuna : Bemerkungen zur Normierung der spätrepublikanischen Bewaffnung und Ausrüstung', in : M. Feugère (ed.), 'L'équipement militaire et l'armement de la République (IVe-Ier s. avant J.-C.)', *Journal of Roman Military Equip.St.* 8, 1997 [1999], 271-6.

Stary, P.F., 'Ursprung und Ausbreitung der eisenzeitlichen Ovalschilde mit spindelförmigem Schildbuckel', *Germania* 59, 1981, 287-306.

Ulbert, G., *Cáceres el Viejo, ein spätrepublikanisches Legionslager in Spanisch-Extremadura*, (Madrider Beitr., 11.), Mainz, 1984.

Verchère de Reffye, 'Les armes d'Alise', *Rev.Arch.* 1864 (2), 337-42.

Waurick G., *Helme in Caesars Heer*, Mainz, 1990.

5 PROTECTIVE EQUIPMENT IN THE HIGH EMPIRE

Beck, F., Chew, H., *Masques de fer. Un officier roinain du temps de Caligula*, cat. exhibition Musée des Antiquités Nationales, 1991-2.

Bishop, M.C., Coulston, J.C.N., *Roman military Equipment*, London, 1993.

Bockius, R., 'Ein römisches Scutum aus Urmitz, Kreis Mayen-Koblenz. Zu Herkunft und Verbreitung Spindelformiger Schildbuckelbeschläge im Gebiet nördlich der Alpen', *ArchKorr.* 19, 1989, 269-82.

Buckland, P., 'A first-century shield from Doncaster, Yorkshire', *Britannia* IX, 1978, 247-69.

Connolly, P., 'The Roman fighting technique deduced from armour and weaponry', in V.A. Maxfield & M.J. Dobson (eds.), *Roman Frontier Studies 1989,*

Proceedings of the XVth International Congress of Roman Frontier Studies, Exeter 1991, 358-63.

Couissin, P., 'Les armes figurées sur les monuments romains de Gaule méridionale', *Rev.Arch.* 1923, II, 29-87.

Couissin, P., 'Les guerriers et les armes sur les bas-reliefs du Mausolée des Jules à Saint-Rémy', *Rev.Arch.* 1923, 1.303-21.

Deschler-Erb, E., 'Ein germanischer Schildrandbeschlag des 1./2. jahrhunderts n. Chr. aus Augst', *Arch. Suisse* 15, 1992 (1), 18-23.

Driel-Murray, C. van, 'A fragmentary shield cover from Caerleon', in J.C. Coulston (ed.), *Military equipment and the identity of Roman Soldiers. Proceedings of the Fourth Military Equipment Conference (BAR S-394)*, Oxford, 1988, 51-66.

Klumbach, H., *Römische Helme aus Niedergermanien (Kunst und Altertum am Rhein, 51)*, Köln 1974.

Robinson, H.R., *The Armour of Imperial Rome*, London, 1975.

Thomas, E.B., *Helme, Schilde, Dolche. Studien über römisch-pannonische Waffenkunde*, Budapest, 1971.

Waurick, G., 'Die römische Kettenrüstung von Weiler-la-Tour', *Hémecht* 1, 1982, 111-30.

Waurick, G., 'Römische Helme', in *Antike Helme. Handbuch mit Katalog*, Mainz, 1988, 327-64.

Wild, J.P., 'A find of Roman scale armour from Carpow', *Britannia* XII, 1981, 305-6,

6 OFFENSIVE WEAPONS IN THE HIGH EMPIRE

Beck, F., Chew H., *Masques de fer. Un officier romain du temps de Caligula*, cat. exhibition Musée des Antiquités Nationales, 1991-2.

Carnap-Bornheim, C. von (ed.), *Beiträge zu römischer und barbarischer Bewaffnung in den ersten vier nachchristlichen Jahrhunderten. Marburger Kolloquium 1994*, Lublin/Marburg, 1994.

Couissin, P., 'Les armes figurées sur les monuments romains de Gaule méridionale', *Rev.Arch.* 1923, II. 29-87.

Couissin, P., 'Les guerriers et les armes sur les bas-reliefs du Mausolée des Jules à Saint-Rémy', *Rev.Arch.* 1923, I. 303-21.

Exner, K., 'Römische Dolchscheiden mit Tauschierung und Emailverzierung', *Germania* 24, 1940, 22-8.

Fellmann, R., 'Hölzerne Schwertgriffe aus dem Schutthügel von Vindonissa', in *Helvetia Antiqua. Festschrift Emil Vogt*, Zurich 1966, 215-22,

Helmig, G., '*Hispaniensis pugiunculus*'? Technologische Aspekte und Anmerkungen zum Fund einer Militärdolchscheide aus Basel', *Arch. Suisse* 13, 1990 (4), 158-64.

Hermann, F.R., 'Der Eisenhortfund aus dem Kastell Künzing', *Saalburg Jahrb.*, 26, 1969, 129-41.

Horbacz, I., Oledzki, M., 'Studien über inkrustierte römische Schwerter, mit besonderer Berücksichtigung eines Neufundes aus dem Bereich der Przeworsk-Kultur in Paiski, Woiwodschaft Piotrkow Trybunalski', *Hambürger Beitr. zur Archäol.* XII, 1985, 147-92.

Kunow, J., 'Bemerkungen zum Export römischer Waffen in das Barbarikum', in *Studien zu den Militärgrenzen Roms III*, Stuttgart, 1986, 740-6.

Lersch, L., *Das sogenannte Schwert des Tiberius. Ein römischer Ehrendegen aus der Zeit dieses Kaisers*, Bonn, 1849.

Lønstrup, J., 'Das zweischneidige Schwert aus der jüngeren römischen Kaiserzeit im freien Germanien und im römischen Imperium', in *Studien zu den Militärgrenzen Roms III*, Stuttgart, 1986, 747-9.

Kellner, H.J., 'Zu den römischen Ringknaufschwertern und Dosenortbändern in Bayern', *Jb. RGZM* 13, 1966, 190-201.

Marchant, D.I., 'Roman weapons in Great-Britain. A case study: spearheads, problems in dating and typology', *JRMES* 1, 1990, 1-6.

Marchant, D.I., 'Roman weaponry in the Province of Britain from the second century to the fifth century A.D', (unpubd PhD, Univ. Durham, 1991).

Martin-Kilcher, S., 'Ein silbernes Schwertortband mit Niellodekor und weitere Militärfunde des 3. Jahrhunderts ans Augst', *Jahresber. ans Augst und Kaiseraugst* 5, 1985, 147-203.

Nylén, E., 'Early Gladius Swords Found in Scandinavia', *Acta Archaeologica* XXXIV, 1963, 185-230.

Obman, J., *Studien zu Römischen Dolchscheiden des 1. Jahrhunderts n. Chr. Zeugnisse und Bildliche Überlieferung* (Kolner St.Arch. röm. Prov. 4), Raden/Westf. 2000).

Quicherat, J., 'Le pilum de l'infanterie romaine', *Mém. Soc. Nat. Antiq. de Fr.*, 1866, 245 sq.

Schulten, A., 'pilum', in *Paulys Real-Encyclopädie der classischen Altertumswissenschaften*, Stuttgart, 1950, 1334-69.

Scott, I.R., 'Spearheads of the British *limes*', in W.S. Hanson & L.J.F. Keppie (eds.), *Roman Frontier Studies 1979* (BAR S.71), Oxford, 1980, 333-43.

Scott, I.R., 'First century military daggers and the manufacture and supply of weapons for the Roman army', in: M.C. Bishop (ed.), *The Production and Distribution of Roman Military Equipment. Proceedings of the Second Military Equipment Research Seminar* (BAR S.275), Oxford, 1985, 195, 160-219.

Ulbert, G., 'Der Meister des silbertauschierten Dolches von Oberammergau', *Bayer. Vorgeschichtsbl.* 36, 1971, 44-9.

Ulbert, G., 'Straubing und Nydam. Zu römischn Langschwertern der späten Limeszeit', in *Studien zur Vor- und Frühgeschichtlichen Archäologie. Festschrift für J. Werner*, Munich, 1974, 197-216.

7 THE CAVALRY

Bishop, M.C., 'Cavalry equipment of the Roman army in the first century AD', in J.C. Coulston (ed.), *Military equipment and the Identity of Roman Soldiers. Proceedings of the Fourth Military Equipment Conference* (BAR S-394), Oxford, 1988, 67196.

Connolly, P., 'The Roman saddle', in M. Dawson (ed.), *The Accoutrements of War. In :Third Roman Military Equipment Seminar* (BAR S-336), Oxford, 1987, 7-27.

Connolly, P., *Tiberius Claudius Maximus, the Cavalryman*, Oxford, 1988.

Connolly, P., 'The saddle horns from Newstead', *JRMES* l, 1991, 61-6.

Craddock, P.T., Lang, J., Painter, K.S., 'Roman horse-trappings from Fremington Hagg, Reeth, Yorkshire, N.R.', *Brit. Mus. Quarterly* 37, 1973, 917.

Dixon, K.R., Southern, P., *The Roman Cavalry from the First to Third Century AD*, London 1992.

Eadie, J.W., 'The development ol Roman mailed cavalry', *Journal of Roman Studies* LVII, 1967, 161-171.

Garbsch, J., *Rönische Paraderüstungen* (Münchner Beitr. z. Vor- und Frühgeschichte, Bd. 30), Munich, 1978.

Giesler, U., 'Jüngerkaiserzeitliche Nietknopfsporen mit Dreipunkthalterung vom Typ Leuna–Hassleben', *Saalburg-Jahrb.* 35, 1978, 5-56.

Hyland, A., *Equus. The Horse in the Roman World*, London, 1990.

Hyland, A., *Training the Roman Cavalry from Arrian's Ars Tactica*, London, 1993.

Jahn, M., *Der Reitersporn, seine Entstehung und Entwicklung*, 1921.

Jenkins, I., 'A Group of Silvered Bronze Horse-Trappings from Xanten (*Castra Vetera*)', *Britannia* 16, 1985, 141-64.

Junkelmann, M., *Die Reiter Roms, I. Reise, Jagd, Triumph und Circusrennen*, Mainz, 1990.

Junkelmann, M., *Die Reiter Roms, II. Der militärischer Einsatz*, Mainz, 1991.

Junkelmann, M., *Die Reiter Roms, Ill. Zubehör, Reitweise, Bewaffnung*, Mainz, 1992.

Junkelmann, M., *Reiter wie Statuen aus Erz*, Zaberns Bildbände zur Archäologie, Mainz, 1996

Lawson, A.K., 'Studien zum römischen Pferdegeschirr', *Jb. RGZM* 25, 1978, 131-72.

Lefebvre des Noëttes, *L'attelage, le cheval de selle à travers les âges*, Paris 1931.

Prittwitz und Gaffron, H.-H. von, 'Der Reiterhelm des Tortikollis', *Bonner Jahrb.* 191, 1991, 225-46.

Rabeisen, F., 'La production d'équipement de cavalerie au Ier s. ap. J.-C. à Alésia (Alise Ste-Reine, Côte-d'Or, France)', *JRMES* 1, 1990, 73-98.

Shortt, H. de S., 'A provincial Roman spur from Longstock, Hants, and other spurs from Roman Britain', *Ant. Journal* 39, 1959, 61-76.

Taylor, A.K., 'Römische Hackamoren und Kappzäume aus Metall', *Jb. RGZM* 22, 1975, 106-33.

Visy, Z., *Die Wagendarstellungen der pannonischen Grabstein*, Pécs [1997], 190 p.

Webster, G., 'A hoard of Roman military equipment from Fremington Hagg', in R.M. Butler (ed.), *Soldier and Civilian in Roman Yorkshire. Essays to commemorate the nineteenth century of the foundation of York*, Leicester 1971, 107-25.

8 THE ARTILLERY

Baatz, D., 'Zur Geschützbewaffnung römischer Auxiliartruppen in der frühen und mittleren Kaiserzeit', *Bonner Jahrb.* 166, 1966, 194-207.

Baatz, D., 'Teile römischer Geschütze aus Rumänien', *Arch. Anzeiger* 3, 1975, 432-4.

Baatz, D., 'Recent finds of Ancient Artillery', *Britannia* IX, 1978, 1-17, pl. I-VI.

Baatz, D., 'Das Torsiongeschütz von Hatra', *Antike Welt* 9, 1978, 50-7.

Baatz, D., 'Teile hellenistischer Geschütze aus Griechenland', *Arch. Anzeiger* 1979 (1), 68-75.

Baatz, D., 'Ein Katapult der Legio IV Macedonica aus Cremona', *Mitt. Deutschen Arch. Instituts, Röm. Abt.* 87, 1980, 283-99.

Baatz, D., Feugére, M., 'Eléments d'une catapulte romaine trouvée à Lyon', *Gallia* 39, 1981, 201-9

Baatz, D., 'Hellenistische Katapulte aus Ephyra (Epirus)', *Mitt. D.A.I. Athen.* 97, 1982, 211-33.

Baatz, D., 'Katapultteile aus dem Schiffswrack von Mahdia (Tunesien)', *Arch. Anzeiger* 1985, 677-91.

Baatz, D., 'Eine Katapult-Spannbuchse aus Pityus, Georgien (UDSSR)', *Saalburg Jahrb.* 44, 1988, 59-64.

Baatz, D., 'Die römische Jagdarmbrust', *Arch. Korr.* 21 (2), 1991, 283-90.

Béal, J.-C., Genin, M., 'Eléments d'arc antique en bois de cerf découverts au Verbe Incarné à Lyon', *Art et Archéologie en Rhône-Alpes (Cah. René de Lucinge)* 3, 1977, 3-10.

Coulston, J.C., 'Roman archery equipment' in M.C. Bishop (ed.), *The Production and Distribution of Roman Military Equipment. Proceedings of the Second Military Equipment Research Seminar (BAR S. 275)*, Oxford 1985, 220-366.

Fougeres, G., 'glans', in Daremberg & Saglio (eds.), *Dictionnaire des antiquités grecques et romaines*, Paris, 1896.

Griffiths, W.B., 'The sling and its place in the Roman imperial army' in C. van Driel-Murray (ed.), *Roman Military Equipment. The sources of evidence. Proceedings of the Fifth Roman Military Equipment Conference (BAR S. 476)*, Oxford 1989, 255-79.

Gudea, N., Baatz, D., 'Teile spätrömischer Ballisten aus Gornea und Orsova (Rümanien)', *Saalburg Jahrb*, XXXI, 1974, 50-72.

Henry, B., 'Les balles de fronde étrusques en plomb', in *101e Congrès Nat. Soc. Sav. Lille 1976, Archéologie*, 9-19.

James, S., 'Archaeological evidence for Roman incendiary projectiles', *Saalb. Jahrb.* 39, 1983, 142-3.

Lafaye, G., 'tormenta', in Daremberg & Saglio (eds.), *Dictionnaire des antiquités grecques et romaines*, Paris, 1919.

Marsden, E.W., *Greek and Roman artillery. Historical Development*, Oxford, 1969.

Marsden, E.W., *Greek and Roman artillery. Technical Treatises*, Oxford, 1971.

Schramm, F., *Die antiken Geschütze der Saalburg*, Berlin, 1918 (new ed.. Saalburg, 1980).

Soedel, W., Foley, V., 'Ancient catapults', *Scientific American* 1978, 150-9.

Vicente, J.D., Pilar Punter, M.A., Ezquerra, B., 'La catapulta tardo-republicana y otro equipamiento militar de 'La Caridad' (Caminreal, Teruel)', in M. Feugère (ed.), 'L'équipement militaire et l'armement de la République (IVe-Ier s. avant J.-C.)', *JRMES* 8, 1997 [1999], 169-199.

Volling, T., '*Funditores* im römischen Heer', *Saalburg Jahrb.* 45, 1990, 24-58.

Zanier, W., 'Römische dreiflügelige Pfeilspitzen', *Saalburg Jahrb.* 44, 1988, 5-27.

9 INFANTRY EQUIPMENT

Baatz, D., 'Lederne Gürteltaschen römischer Soldaten?', *Arch. Korr.* 3, 1983, 359-61.

Bishop, M.C., Coulston, J.C.N., *Roman Military Equipment*, London 1993.

Busch, A.L., 'Die römerzeitliche Schuh- und Lederfunde ans der Kastelle Saalburg, Zugmantel und Kleiner Feldberg', *Saalburg Jahrb.* 22, 1965, 158-210.

Driel-Murray, C. van, 'Leatherwork in the Roman army', *Exercitus* 1986, 2 (1), 16.

Driel-Murray, C. van, 'Footwear in the North-Western Provinces of the Roman Empire', in '*Stepping through time. Archaeological footwear from prehistoric times until 1800*', Zwolle 2001, 337-76.

Gansser-Burckhardt, A., 'Die Lederfunde aus dem Schutlhügel von Vindonissa 1951', *Ges. Pro Vindonissa* 1952, 57–65.

Kunzl, E., 'Cingula di Ercolano e Pompei', *Cronache Poinpeiane* 3, 1977, 177–97.

Oldenstein, J., 'Zur Ausrüstung römischer Auxiliareinheiten. Studien zu Beschlägen und Zierat an der Ausrüstung der römischen Auxiliareinheiten der obergermanisch-raetischen Limesgebietes aus dem zweiten und dritten Jahrhundert n. Chr.', *Ber. RGK* 57, 1976, 49–366.

Petculescu, L., 'A note on military equipment of Roman officers in the 3rd century A.D.', *Bayer. Vorgeschichtsbl.* 56, 1991, 207–12.

Unz, C., Deschler-Erb, E., *Katalog der Militaria aus Vindonissa (Veröff. Ges. Pro Vindonissa 14)*, Brugg, 1997.

Voirol, A., 'Les militaria d'Avenches/Aventicum', *Bull. Pro Aventico* 42, 2000, 7–92.

10 THE LATE EMPIRE

Aurrecoechea Fernandez, J., *Los cinturones romanos en la Hispania del Bajo Imperio (Monogr. Instrumentum, 19)*, Montagnac, 2001.

Böhme, H. W., *Germanische Grabfunde des 4. bis 5. Jahrhunderts*, 2 vol., Munich, 1974.

Böhme, H. W., 'Das Ende der Römerherrschaft in Britannien und die angelsachsische Besiedlung Englands im 5. Jahrhundert', *Jb. RGZM* 33, 1986, 469–574.

Bullinger, H., *Spätantike Gürtelbeschläge. Typen, Herstellung, Trageweise und Datierung*, 2 vol., Bruge, 1969.

Casey, J., *The Legions in the Later Roman Empire*, Cardiff, 1991.

Coulston, J.C.N., 'Later Roman armour, 3rd–6th centuries AD', *JRMES* 1, 1990, 139–60.

Ferrill, A., *The Fall of the Rmnan Empire. The Military Explanation*, London, 1986.

Feugère, M. 'Apollon et Daphné sur une boucle de ceinture tardo-romaine en argent doré', *Arch. Korr* 22, 1992, 125–36.

Heurgon, J., *Le Trésor de Ténès*, Paris, 1958.

James, S., 'Evidence from Dura-Europos for the origins of Late Roman helmets', *Syria* 63, 1986, 107–34.

James, S., 'The *fabricae*: state arms factories of the Later Roman Empire', in J.C.N. Coulston (ed.), *Military Equipment and the Identity of Roman Soldiers. Proceedings of the Fourth Roman Military Equipment Conference (BAR S.394)*, Oxford 1988, 257–331.

Klumbach, H. (ed.), *Spätrömische Gardehelme*, Munich, 1973.

Sommer, M., 'Die Gürtel und Gürtelbeschläge des 4. und 5. Jahrhunderts im römischen Reich', *Bonner Hefte zur Vorgeschichte* 22, 1984.

Schnurbein, S. von, 'Zum Ango', in *Studien zur Vor- und Frühgeschichtliche Archäologie. Feststhrift fur J. Werner*, Munich 1974, 411–33.

Schulze-Dörrlamm, M., 'Germanische Kriegergraber mit Schwertbeigabe in Mitteleuropa aus dem späten 3. Jahrhundert und der ersten Hälfte des 4. Jahrhunderts n. Chr.', *Jb. RGZM* 32, 1985, 509–69.

Stephenson, I.P., *Roman Infantry Equipment. The Later Empire*, Stroud, 1999.

Swift, E., *Regionality in Dress Accessories in the late Roman West (Monogr. Instrumentum 11)*, Montagnac, 2000.

Swift, E., *The End of the Western Roman Empire*, Stroud/Charleston 2000.

Tomei, M.A., 'La tecnica nel tardo impero romano: le machine da guerra', *Dial. di Arch.* 4, 1982, 63–88.

11 THE ARMY AND ROMAN SOCIETY

Bernard, H., Bessac, J.-C., Mardikian, P., Feugère, M., 'L'épave romaine de marbre de Porto Novo', *Journ. Rom. Archaeol.* 11, 1998, 53–81.

Breeze, D., 'The ownership of arms in the Roman army', *Britannia* 7, 1976, 93–5.

Feugère, M., Freises, A., 'Un casque étrusque du Ve s. av. n. ère trouvé en mer près d'Agde (Hérault)', *Rev. Arch. Narb.* 27/28, 1994–5, 1–7.

Feugère, M., 'Militaria de Gaule méridionale, 3. Hyères (Var): nouveau casque de type étrusco-italique', *Arma* 8, 1996, 20–1.

Gianfrotta, P.A., 'Commerci e pirateria: prime testimonianze archeologiche sottomarine', *MEFRA* 93, 1981, 227–42.

Künzl, E., 'Politische Propaganda auf römischen Waffen der frühen Kaiserzeit', in *Kaiser Augustus und die verlorene Republic*, Berlin, 1988, 541–5.

Le Bohec, Y., *L'armée romaine*, Paris, 1989.

MacMullen, K., 'Inscriptions on Armor and the Supply of Arms in the Roman Empire', *AJA* 64, 1960, 23–40.

Speidel, M., 'The weapons keeper, the fisci curator, and the ownership of weapons in the Roman army', in *Roman Army Studies II (Mavors Roman Army Researches, VIII)*, Stuttgart, 1992, 131–6.